GIGI PADOVANI

Nutella World

50 Years of Innovation

First published in the United States of America in 2015 by
Rizzoli Ex Libris, an imprint of
Rizzoli International Publications, Inc.
300 Park Avenue South
New York, NY 10010
www.rizzoliusa.com

Originally published in Italy as *Mondo Nutella: 50 anni di innovazione* in 2014 by
RCS Libri S.p.A.

Translation from Italian by Aaron Maines (chapters 1-10) and Sylvia Notini (chapters 11-12). Translation revised by Sylvia Notini.

Photographs courtesy Ferrero Archive except:
Giovanni Ferrero, courtesy Centro Studi Beppe Fenoglio (Alba)
Photos of World Nutella Day, courtesy Sara Rosso
Machine à tartiner, courtesy Henri Gallot-Lavallée
Every effort has been made to cite all copyrighted materials. Any inaccuracies brought to the publisher's attention will be corrected for future editions.

Second printing, 2015
2015 2016 2017 2018 / 10 9 8 7 6 5 4 3 2

ISBN: 978-0-8478-4585-9

Library of Congress Control Number: 2014958348

Printed in Italy

Contents

Part one
NUTELLA CULT

Part two
NUTELLA SOCIAL

Part three
NUTELLA COMPANY

Part four
NUTELLA GRAFFITI

PART ONE
Nutella cult

1

It's all Napoleon's fault

It's been described as an expression of the soul, a consuming passion, and the symbol of a generation. It has been a fixture in people's kitchens in countries across the world for decades, becoming a cult object. In part due to its international-sounding name, it has won over a hundred million families, becoming more than a simple brand: a lovemark. Nutella—pronounced *new-tell-uh*—is a hazelnut and cocoa spread, a commercial specialty first created in 1964, although the act of blending hazelnut and cocoa is deeply rooted in the history of chocolate. This little jar with a white top, today a citizen of numerous nations, was first created in Italy. More precisely, in Piedmont, a region in the northwest corner of the Italian peninsula that is surrounded by mountains and borders both France and Switzerland. Nutella's oldest ancestor is a small, delicious brown ingot: the *gianduiotto*. This small chocolate, shaped like an overturned canoe, was created in Turin halfway through the 1800s. First it seduced what was then the capital of Italy, and ultimately all of Europe. Right from the start, consumers appreciated its creamy consistency, its flavor—neither too sweet nor too bitter—and its intoxicating hint of hazelnut. But it was impossible to spread on bread.

The gianduiotto's shift from solid to creamy took place in the wake of World War II in a small factory in Alba, roughly forty miles from Turin. Alba is an elegant town of red-roofed medieval towers, famous for its white truffles and superior wines. It is the capital of the Langhe region, an area celebrated by writers like Cesare Pavese and Beppe Fenoglio and recently declared a UNESCO World Heritage Site. In the 1940s working for the factory was a talented pastry chef: Pietro Ferrero, founder of a company that today produces dozens of sweet specialties, including Nutella, Tic Tac, Ferrero Rocher and Kinder. As had happened a century earlier with the creation of the gianduiotto, during the difficult postwar period, this artisan turned to a small, aromatic, rich nut that had many characteristics in common with cocoa: the hazelnut. Hazelnuts were cheap and easy to find, cultivated by the farmers in the hills around Alba.

The felicitous fusion of hazelnut and cocoa was born to satisfy a need—premium raw ingredients were scarce in the wake of war. Similar circumstances had occurred midway through the 1800s, when the Napoleonic Wars had caused a sharp decline in goods imported from the Americas, cocoa and sugar in particular. You might say that the first person responsible for the creation of the gianduiotto was Napoleon Bonaparte, the Corsican-born general who seized power in France in 1799 and proceeded to set most of Europe on fire.

Hence Napoleon is the real "father" of Nutella. In order to understand why, we have to go back to Germany in 1806. Holed up in Hohenzollern castle in Berlin, the French emperor wanted to take revenge for the naval defeat he'd experienced the previous year at Trafalgar. From that Prussian city, which Napoleon had only just conquered, the emperor issued a decree that put a total embargo on the British Isles: any and all ships flying the Union Jack were forbidden to moor in any French-controlled port, which included southern Italy. England's reaction was equally severe: His Majesty's gunships began stopping even neutral ships headed for French ports. The power of the British navy made England's embargo even more effective than France's. One consequence of the Continental Blockade, as this standoff would be called, was that colonial goods all but disappeared across Europe. The prices of the few imported foodstuffs still available on the open market increased exponentially. As Canadian historian Jack Galloway—one of the authors of *The Cambridge World History of Food*—explains, cane sugar disappeared entirely from French and European markets. In order to make up for its absence, which was driving the Parisian well-to-do to desperation, Napoleon encouraged the cultivation of sugar beets and the building of factories capable of transforming them into sugar by using a method that had been perfected in Prussia by the chemist Franz Karl Achard. But cocoa was another story. It wasn't yet being cultivated in Africa (where most cocoa cultivation takes place today); which meant that its importation from South and Central America was the only possible supply option.

In Turin, as in Paris, people ate lots of sugar and cocoa. By the late 1700s, the city had become one of the most important centers for chocolate production in all of Europe. In the eighteenth century, Turin's master chocolatiers were producing roughly 350 kilograms (750 pounds) of chocolate every day and exporting it to Austria, Switzerland, Germany, and France. This "food of the Gods" had reached Piedmont thanks to marriages between the dynasties: the dukes and counts of the region's ancient royal family, the Savoia (first established in 1003 in the Savoie region in France) had wed French and Spanish princesses. In the 1800s there was even a "Chocolate Department" in the royal court in Turin, and royal licenses for its sale—similar to today's commercial licenses—were given by the court to the best confectioners so that the nobility might continue to enjoy their hot coffee with their beloved brown gold. Many young Swiss citizens moved to Turin to work in these chocolate shops and learn the trade, including François Cailler (one of the founders of Nestlé) and Philippe Suchard (another storied Swiss chocolate brand name). Cocoa traveled from South America to Spain or Portugal, then on ships to ports in Nice and along the Italian coast, at the time owned by the Piedmontese. At first chocolatiers pounded the cocoa on a hot *metate*, a concave sheet of stone first used by the Aztecs. Later the first hydraulic machines, large *mélangeurs* (mixers) with granite wheels were used. Thus was the confectionary industry born in Turin, Italy.

THE FIRST SURROGATE

Once Napoleon instituted the embargo, everything became more difficult, even though the Continental Blockade was lifted in 1814. The prices of raw ingredients shot sky-high and therefore Italians, just like the French, had to adapt. Although there are some who consider the influence of Napoleon Bonaparte's embargo on the birth of the gianduiotto to be something of a myth, there is proof that it caused a sweet revolution in agriculture, insofar as cane sugar became all but unavailable across the European continent. In Italy the issue was addressed by a young Piedmont politician who eventually became the country's first prime minister: Camillo Benso, the Count of Cavour. An agricultural producer and the minister of agriculture, Benso, promoted the cultivation of sugar beets in Piedmont. At the same time, hazelnuts began to substitute cocoa, and sugar beets and hazelnuts were used, together with other dried fruits, to make a chocolate surrogate. Documentary proof can be found in a short, fifteen-page booklet published in 1813 in Venice by Stamperia Domenico Fracasso, entitled *Piano teorico-pratico di sostituzione nazionale al ciocco-lato* (A theoretical-practical plan for the national substitution of chocolate) and written by Antonio Bazzarini. The eclectic proposal presented by the author (who would later write an encyclopedia and a dictionary, and who left Venice to settle in Turin) was actually quite simple: given that the "nut of the cocoa tree has unfortunately milked European markets dry," it was necessary to substitute it with "those kinds of native species" that had been long forgotten. Bazzarini invited his readers to use other kinds of "rather nutritional vegetables" instead, like the "western hazelnut," or toasted almonds, lupines, or corn. Once the raw ingredients have been processed, the booklet explained, confectioners could add up to one-third cocoa, which they were advised to use "like paint." In addition to making "the piece enjoyable and fragrant, this will make it equally solid and more like the more perfect usual product, including its looks." It was a full-blown surrogate, and the book included a recipe for its creation: 2.25 kilograms (4.96 pounds) of almonds (or hazelnuts); 40 grams (1.41 ounces) of roasted lupines; 900 grams (31.74 ounces) of corn; 40 grams (1.41 ounces) of powdered cinnamon and vanilla; and 1.52 kilograms (3.35 pounds) of sugar.

While we can't be sure of whether the young Turin chocolatier Michele Prochet, considered to be the inventor of the gianduiotto, had the chance to read Bazzarini's booklet, we do know that Italy's masterchefs were familiar with hazelnuts, and that they used them to create *torrone*, a type of nougat, as well as pastries and pies. In his book *Dolci delizie subalpine* (Sweet Subalpine Delights, 1995) food writer Mario Marsero maintains that the first prototypes of chocolates made with the new surrogate were already being prepared as early as 1852 by Prochet, one of many young Waldensians—like Gay-Odin, Talmon and

Caffarel—who had traveled to the Italian city to start up confectionary businesses after King Carlo Alberto of Piedmont-Sardinia recognized the right to religious freedom in 1848.

The Waldensian community, which was linked to Switzerland, had been persecuted for centuries by the House of Savoia, all the way to King Carlo Alberto, who, influenced by liberal French thinking and the Napoleonic Code, gave the cult his blessing. As a result numerous artisans descended into the city from the surrounding valleys in order to found their companies. According to some, the Waldensians deserve recognition for having invented the first "clothed"—packaged or wrapped in paper—chocolates in the world. In an issue of the magazine *Il Dolce* (The Dessert), published in 1932, one author wrote that "gianduia paste is nothing more than a chocolate with toasted hazelnuts," explaining that the first company to create it was Prochet, Gay & Co., although there is still some doubt about the date.

One thing we do know for sure is that in 1878 the chocolatiers Caffarel and Prochet joined forces, merging their companies under one brand name. While Caffarel is currently part of the Lindt group, it has maintained its proud Italian roots, and preserved in the former company's archives a document that attests to the fact that the "baptism" of the cocoa and hazelnut chocolate took place in Turin in 1865 during Carnival time. It was during the "Fiera Fantastica" (Fantastic Fair) held over a fifteen-day period along the streets of the capital of Piedmont, that a sort of town jester named Gianduia was given a taste of the *givu* ("butts" in Piedmont dialect, or the first small chocolates) and liked them—so much so that he awarded their maker "a special certificate attesting to the merit of the company, authorizing it to call this Turinese product by the name, 'Gianduia.' This document can still be found in the Caffarel, Prochet & Co. branch offices in Turin."

And thus gianduiotti were born. In 2001 this name was registered in the global Codex Alimentarius, used by the World Trade Organization to define the rules of international commerce, following intense negotiations conducted by representatives from the Italian confectionary industry. Today there are four types of chocolate in the world: white chocolate, milk chocolate, dark chocolate, and gianduia (or one of the derivatives of this word).

But who exactly was Gianduia? The name was attributed to a type of mask used in Italian commedia dell'arte, created in the early 1800s for street theater puppetry, and was derived from *Giôan d'la dôja*, which meant *Giovanni del boccale di vino* ("John of the wine jug"). The character was a happy-go-lucky gourmet who eventually became a symbol of the Italian Risorgimento—a nationalist revolt that led to the birth of a unified Italy. He was a beloved character in Italy, at least up until a few generations ago. In the book *Torino e i torinesi* (Turin and the Turinese), a chronicle of anecdotes published toward the end of the 1800s, Alberto Viriglio wrote that "Gianduia is not a mask: he's a character. Beneath a superficial appearance of ingenuousness and roughness, he hides talent, readiness, practicality, and a grand heart". The actor who played Gianduia during the carnival was symbolically crowned "king" of the city. And in fact it was none other than *Giôan d'la dôja* who led the popular uprising in 1865 that opposed plans to move the capital of the Kingdom of Italy from Turin to Florence.

THEY CALLED HIM *GIANDUJOT*

A century later, this odd element—the mask—most likely inspired an ambitious artisan confectioner who grew up between the Langhe region and Turin during the 1930s and 1940s: Pietro Ferrero. In 1946 he decided to print Gianduia's face on the packaging for his specialties, with two happy children alongside and a catchphrase that read, "I was the first, and I'm still the best." The difficulties that Monsù Pietro (a respectful appellation, the equivalent of "Signor Pietro" in the Piedmontese dialect) encountered in obtaining raw ingredients immediately after World War II were not entirely the same as those his colleagues grappled with at the beginning of the 1800s. Italy was on its knees. Very few people could afford sweets or children's snacks. Everything was rationed. But blending cocoa and hazelnut together proved his good fortune and created the necessary conditions for the birth of Nutella.

Pietro Ferrero was a farmer's son. The town he was born in, Viaiano Soprano, is located in the Langhe region, twenty miles south of Alba: a huddle of houses hugging woods, vineyards, and corn fields overlooking the Tanaro River, between hills that have only recently begun to enjoy economic prosperity thanks to fine wine, tourism, and the solid economic foundation offered by nearby industries. When the Ferrero brothers were born (Pietro in 1898; Giovanni in 1905), life was hard in that part of the world. Their little town was a place to escape from as quickly as possible, and that's just what the two young Ferrero brothers did once they realized they had no desire to work the land the way their parents had. Pietro learned the confectioner's trade in Dogliani, a lively town of five thousand, famous today for its Dolcetto wine and the estate of Luigi Einaudi, the first president of the Italian Republic. Giovanni instead joined the carabinieri, and later worked in sales in Alba.

In the beginning, destiny tore the two brothers apart. They had entirely different personalities, and they also looked nothing alike: Pietro was small, taciturn, a loner; Giovanni was big and exuberant, sporting the cocky mustache of a Hollywood actor. The former knew how to cook extraordinary dishes, amidst pots and ovens, making do with whatever he had available. The latter was skilled at buying and selling food products. In the years following World War II, that sweet surrogate made of hazelnut, chocolate, sugar, and coconut butter changed their lives, transforming the tiny shop they started into an industrial empire.

The main street in Dogliani is lined with traditional Piedmont porticoes. This is where it all began: in 1923 Pietro Ferrero opened his first pastry shop here. At that time, the Italian National Fascist Party had just abolished Mayday festivities, substituting them with celebrations for the birth of Rome, which was established as having taken place on April 21. Pietro had skill and, thanks in part to the beautiful cakes and pies he displayed in his shop window, he managed to win the affections of Piera Cillario, a twenty-something-year-old woman, and the youngest of eight brothers and sisters. This woman would become his wife in 1924 and prove to be a pivotal figure in the success of the company her husband founded. Two years later they moved to Alba to work in Rava, a confectionary shop owned by one of Piera's nephews. In the 1930s they moved to Turin, where they opened two pastry shops in less than a decade: the second was the more elegant of the two, and boasted no fewer than seven display windows and a refined clientele. But when the war broke out, the Ferrero family was forced to flee, and decided to return to the Langhe region.

In the meantime they'd raised their son, Michele, who had been born in 1925. Michele studied accounting at boarding school, where he was tutored by his uncle, the priest Eugenio Cillario, and once the war was over, decided to stay at home and help his parents. Business was doing well, and the beautiful little pastry shop in Alba had become family property, even though it wasn't easy selling sweets during those days. The general population had next to nothing to eat, let alone chocolate, which was a genuine luxury and cost around 3,000 lira per kilogram/2.2 pounds (equal to roughly 90 euros or $120 today). Pietro knew that, in order to increase production, he had to invent special, low-cost products—something that cost no more than 600 or 700 lira per kilogram/2.2 pounds (less than 20 euros or $26 today). His brother Giovanni came to his aid. At the time, Giovanni was earning a decent living, buying and selling foodstuffs out of his little Balilla—a car built by Fiat that helped bring automobiles to the Italian masses—and supplying yeast to all the bakers in the region.

"You know what, Pietro?" said Giovanni one day in his brother's shop. "They just sold me this barrel full of molasses for next to nothing. It was drawn from sugar beets while they were making sugar. It's not as sweet as sugar, but it's good. They use it to make yeast too. . . They gave me some practically for free. Why don't you try it out and see what you can do with it?" Monsù Pietro got to work, rolling up the sleeves of his crisp white pastry chef's jacket. As chance would have it, he had some hazelnut *panello* (oilcake, or solid residue from the refining process) lying around the shop. He drew some hazelnut oil from it, added a little coconut butter (because cocoa butter was too expensive and impossible to find) and some powdered cocoa. Simple but healthy ingredients. He experimented over and over again with the mix, managing to create a sort of semisolid paste, sweet and pleasant to eat. Then he set his creation in rectangular molds in order to shape it. From the local butcher he got some yellow wax paper with which to wrap his mouthwatering little ingots.

According to a reconstruction of events put together by Italian journalists De Vecchi, Di Nola, and Tonelli in their book *Storia di un successo* (A Success Story, 1967), this episode took place toward the end of 1945 or the start of 1946. They wrote:

"When the paste cooled down, Pietro Ferrero called his wife in and asked her to try it. 'I think it's delicious,' said Signora Piera, who loved chocolate and could never get enough. 'Dad, it's delicious!' exclaimed their son Michele, smacking his lips. [. . .] 'I love it,' he insisted. Curious, Michele asked, 'What did you put in it?'"

Smiling and happy-go-lucky as always, the next day Giovanni dropped by to pick up Pietro's creation and try to sell some to the bakers he supplied with yeast. He didn't even manage to finish his rounds before some of his first clients caught up with him again. "Listen, Signor Ferrero, do you still have some of those sweets? Cut up and spread on bread it's delicious. . . We've already sold it all!"

The most authentic retelling of that memorable invention was provided by Pietro's son Michele, when Nutella was already an industry, during one of the few interviews he gave over the course of a life lived far from the spotlight, responding to questions from Italian journalist Alfredo Pigna for the book *Miliardari in borghese* (Undercover Millionaires, 1967).

"Do you know what the '*pastone*' is? Some people called it 'the poor man's chocolate,' but I'd say it's a sweet for the humble. [. . .] My father invented a *pastone*, a sort of gianduiotto, that was very good and relatively inexpensive. My father and my uncle Giovanni, who was his partner, thought that our best clients would be those thousands of workers, builders, carpenters, and farmers who were used to buying a couple of tomatoes and some cheese to make a simple sandwich for breakfast. What if, thought my father and uncle, we give them a chance to eat something sweet, something that costs the same or even less than what they usually buy? They were right. That idea was so successful that even today we have trouble comprehending the extent of its success. Ferrero was born of that simple *pastone*."

The product passed the market test, becoming a close competitor with chocolate: it had the same nutritional characteristics, since hazelnuts have a composition quite similar to cocoa, and was delicious to eat. Most importantly, everyone could afford it.

People liked to say that Giovanni Ferrero could sell sand from the Tanaro River for gold. But the truth is there was no need for a golden tongue to sell that sliceable surrogate: it was selling as fast as his brother could make it. So the two brothers formed a company, hired a few workers, bought new machinery, and began working day and night in order to keep up with orders that were pouring in from all over the Langhe region, all the way to Turin. They had to give the invention a name, and naturally the first thing that came to mind was that chocolate invented under Napoleon's regime, so they called their creation "Giandujot."

Graziella Borello was one of the first workers hired in 1946. Back then just six or seven people worked in the Ferrero facility, all of them quite young, and only two or three men. As Graziella notes, "There were only two machines that ran on electricity. Everything else we did by hand. Hazelnuts would come in from the countryside: we had to toast them, shell them, and reduce them to mush. Then they were mixed in with other ingredients, sugar, cocoa and vegetable fats, until the paste was ready to go into the molds. When everything was done, each one-kilo (2.2-pound) loaf of Giandujot was wrapped in aluminum foil and packed in cardboard boxes. As soon as they came off the production line, there were clients waiting to buy them and take them away." Every once in a while Mamma Piera stopped in to make sure everything was proceeding smoothly, even though her job was to run the cash register at the pastry shop on via Maestra, located just a short walk away. In the beginning, the company registered amazing numbers: in November alone they sold 1,100 quintals (121 tons). The small rooms of the first factory in downtown Alba quickly proved insufficient, and in December 1946 the company moved everything to a large warehouse near the Tanaro River that the Ferreros had bought during wartime, in 1944. By the end of the year, the number of employees had risen to around fifty, and it would soon double again.

For poor farmers living in the hills around Alba, that small factory became a sort of mecca, a place where people aspired to work. "They're hiring workers and letting them spend a few months at home so that they can work the fields too," it was rumored around the region. In fact, production was seasonal. In 1951, 70 percent of Alba's population worked in agriculture, which was not very profitable, and the entire area had depopulated in the period between the two world wars. The Ferrero factory, in the same area where its larger, more modern facilities are located today, was growing at a breakneck pace: by the end of 1951 the number of employees had risen to 300; just ten years later, in 1961, no less than 2,700 people worked at Ferrero.

THE ATTEMPTED SALE

Marketing expert and author Philip Kotler familiarized the world with the "four P" model, theorized in 1960 by E. Jerome McCarthy and considered an essential formula for strategizing how to satisfy market needs while making a profit. The four lynchpins of his "marketing mix" system were: product, price, place, and promotion. In the 1950s, Giovanni Ferrero actually used an approach that put McCarthy's first three Ps together. This was the "attempted sale," a system halfway between wholesale and a traveling salesman's market stall, and it worked well in difficult circumstances, such as those the

Italians were experiencing in the postwar period, when demand was low. Giovanni drove around Piedmont and Lombardy in his fire-red Fiat 1100. One morning he traveled to Milan to bring a client a load of Giandujot, but when he got there he found the warehouse wasn't open yet, so he walked over to a café in order to call the client. When Giovanni got back to the car he discovered a small crowd of people clamoring to buy some of his precious delight: "The smell of hazelnut was our best ambassador"—or as Kotler would call it, "the fourth P." That episode inspired the brothers to sidestep the wholesalers. Sales representatives at Ferrero began visiting shopkeepers, delivering merchandise directly to them. Given that these agents only received a percentage on sales, this led to a considerable increase in orders. In 1947 Ferrero had a dozen hazelnut-and-cocoa-colored company vehicles, Gianduia's merry face painted on the sides. But by 1950 this number had grown to 154, and to 1,624 in 1960. In Italy, the Ferrero company car fleet was second only to the military. Each salesman had a full warehouse in his little van, and the company also organized a network of dealerships in order to avoid the wholesalers who were monopolizing the market. Giovanni Ferrero was fully familiar with sales mechanisms: he had a wholesale company of his own in Alba, separate from the company he had founded with his brother.

These were "heroic" times. Amilcare Dogliotti, who became CEO of Ferrero in the 1990s and for a long time was Michele Ferrero's main collaborator, says that when he joined the company in 1954, fresh out of college, they put him in one of these little vans and sent him out to accompany a salesman. "When he saw me there, he gave me a dark look, because with me in the van he had less space for product. So we reached a compromise. We removed the passenger seat and set up a stack of boxes full of Giandujot so that I had a sort of stool to sit on."

SUPERCREMA

Not even a disastrous flood on September 1948 could hamper the company's unstoppable growth. But the following spring the Ferrero family was struck by tragedy: the company founder, Pietro, died of a heart attack. He was just fifty-one (and the same tragic destiny would strike the grandson who bore his name in 2011, when he was just forty-seven). In 1949 Pietro's widow, Piera, his son Michele—barely twenty years old—and his brother Giovanni took the company in hand. Ferrero began offering new products in addition to the Giandujot, all characterized by reasonable prices: the Cremino, Sultanino, and Cremablock. In Italy, per capita consumption of sweets remained extremely low, around 2 kilograms (4.4 pounds) per year, so Ferrero always tried to offer consumers small product sizes in order to keep prices low.

But when did the ritual of spreading Nutella on a slice of bread begin?

There are still a few retired milkmen in Turin who remember that steamy summer of 1949, when Italian cycling champions Fausto Coppi and Gino Bartali were battling one another in the Giro d'Italia, American actor Tyrone Power was all the rage at the dawn of the Roman *dolce vita*, and the Giandujot melted like snow in warm sunlight. The Ferrero agents withdrew their product as quickly as possible, storing them in a warehouse and only then realizing that when reduced to a cream, Giandujot could be spread on bread. Urban legend or a real stroke of luck? The history of pastries and sweets is rife with examples of "fortunate" mistakes. Pralines were created in 1636 when a pastry chef in the service of the Count of Plessis-Praslin became distracted. The tarte tatin was a product of the carelessness of the Tatin sisters, while working in a restaurant in the French countryside toward the end of the 1800s. Beginning in autumn of 1949, Supercrema started showing up in shops around Italy. The creamy consistency of that "food preserve" made of hazelnuts and cocoa was achieved using a substance that the young Michele Ferrero discovered reading an American magazine: soybean lecithin, a substance that can retain fats. Some shopkeepers had complained that the Giandujot would "sweat" at times. Adding lecithin rendered the product more stable, making it possible to start producing Supercrema, or Nusscreme, as it was called in the early days. Ferrero's entrepreneurial founders immediately got the idea of packaging it in various useful and reusable containers: sealed cans, aluminum pots, toy wooden boxes for kids, glasses, jars, and more.

In small towns in southern Italy people started organizing a sort of public service: the "spreadfest." Children ran to the milkman or baker with a slice of bread in hand, and for five lira (mere pennies) they were given a thin spread of Supercrema; for double that, a thick spread. Advertising was aimed at "intelligent housewives" who knew well enough to choose a product with "high energy value," given that it provided "no less than 5,100 calories" for a mere 600 lira per kilogram/2.2 pounds (around $25 today), and could be eaten with as much or as little bread as one liked. This was the practical application, in a simple and perhaps unknowing manner, of the main function of modern marketing: not a promotional or advertising activity, but, as Kotler describes, a process through which the company "creates value for the client and establishes a solid relationship with them in order to achieve added value in exchange."

Back in the factory in Alba people were at work day and night, including Sundays, in order to meet rising demand. It was easy to find people willing to work among the small farming towns in the surrounding hills, while allowing employees to continue to live in their rural homes without having to move into town. This meant the countryside wasn't depopulated, and at the same time the town was able to develop. In 1957 there were already seven Ferrero bus lines running routes for employees. There was even some friction, at least initially, with the local parish due to the company's decision to have people work on Sundays, but Giovanni Ferrero managed to convince the priests that the sacrifice was necessary in the name of a greater good for all.

It's important to recognize how the company's management was able to take advantage of Italy's economic miracle without overwhelming the territory, as instead happened in Turin with the automobile industry. As sociologist Francesco Alberoni emphasizes in his book *Lavorare Creare Donare* (Working Creating Donating, 2003), published by Ferrero Foundation: "There are places where, almost miraculously, at a certain point in history, an extraordinary social and culture dynamic is created. That's when exceptional people arise, and great works are accomplished. We all know about glorious periods like those enjoyed by Athens or Florence. But the same processes take place on smaller scales as well, in small cities, or towns, during particularly fertile and fortunate moments in history. Take Maranello for example, where Ferrari was born; or Ivrea in Adriano Olivetti's day. The same thing happened in Alba, where Ferrero was founded: the only true Italian multinational corporation. Ferrero is not only a business; it's a family, a community. In truth it is even more, because it has interacted with its surrounding territory, with the civil society from which it arose, drawing energy from it while at the same time enriching it, helping it to grow." Giovanni Ferrero helped found professional schools to train mechanics, electricians, and designers, and already in 1956 hired a social assistant who could help identify and fulfill the needs of the people working for Ferrero.

This way, he began to develop an Italian brand of company

assistance that included housing, hospitals, nursery schools, vacations, recreational clubs, and more, and continues to function today.

IN EUROPE: GERMANY AND FRANCE

Michele Ferrero loved sneaking into supermarkets incognito and, together with a collaborator, tasting his company's products as well as those produced by its competitors. It's a habit he'd started with his uncle Giovanni, when he was still alive, and the young entrepreneur soon began exploring different markets, buying raw ingredients and trying to figure out the "secrets" of other European producers. Confirmation comes from Francesco Rivella, a chemist the company hired in 1952, and who remained with Ferrero for forty years. A little chemistry lab was created in Milan specifically to analyze the raw ingredients that Giovanni and Michele went out and bought. From that moment forward the two began traveling around Europe. "We have to move beyond Alba," Michele always said back then. Before making a decision on Ferrero's investment in Germany, he left with Rivella on a long trip through northern European countries. They didn't leave so much as a German *süsswaren* or French or Belgian *pâtisserie* untouched. They bought chocolates, chocolate creams, wafers, and snacks of all kinds, analyzing the foodstuffs not so that they could copy them, but to improve them. They wanted to leave the surrogates behind and toast their own cocoa beans. The first dark chocolate Ducalba bars were produced and this quality chocolate proved an immediate success. The air around the medieval towers of Alba became infused with the rich aroma of freshly toasted cocoa beans emerging from a modern facility set up on the banks of the Tanaro River.

Those voyages into northern Europe helped Michele Ferrero realize that they needed to look for opportunities in new markets, to win over the high per capita consumption connected with chocolate. When he was barely thirty years old, Michele Ferrero, in a stroke of genius, managed to convince his somewhat reluctant family of the importance of opening a factory in Germany. Today the average German eats more than 8 kilograms (17.63 pounds) of chocolate per year, while Italians eat barely half that. And back in the 1950s this difference was even greater. Michele's decision was a winning idea, as ex-CEO Amilcare Dogliotti notes, "Signor Michele said to me, 'If we're not someone in Europe, we'll never be anyone in Italy either.' His words proved prophetic." When Ferrero inaugurated a new factory in Allendorf, Germany, the then-CEO of Motta—an Italian confectionary company founded in 1919 that was a direct competitor and had single-handedly introduced Italians to the *panettone*, a rich dessert bread cake—declared, "The Ferrero family has found a way to put itself out of business." To be honest, demand was greater in northern Europe, and that's where the business needed to go. From that moment onward the strategy embraced by the company in Alba has always been to expand in foreign markets: not as part of a search for competitive advantages in production costs (what people mean today when they talk about "delocalization"), but simply to respond to a greater market demand with respect to the products offered.

The factory was founded a little over ninety miles from Frankfurt, in a hilly area of the Hesse quite similar to the Langhe, and can be considered the first example of internationalization in the Italian confectionary industry. It was 1956, and the Treaty of Rome—officially the Treaty establishing the European Economic Community (TEEC), a forerunner to the modern-day European Union—would not be signed until

March of 1957, but things were moving in that direction. For the first facility in Allendorf, Ferrero bought several factories abandoned after World War II, in which Hitler had originally built V1 missiles. There, company pioneers sent from Alba, like Severino Chiesa and Giuseppe Faussone, created an industrial hub out of thin air. The life of these "exiles" from Alba is told autobiographically by Marisa Fenoglio, sister of the writer Beppe Fenoglio and the wife of Faussone, in her book *Vivere altrove* (Living Elsewhere, 1997): "Germany was waiting for me the day of my wedding. Surrounded by a small crowd of friends and family, I'd heard the voice of one of Sergio's best men. He was Sergio's employer, a man who entertained grand European expansion plans for his family company, and which he shared with me just outside the church, with people still standing in the sacristy: 'Signora Faussone, how would you like to go to Germany with your husband?'"

Michele Ferrero thought he would be successful with Cremalba, a sort of sweet snack roughly the size of a stick of butter. Instead, the Germans fell in love with a praline with a liquor cherry heart: the Mon Chéri, sold individually rather than in pricey boxes. In spring 1957 the Ferrero company in Germany had sixty employees. It had started with just five. By the end of that year, thanks to the success of Mon Chéri, the employees numbered one hundred and fifty.

Keeping in mind the excellent results the company had obtained in Germany, Michele Ferrero decided to broaden his horizons to France as well: he established the company Dolcea, and in 1959 that company bought an old textile factory in Villers-Écalles, in Normandy, on the border of Pays de Caux and the Austreberthe valley. It wasn't easy to turn a factory that produced textiles into one that made chocolate, but a team sent from Italy fine-tuned the machinery and trained the French employees to perfection. Success and development moved quite quickly in France, and in 1964 the company's commercial services and general management moved to Mont-Saint-Aignan, a town near Rouen, setting up shop in a small villa. In 1978 they opened a new warehouse for products that reached Grand-Quevilly, on the banks of the Seine River, not far from the hills of Mont-Saint-Aignan, where in 2000 the company built the general headquarters for Ferrero France.

In the meantime, Supercrema was starting to register impressive results. It was an unexpected success in Italy, where it was sold in bulk in special pots, and the container helped promote the product. The buyer could keep the pot, taking it back to the store where it would be filled with Supercrema sold by weight. As Dogliotti notes, "Then the first special packaging was created: little colored boxes that children could play with, inside of which we put the cream they could spread on bread at snack time. Glasses only came later, and then the jars. These could be reused as well, and helped us win over the housewives."

The small artisan company from Alba was becoming an international reality. But Giovanni Ferrero, whose commercial intuition and managerial skills had brought them this far, didn't get a chance to enjoy their success. Like his brother, Giovanni was struck down by a heart attack at a young age, when he was just fifty-two, on March 25, 1957. A year later the company bought out the remaining portion of the company inherited by his wife Ottavia Amerio, through a special arbitration process that established the selling price. Thus "Signor Michele," now just thirty-three years old and with only his mother at his side, found himself at the head of a company in the full throes of international development.

Up until this point, competing companies had been unable to match Ferrero's growth. But now they began to respond with price-reduction policies and by introducing small-portion products of their own into the market. Then, in 1962, Michele Ferrero had another winning idea: moving away from surrogates and into chocolate, increasing the quality of raw ingredients adding cocoa and cocoa butter. By this time, Italy and the rest of Europe had left behind the hunger experienced during the war years. A baby boom was underway, and it was time to offer new specialties. They also needed brand names that could be recognized everywhere, because now brands were no longer simply a producer's signature; they'd evolved into a tool for interacting with the world at large. In order to make a name for good products it was no longer enough simply to know how to sell—you had to know how to get your name out there too. And how was that possible? Through marketing and advertising.

Napoleon is relevant here once again, but not for his 1806 Continental Blockade and the legend of the birth of gianduiotto, but for his ability as a grand communicator, someone who was able to spread his image across France and all over Europe in bronze busts and painted portraits and the first logo in modern history. Advertising experts agree: when compared to the intricate allegories of noble medieval coats of arms, his simple "N" wreathed with laurel branches is an essential, modern image.

Today it's amusing to think that Nutella's epic story, from raw materials to market, is all Napoleon's fault.

2
Brand naming: 1964

In the Christian church, baptism was originally referred to as the "sacrament of illumination." Nowadays brands and logos have increasingly become guiding lights for many consumers and can determine the success of people, products, and events. Marketing experts maintain that a brand name has to withstand the test of time to be able to establish a stable relationship with the consumer. In order for a name to prove successful, it has to be original, unique, and distinctive, insofar as it establishes a sort of bond of faith with the purchaser. The most successful brand names are generally short and made up of just two or three syllables. They have to be easy to pronounce in more than one language, and easy to remember. Sophisticated brand-naming techniques exist that analyze the expressive values of a word or letter of the alphabet through complex investigations into phonosymbolism. People who use them maintain, for example, that nasal consonants like "m" and "n" evoke feelings of warmth, softness, and slowness, reminding people of their childhood. Who can really say whether Forrest Mars and Bruce Murrie were aware of this when, in 1954, they began selling their first packages of chocolate M&M's? In any case, from this point of view Nutella makes a perfect brand name.

In the early 1960s, when Ferrero's management was grappling with the best way to launch the company's Supercrema—a specialty that was extremely popular with consumers and was actually creating new consumer habits—in France and Germany, brand value studies were nowhere near as developed as they are today. For decades industries had moved forward through trial and error. A fortunate name choice was part of what had helped immortalize certain products: the Montblanc fountain pen (1910); Lego toys (1916); Chanel's No. 5 perfume (1921); 3M's Scotch tape (1925); Nescafé (1937); and Vespa (1945). And who could forget the fortuitous example of the strongest, most famous brand name in the world? Coca-Cola appeared for the first time in an ad published in the *Atlanta Journal* on May 29, 1886; as Jean-Pierre Keller reminds us in *La Galaxie Coca-Cola* (The Coca-Cola Galaxy, 1980), the product was presented as a "Refreshing! Exhilarating! Invigorating!" drink, thanks to the properties inherent to the "marvelous coca plant" and the "famous kola nut." One hundred and thirty years later no one associates the drink invented by the pharmacist John Stith Pemberton with those ingredients anymore because the brand's intangible dimension has superseded everything else: Coca-Cola is at once form (the bottle) and fun. Similarly, Nutella is at once form (the jar) and conviviality. These are two typical examples of the way a well-chosen brand name can provide its product with something more: satisfy not only a functional need but also a cultural and emotional desire.

Sometimes brand naming is the result of a careful market strategy, other times it is merely the result of chance choices. Google, the most popular search engine in the world, is together with Apple and Coca-Cola one of the most valuable brand names on the planet, according to a list put together by Interbrand. The name derives from a mathematical term—a googol—that stands for the number 1 followed by one hundred zeroes (10^{100}). This term was first coined by the nine-year-old grandson of the American mathematician Edward Kasner, who was trying to explain the difference between an enormous number and the concept of infinity. Danon, the name of the top-selling French yogurt brand, got its name from a child's nickname: Daniel Carasso, or "Danon" to his friends. His father dedicated the first yogurts he produced to his son, registering the brand in Barcelona in 1919 and later producing the yogurt in France. Then there's Schweppes, a name that adorns a number of different soft drink labels and usually brings to mind an onomatopoeic reference to the liquid's effervescence. But the name actually comes from the last name of the drink's producer, Jacob Schweppe, a German chemist who discovered a way to create effervescent water and founded a company to produce it in London in 1792. Even the company that has changed the way the world goes shopping, becoming the most important e-commerce website in the world, owes its brand name to the fortuitous intuition of its founder Jeff Bezos. As Brad Stone notes in Bezos's biography *The Everything Store*, Jeff was sitting in a garage in Seattle in 1994, leafing through the "A's" in a dictionary, looking for a name that would put his website at the beginning of the list of what's available on the Internet, when he was struck by the word "Amazon." "The Amazon River is the longest river on the planet," thought Bezos, "and I'll make it the biggest bookstore on the planet too."

In much the same way, the process through which Ferrero's hazelnut spread with cocoa was baptized "Nutella" was at once fortuitous and deliberate. Sometimes an obstacle can make someone change course and lead to a brilliant idea: in this case the obstacle was an Italian law about food packaging that threatened the brand name "Supercrema." Furthermore, Ferrero was fully conscious of the need to find a brand name that would be recognizable the world over.

LOOKING FOR A BRAND NAME

When people in Alba read Article 10 of a new Italian law, they got worried. "It is forbidden to sell or advertise in newspapers or any other media, brand names or certificates of quality or genuineness from any source, as well as illustrations and/or drawings, that can mislead good faith or trick potential purchasers as to the nature, substance, quality or nutritional properties of said food product, or that vaunt any particular medicinal actions." This normative was part of the new Italian law no. 441/63, approved in 1962 and modified the following year, concerning the "hygienic disciplines covering the production and sale of foodstuffs and drinks." The company's legal offices were quick to offer an opinion: this new wording put Supercrema at risk. In fact, adjectives like "super" and "extra," used to identify an added value, were permitted only if the product put on sale could vaunt objective qualities that differentiated it from other, similar products: if, for example, a Giandujot cream with 10 percent hazelnut existed already, and Supercrema offered more.

At the same time, the news arriving from Germany wasn't good. Germans were crazy about chocolate and they loved the Mon Chéri, but Ferrero's cream wasn't putting a dent in their traditional breakfast: bread with butter, jam, or honey. In 1961 a new spreadable cream was released in France, displaying a new name that may have been too functional: Tartinoise. The brand name was born of the union of two French words, *tartiner* (to spread) and *noisette* (hazelnut), and the product enjoyed a small measure of success. But Ferrero wanted to find a European brand name that was evocative as well as easy to pronounce and remember. The company chief of Ferrero's German division, Severino Chiesa, was adamant about it, and back in Alba they were starting to realize that there might be a way to turn the ugly Supercrema duckling into a swan. Experts were called in and numerous meetings were held in Hesse and the Langhe. We mustn't overlook the fact that Philip Kotler's book *Marketing Management: Analysis, Planning, and Control*, considered to be the first theoretical textbook on this new economic science, was published in 1967. In Italy, the group of managers surrounding the young Italian entrepreneur didn't have many scientific tools available, but they'd intuited what they needed in order to be successful. One of those managers, Amilcare Dogliotti, sums up that fervent period as follows: "Signor Michele said, 'We have to find a name that doesn't just work in the German market. It has to work all around the world.' That was always his credo: to make products not just for the national market, but for at least an entire continent. The packaging had to be the same everywhere. There were lots of meetings, encounters, discussions. We wanted to link the new name to hazelnuts, so we focused on the English and German root words *nut* and *nuss*. Some people got behind the world 'Nussly,' but it was abandoned because people thought it would only work in Germany."

The focus had to be on the hazelnut—*nocciola* in Italian, *noisette* in French, *hazelnoot* in Dutch—a nut that was the pearl of Turkish, Italian, Georgian, and Chilean hills, because Ferrero's destiny had always been connected with this valuable, healthy foodstuff. Some people put forward a range of new proposals: Nutsy, Nussly, Nutosa, Nutina. . . As always, the final decision lay with Signor Michele, who finally came up with the winning idea while he was in Frankfurt, where he had gone to inaugurate the company's new German headquarters. After a late evening walk, Michele went back to the hotel and said to his wife Maria Franca, "What do you think about 'Nutella'? I like the way it sounds. . . Let's see if other people like it too." Even though he'd never studied economics or communications, and was famous for his direct, almost rushed manner of speaking, Michele Ferrero had vision. He knew where he wanted to take his company, and he knew how to surround himself with people who could help him achieve his objectives. One of these was the sociologist Giampaolo Fabris, who worked at Doxa. Doxa was the first market research company established in Italy, where it was founded in 1946. Here's what Fabris had to say about the experience: "I started working when I was still quite young, barely past twenty. I had just finished university and earned my degree when I was asked to test the new name they'd come up with to relaunch Supercrema, Nutella's predecessor, across Europe. Back then the absolute *deus ex machina* of the company founded by his father was Michele Ferrero, an extraordinarily open-minded man and an ingenious product manager who understood, long before the other big multinationals, the rule of non-clonability. This was already a constant for most of Ferrero's products, and a simple yet extremely important part of the company's success. At the same time, he'd understood Nutella's enormous potential, even though most of the company's energies were being directed at promoting Mon Chéri, then considered Ferrero's top-tier product. Back then, market studies—most of which were transnational and concentrated on product names—weren't standard yet. We conducted careful analysis of how consumers in Germany, France, and England were responding to that brand, to see how it was being interpreted and decoded. At a time when Italian companies, even the biggest, most modern ones, were just taking their first baby steps in marketing, this was an operation that would have held its own even against today's strategies. The launch campaign was created by a Milanese design studio and got underway with a widespread series of ad posters that displayed a slice of bread slathered [with the cream]."

Once the choice was made, the Jacobacci-Casetta studio in Turin, a company that specialized in brands, presented a request to register the name at the Italian Ministry of Industry in Rome on October 10, 1963. A certificate of approval—no. 164,196—provided by the main patent office didn't arrive until March 17, 1964, but based on the Madrid accords, which made it possible to extend brand name patent protection to all member countries (today more than ninety, and constantly on the rise), it was extended internationally at once. In the early part of April 1964 the offices in Alba released "Official Notice no. 20," entitled "NUTELLA," directed at all affiliated departments and inspectors and signed by the company's management. "From this time forward," read the first lines of the notice, "packaged Supercrema will be renamed NUTELLA. This change has been prompted by the need to use a name with European reach; one that expresses a precise concept that can be understood not only in Italy, but in all countries in which our products are sold [. . .] The name NUTELLA will provide us with interesting publicity options in a larger area. [. . .] Current production with labels using the 'Supercrema' name will continue until we have finished our packaging, label, and capsule supplies: probably up until 20 April."

This is the reason why Nutella's official birthdate has traditionally been set on that rainy spring Monday, when the first jars sporting the new label were filled with the hazelnut cream. In truth, the date April 20, 1964, has gone down in history as the day the United States and the Soviet Union reached an agreement to reduce nuclear arms. Italy was experiencing its first economic crisis in the wake of its happy economic boom (during which the gross domestic product grew by 5 percent per year until 1963). But the country remained optimistic. People were still buying things: Procter & Gamble detergents; Zanussi washing machines and refrigerators; Fiat cars; and Ferrero products. Fortunately, Nutella had finally arrived.

LOVABLE LETTERING

Three syllables: Nu-tel-la. A name neither too short nor too long, and equipped with a sweet suffix—"ella"—that influenced its fortunate destiny. English speakers were reminded of Cinderella. Italians were reminded of their childhood through the assonance with caram-ella (candy in Italian). The French pronounced it placing emphasis on the "a." In the United States it became a lighthearted play on words: to go nuts about Nutella. The sound of the name worked, as a psycholinguist might say, especially for a foodstuff that brought to mind childhood and snack time. Ferrero had played with this suffix in the past, with its "Naturella" candies and "Cerasella" pralines, before Mon Chéri took over due to its success in Germany.

Now it was time to dress the brand name in appropriate clothing, identifying a logo that could make it a true product achievement: the company decided to make room for this new project, destined to become a huge success all over the world. This too was a choice motivated by precise marketing concerns that are as valid in today's world as they were back then.

Today Ferrero enjoys an excellent global reputation. It is considered a place any young person would be happy to work. But back in 1964 this wasn't the case. After having won over so many consumers thanks to the low prices it charged for surrogate-based products, brands like Mon Chéri, Nutella, and Duplo were being positioned in a new, higher market segment thanks to the ingredients they contained. This meant the company needed to avoid emphasizing the Ferrero name and concentrate on the individual names of its specialties.

Two elements in Nutella's brand equity have remained unchanged for over fifty years, ever since they were first designed by Carmelo Cremonesi and Gian Rossetti's company, Studio Stile, in Milan: the lettering, in other words the font chosen for the logo, set against a white background; and the image of a slice of bread spread with hazelnut and cocoa cream impressed upon the label. Cremonesi was an artist and photographer, while Rossetti was a hyperrealist designer who could make any foodstuff—from snacks to candies and pralines—look appetizing. All the images that appeared on Ferrero products during the 1960s and 1970s were created by Rossetti, and the style has remained unchanged even after his death (in 1993): simple, sunny lines that are rich in color and optimism. The knife with a dollop of cream dripping off the edge, about to drop onto a slice of homemade bread, carefully spread with a bright, delicious-looking cream . . . It all works to bring Nutella's wonderful taste to mind even before it hits your taste buds.

At the time, Olivetti was the leader in Italian industrial design, having presented a brand with tiny lettering already back in 1938, created by the painter Xanti Schawinsky. Later the graphic artist and architect Marcello Nizzoli, a protagonist in the creation of the famous Lettera 22 typewriter in 1960, perfected the Olivetti logo and created the brand identity so many are familiar with today. Studio Stile drew inspiration from his work, and was at the time the first international advertising agency to be headquartered in Milan, working with Plan International in Europe and Grant Advertising in the United States. Michele Ferrero first learned about them from one of his suppliers: they'd become famous for a few posters dedicated to detergents, fabrics, and Band-Aids. Cremonesi says, "Signor Michele was a volcano; he'd stay awake all night thinking up new ideas. We always enjoyed direct contact with him. We were charged with studying the company's logos and packaging. We designed the paper wrappings for the Mon Chéri very carefully: he wanted people to be able to see the ribbons clearly, giving them the sense of a pretty little gift. Then we moved on to the Supercrema. We presented a few proposals with red lettering, all in capitals, then in the end everyone decided to use a logo with all lowercase letters. The move to Nutella, after they'd chosen a name that was recognizable all over Europe, was quick."

Studio Stile chose a Helvetica Medium font. Cremonesi made the final decision, selecting "wooden club" characters that were quite popular during those years, with small, sans serif letters, meaning they lacked any terminations at the end of the typeface form. These are the terminations used in the classic Times font, which many books were printed in, because it is easier to read in long texts. Helvetica, on the other hand, is a font designed to draw attention to a logo. It was first created in 1957, in Switzerland, by the graphic artist Max Miedinger. After it was chosen for Nutella, it would be used throughout the 1970s by numerous companies for corporate logos, including 3M, BMW, Jeep, Panasonic, Tetra Pak, Toyota, and many others.

A DELIGHT TO SPREAD ON BREAD

The slogan for the first advertisements read: "A delight to spread on bread." Rossetti set that thick slice of bread on top of the jar filled with hazelnut cocoa cream in order to reassure mothers, who were distrustful of chocolate's nutritional value. "Bread and Nutella" is a binomial that Ferrero never questioned. The first advertisements in Italy, France, and Germany started with an image of a mother spreading the hazelnut cream on a slice of bread and offering it to her son. "*Nutella auf's Brot*" were the words on the label in Germany, which were meant to emphasize the connection with *Brot*, or bread, for the consumer right from the start. The ritual of spreading made it impossible for children to eat just the chocolate and not the bread. Giampaolo Fabris has this to say about this fundamental move, that experts today would refer to as a key marketing mix: "This changed the way people viewed chocolate in Italy. It was no longer thought of as a small, dark, expensive square of foodstuff, but as a cream to be spread on bread. This reassuring, homemade, protective, and maternal bread was to Nutella what milk was to other Ferrero products, with the famous slogan 'More milk and less cocoa.' Even the words 'vegetable preserve' were interpreted as confirmation of the product's innocuousness. It was an extremely intelligent choice, because Italians' relationship with chocolate was problematic to say the least. It was considered a food appropriate only for important occasions; one that was generally bad for you, and for children in particular."

In some European countries there was a strong prejudice against chocolate, especially in Italy and France. People said that chocolate "heated you up," "gave you pimples," and caused cavities. Science had already disproven these misconceptions, but they remained deeply rooted in the public consciousness all the same. Spreading Nutella on bread—a hearty healthy foodstuff—helped offset people's doubts. With Nutella, the eventual negative effects of cocoa were in some ways exorcized by the presence of bread. The company also focused on hazelnuts as a characteristic ingredient. But snack time wasn't the only moment attracting advertising agencies' attention. Breakfast was considered an appetizing moment for consumption right from the start. One ad read: "Serve it in the morning: Nutella provides a portion of the healthiest ingredients nature has to offer: sugar, hazelnuts, milk, and chocolate flavor. Spread on bread, it provides an excellent breakfast and puts people in a good mood. Work harder and feel more energized with Nutella in the morning!"

The initial decision to distribute the product in glasses or little jars designed specifically for Nutella is also worth appreciating. There were two reasons for this. First, it was a way to provide all families with a small, light portion that would keep the cost of the product down so that more people would be encouraged to try it as a morning spread. Second, it was a way to add further value to the product. Once the spreadable cream was finished, the glasses and jars could still be used at the dinner table.

Not long after the six-sided glass containers debuted in Italy, the company released as many as fourteen different versions: glasses for water, wine, even a beer mug. Every package was linked with the idea of reuse. In this manner Nutella containers, which became more and more beautiful and colorful with each new series, boasting new designs and images, remained on the family table at breakfast, lunch, and dinner: a constant product reminder. Today collectors exchange these early Nutella glasses, each with its own distinctive yellow, red, or blue decorations. Given that only one or two series were released each year, with different models available in each series, over a fifty-year period Ferrero released some seven or eight hundred different kinds of glassware containers. Therefore it is very likely that every Italian has drunk out of a Nutella glass at one time or another. And while Nutella glasses worked well in Italy, in France the cream was sold in glass *coupelles* that were perfect for fruit salad. In Germany the company decided that people wouldn't be drawn to these gift packages—in part because mustard was traditionally sold in similar, reusable glasses—and decided to try marketing a container that characterized the product.

One or two years after Nutella's debut, it began to be sold in a small, sleek, distinctive jar that has become a symbol of the product, as much as its Helvetica font lettering and the red "n" set against black lettering. The Pelikan jar, as this container was called inside the company owing to its vague resemblance to glass inkwells, was launched when people inside Ferrero realized that selling the product in glasses wasn't enough to give Nutella its own, specific product identity. Anyone could copy the system, filling glass jars with a similar hazelnut cream and thereby competing with Nutella. They had to design packaging that distinguished the product, custom-tailoring the look for a substance that had no inherent form of its own. They chose an appealing plastic jar, one for which it was easy to get the cream out of with a knife or a spoon. At first the Pelikan wasn't the best seller it is today (where it covers between 70 percent and 80 percent of the market share). In fact, less than a quarter of all Nutella sold was packaged in the Pelikan container. But it nevertheless became a fundamental communications tool, transforming the product into a recognizable icon, like the famous Coca-Cola bottle.

Starting with the official creation of Nutella in 1964, Ferrero used three key tools to build long-lasting success: marketing mix, packaging, and communications. The company paid constant attention to the consumer so that people were made aware of the value they'd receive by buying Nutella. In the beginning, the company gave its marketing campaigns a "foodstuff" approach, concentrating more on portions and ingredients than on relationships or the social aspect of its product. Nutella hadn't yet developed into the lovemark it is today. But once this new brand-identity position emerged, Ferrero would be ready to recognize and respond to it in the best way possible. The company knew how to adapt to the *zeitgeist*, the spirit of the times.

3

Building the Nutella lovemark

In today's "culture of desire," some products have the power to make us dream. But not all of these are transformed into iconic brands. A top brand doesn't automatically become an icon and even a huge investment by its producing company won't necessarily make a difference. The process is at once spontaneous, complicated, and determined by the consumers who take possession of a given product. Often a simple, well-chosen logo design—although unquestionably important—isn't enough either. This is most clearly the case in immediately recognizable brands, as the global analyst for Millward Brown, Nigel Hollis, notes in the book *How Brands Become Icons*: "The shape of a VW beetle is unique, Lego bricks are familiar from childhood, and McDonald's arches are readily identifiable in any landscape." But most of these are products that have become deeply rooted in the culture of one or more countries—consumer goods that manage to satisfy the collective needs, anxieties, and desires of a great number of people because they offer something more than merely functional benefits. Analysts, for example, have even included the Red Cross among such lists: everybody everywhere knows what that red cross on a white background represents. Other classic examples of instantly recognizable brands include Coca-Cola, Apple, Google, Subway, Zippo, Veuve Cliquot, Adidas, Ikea, Nike, and others.

But it takes a fair amount of time in order for a brand to embody its myth. And while pop icons also stem from personalities in music or politics—such as the Rolling Stones, Madonna, Elvis Presley, Gandhi, or Che Guevara—contemporary culture isn't the only place where certain figures are identified as models worth emulating. The phenomenon is as ancient as mankind, with rituals and tales that have helped real events withstand the tests of time. Classical mythology, from the Greek word *mythos*, meaning a fable or tale, has offered immortal protagonists and the stories that belong to them: Aphrodite (or Venus, for the Romans), a goddess born of sea foam who embodies beauty; Dionysus (or Bacchus), who is related to wine and partying; King Midas, who stands for wealth; Icarus, who symbolizes man's presumptuousness. Can simply anything become myth? French philosopher and semiotician Roland Barthes (1915–1980) believed so. In his classic book *Mythologies* (1957; English trans. 1972), he wrote that every object can pass from a mute existence to an "oral state": "Myth is a system of communication; it is a message."

Iconic brands manage to stay forever young because they bridge generations and establish an emotional relationship with the consumer. Cult products speak to the heart as well as to the mind. They even go so far as to create an affectionate connection, becoming "lovemarks," as Kevin Roberts, CEO of Saatchi & Saatchi, writes in his book *Lovemarks: The Future Beyond Brands* (2004), published as a crisis in global brands was just beginning. Roberts maintained that brands had run out of juice. There were a number of reasons for this, for example brands being overused and companies being unable to understand new consumers, as well as brands being "smothered by creeping conservatism."

It may sound hard to believe, but even though Nutella has been on the market for over fifty years, it has never risked "running out of gas." The people who take care of its image, who have chosen its ad campaigns or modified its market position, have always known how to adapt the marketing mix to the times, as well as to the brand's identity and experiences. And once that spreadable cream became a lovemark—at different times in different national markets—the work Ferrero's managers had to face may have become even more difficult. There's always a risk of messing things up, as Roberts stated all too clearly: "Lovemarks inspire loyalty beyond reason and are owned by the people who love them."

A LOVEMARK IS BORN

Sometimes, in order for a successful brand to be transformed into a brand people love, a generational shift is required. This is what happened to Nutella in Europe. But, today, thanks to social media, everything happens much more quickly. Even in the world of technology, the process is far more rapid, as smartphones and iPads—devices few can live without today—have shown. The same is true of cars, sometimes the object of "blast from the past" intuition on the part of companies, for example the Volkswagen Beetle and the Mini Minor in Europe, or the Chevrolet Corvette in the United States, an American sports car produced by GM that has now reached its seventh generation. But we mustn't confuse nostalgia with an authentic cultural and emotional identity, one that is capable of extending beyond mere useful value. When it comes to foodstuffs, during the design and launch phases of a new specialty people are often unable to predict the way it will be welcomed by consumers, even when the most sophisticated techniques have been used to create them. This was the case for Coca-Cola, but also for Pringles potato chips, Chupa-Chups lollipops, Martini vermouth, Oreo cookies, and lots of other popular consumer products that have become iconic in our times by word of mouth. As Italian photographer Oliviero Toscani, who became famous for the ad campaigns he created for Benetton, writes in his preface to *CoolBrands*, a book that brings together a selection of the coolest brands chosen by Superbrands for Italy (and which includes Nutella): "No great brand is born of the banal presumption that it will have mass appeal, but of the drive and quality of an individual, or of a niche, that over time spontaneously spreads to everyone."

This brand has to have a cultural and cerebral dimension as well. In other words, it has to carve out a niche for itself in people's minds through names, slogans, logos, packaging, and advertising. Sometimes images are enough: for example the Swoosh, Nike's logo; the golden arches outside McDonald's; or the two superimposed arrowheads of Citroën. Sometimes it needs a timely idea. This is true of several retail brands that are based on value aspirations: Whole Foods Market, an American chain store selling natural and organic foods; Starbucks, the most popular coffee shop among young people the world over; Eataly, the "high-quality Italian food" chain created by Oscar Farinetti, inaugurated in Turin in 2007 and now also established in Chicago, New York, Dubai, Istanbul, and all over Italy.

Sometimes a carefully planned marketing mix makes it possible to "build" an icon brand in a very short time. This is what happened in Italy with Mulino Bianco cookies, created by the Italian company Barilla—a brand famous for its pasta, but that also specializes in oven-baked goods—in 1975, during a period when the company had American owners. A fortuitous Italian ad campaign that ran during the 1990s even managed to turn the ancient Tuscan mill in the Siena province where the commercial was shot by Academy Award–winning Italian filmmaker Giuseppe Tornatore into a tourist destination. Giovanni Ferrero, the current CEO of Ferrero, focused on this event in his book *Marketing Progetto 2000* (Marketing Project 2000), which he wrote in 1990: "Even before it was a marketing operation, Mulino Bianco was a cultural operation. To be precise, one should say that Mulino Bianco became an important marketing operation precisely because it was presented as a cultural operation. With respect to traditional marketing philosophy, Mulino Bianco was a revolution: instead of offering a greater quantity of products, or betting on merchandising formulas and contents, Barilla presented the market with an unexpected set of values and a rich symbolic world with reference to the food market and confectionary in particular." The mill was transformed from mere *sign*, to *symbol* of goodness, health, and naturalness thanks in part to cookies sold in bags made of loose, soft paper like the kind bakers used generations ago.

But for a product to become legendary there has to be something more. It's not enough for it to be famous, it has to be venerated. These are objects that are neither "in vogue," nor appear as status symbols. They are not best sellers, but become iconic. They can be cult objects produced by a brand—like Ferrari cars—or individual models (like the Adidas flip-flops worn by Mark Zuckerberg, the founder of Facebook). Sometimes cult objects are released in small batches and intended as luxury products, like Chanel's No. 5 perfume, first created in 1921, or the Omega Seamaster Diver 300 wristwatch, associated with James Bond. Sometimes, as with Nutella and Swatch watches, they number in the millions. In order to understand the phenomenon of Nutella, you need to remember that cult merchandise can provoke an emotional response that continues over time, even for fifty years or more.

At this point, what does the marketing team need to do in order to protect and conserve this patrimony? Kevin Roberts explains this as well in his book: "Lovemarks could not be constrained by the world defined by brands and marketing. Sure, this world was important, but Lovemarks had to be open to more. Open to the local and to the global. To connect with people as well as services. Places as well as products. The object people make themselves as well as what they buy."

Hence, the legendary character of a product does not merely depend on its usefulness or intrinsic qualities. But is that really the case with Nutella? Not exactly. Nutella's properties—a soft, spreadable cream that hints at the magical world of chocolate even though it's not actually chocolate; the inviting smell of hazelnuts, a delicious daily breakfast treat—exist alongside its legendary connotations: a memory to spread on bread; a jarful of desire that placates daily anxiety; the Holy Grail of indulgence. If it weren't so good, it would have never become what it is today. A legend needs ritual if it is to spread. And, in fact, Nutella Parties gather together people who share the same credo; people exchange expressions of adoration for Nutella on social networks; symbolic simulacra appear on T-shirts, baseball caps, and other objects destined for daily use (such as mouse pads, teacups, and even toasters); associations that unite people with a single passion are created, both online and in public manifestations.

To paraphrase Marshall McLuhan, the jar becomes the message, before ascending to myth. The hazelnut cream has by now become a medium, like radio, press, television, electricity, photography, comic strips, games. And so over the past fifty years filmmakers, theater directors, artists, singers, writers, journalists, and politicians have appropriated Nutella as their own to express other concepts: indulgence, happiness, nostalgia, sharing.

THE FIRST ICONS IN ITALY

An enormous, six-sided glass, standing taller than a dinner table, filled with enticing, spreadable cream. On a table, a white-and-red-checkered tablecloth, a bowl with homemade bread cut into thick slices, and a large knife. It's nighttime, and a young man sits in the kitchen, completely naked, his face unshaved. Sighing with pleasure, he starts spreading the bread with that cream and devouring his consolatory meal. The actor, Nanni Moretti, is also the director of the movie, called *Bianca* and released in Italy in 1984. He was around thirty at the time, and would later release *La stanza del figlio* (*The Son's Room*; winner of the Palm d'Or at the Cannes Film Festival in 2001) and *Habemus Papam* (*We Have a Pope*), a 2011 film that presaged Pope Benedict XVI's decision to abandon the papacy. The main character here is Professor Michele Apicella (played by Moretti), who falls in love with his colleague Bianca (Laura Morante), only to be overwhelmed by doubts and guilt after making love to her. He copes with these feelings by eating bread and Nutella which he gets out of a huge jar.

Whenever they think of Nutella, Italy's baby boomers can still see that scene: it made the movie *Bianca* a key step in the building of a legend. Nanni Moretti was eleven years old when the hazelnut cream first went on sale, and Nutella was deeply rooted in his childhood memories. The director has never been fond of talking about his movies, but during a meeting with students in Rome, he did admit that Nutella should be understood as a sort of youthful internationalization; a passport to the world. Then he laughed, adding: "In Paris they asked me, 'Is Nutella this famous in Italy, too?'"

Nutella took another important step toward longstanding celebrity when it was included (and exalted) in a number of books. In *Qualità: scènes d'objets à l'italienne* ("Quality: Scenes of Objects Italian-Style"; published in France in 1990), Italian journalist Rita Cirio selects roughly seventy objects that are part of Italian life: the Ferrari, the Olivetti 22, the Moka-Express, pizza, Parmigiano-Reggiano cheese, mortadella, breadsticks, and, of course, Nutella. "If a pop artist wished to paint a contemporary version of a Renaissance banquet, the sumptuously laden table would be covered with foodstuffs connected with mass consumption, reflecting the leveling of international tastes: a Campbell soup can, a hamburger dripping with bloodred ketchup, a bottle of foamy Coca-Cola, and, for dessert, in a minor digression from American flavors, a jar of Nutella." After mentioning Nanni Moretti's film, Rita Cirio continues: "Entire generations have been raised on its flavour that tastes like chocolate, but isn't chocolate, as well as its soft, sweetish, and slightly sticky consistency, a sort of Proustian madeleine, both spreadable and collective." This is a cult quote, an allusion to the novel *À la recherche du temps perdu (Remembrance of Things Past)*, in which Marcel Proust recalls the madeleines he once enjoyed with tea in the house of his Aunt Léonie in Combray, France.

Among the many explanations for Nutella's success, the connection with childhood memories takes center stage. Of course, it all depends on one's age. Italian writer Umberto Eco once noted, "For people like me, who experienced childhood before the War, Nutella is not a fetish object, and doesn't inspire any Proustian reflections. But I imagine it does for my children."

In Italy, Nutella's fame was further reinforced by two books written in 1993 and 1994 by a celebrated cabaret performer, Riccardo Cassini. The two books sold a total of one million copies, enjoying unexpected success, thanks to a parody of *sbafatio* ("eating") in mangled Latin (*Nutella nutellae*, the first) and twisted English (*Nutella 2—La vendetta*, the second). The second piece artfully blended broken English and Neapolitan dialect: "Once upon a time, many many many, ma *'na cifra* [an expression that means 'a whole lot' in Neapolitan dialect] of many years ago, at the beginning of the initiation of the *mond* [world], there was the chaos. One day, God—God is the *nome d'art* of *Dio*—, God, who was *disoccupated* [unemployed] had a *folgorant* [dazzling] idea and so God created the *Nutell* [Nutella]. And God saw that the Nutella was good, very good, good *'na cifra*." In 2001 maestro Antonello Lerda even produced an opera, *Nutellam Cantata*, featuring soprano and baritone singers and a Bacchanalian-style parody set to music by Stravinsky and Kurt Weill.

During those same years the underground rock group Susy Likes Nutella was founded in Florence, and in 1995 two famous Italian singers—Giorgio Gaber, a darling of shrewd, cultured intellectuals; and Renato Zero, a pop icon for more than one generation of fans—mentioned Nutella in their songs. In "Destra-sinistra" ("Right-left") Gaber sang about Nutella as an icon of the Italian left wing, as opposed to Swiss chocolate, which was a symbol of the right wing.

Only in Italy could people create an ideological dispute over a hazelnut cream, as the Italian correspondent for the *International Herald Tribune* would note a few years later in an article published on December 10, 2004, entitled "The Politics of Nutella." It began with a question that may appear strange to the uninitiated: "Is Nutella, the chocolate hazelnut spread, left- or right-wing?" A few lines later, the journalist noted that Nutella is actually "nationalpopular," and that, in fact, of the many Nutella Parties held in the 1990s in Italy, the first was "organized by Prime Minister Silvio Berlusconi's rightist Forza Italia party."

From film to books and music, by the mid-1990s Nutella's bipartisan immortality had come full circle, and the figurative arts and public celebrations were soon to follow.

IN THE ITALIAN DICTIONARY

Marketing experts all fear the vulgarization of the brand. This happens when a brand becomes such an intrinsic part of everyday language that it is identified with a type of product; when consumers and the media use it in antonomasia to refer indiscriminately to a kind of product, no matter which company makes the original. This happened to Biro pens, the Jacuzzi, the Jeep, and many other famous products. The Sony Walkman is an extreme example: once "walkman" became part of the common vernacular, Austria's Supreme Court ruled that it could be used to indicate any portable device designed to reproduce music, denying the multinational company exclusive rights.

Nutella's official consecration came with an entry in Devoto-Oli's *Dizionario della lingua italiana* (Dictionary of the Italian language), included in April 1995: "*nutella* s.f. (nu-tél-la) *Nome commerciale di una diffusissima crema a base di nocciole e cioccolato* [The commercial name of a popular cream made with hazelnuts and chocolate]." The publishing company that produced the dictionary—Le Monnier in Florence—immediately received a letter from Ferrero, asking that the publishers add a note indicating that Nutella is an official trademark, insofar as it "cannot be used generically as a term for all hazelnut-and-cocoa-based creams." According to Ferrero's legal department, "The expression 'Nutella' is a globally registered trademark produced by Ferrero, and used by the company to identify its own specific product produced with hazelnuts and cocoa, and as such this trademark can only be used exclusively for Ferrero's product."

The publishing house in Florence received similar letters of protest from Jacuzzi and Dow Italia for having included "Jacuzzi" and "Domopak" in the entries in its *Devoto-Oli*. Le Monnier moved quickly in its own defense, communicating (through its own lawyers), that the definition of these entries as "commercial names" was not intended to indicate general terms, but included the concept of "registered brands," which would be added in the next edition of the dictionary.

Debate sprang up among linguists as well. Interviewed by the Italian daily *Corriere della Sera*, Gian Carlo Oli replied that "the line and a half I've dedicated to the entry 'nutella' reads: the commercial name of a popular cream made with hazelnuts and chocolate. The use of the term 'commercial name' is precisely what protects me from dispute. Then again, what would you say about aspirin? It's the commercial name of acetylsalicylic acid, registered in 1899 by a well-known German pharmaceutical company, but at this point it has become a part of everyday language, and you can quite reasonably write it in lowercase letters." Some people spoke up, defending the Devoto-Oli dictionary in various newspapers, emphasizing their view that the word "Nutella" belonged to everyone. And that's precisely the point: it had become a lovemark. But it was nevertheless a brand. And in fact in the end, the company won. In the next edition of the dictionary, the entry read: "*nutella* s.f. (nu-tél-la) The commercial name of a popular cream made with hazelnuts and chocolate (*registered trademark*)."

FRANCE'S NUTELLA GÉNÉRATION

Media and technology have made it possible for every brand to take advantage of the imaginary dimensions of consumption, especially in the era of Internet and social media, when production and consumption live side by side. Today, people calculate a brand's value through various parameters, the first of which is brand awareness, or, in other words, how well a consumer is familiar with a given product. This, in turn, is measured based on recognition of the brand when a person sees it, and on the spontaneous memory of it when he or she thinks of a product category. Nutella is an almost automatic connection among spreadable creams, but the brand isn't always mentioned for the reasons Ferrero might like. In the cases of Nanni Moretti and Riccardo Cassini, people around Italy were putting emphasis on a sort of gluttonous and not particularly "nutritional" consumption.

But once Nutella became a muse for art, its brand equity grew more easily. During the 1990s European painters and musicians began to mention Nutella in their work, helping the product acquire a legendary kind of aura. The forerunner of this trend of using products in the figurative arts was Andy Warhol, who in 1962 exhibited his painting *Big Campbell's Soup Can, 19¢ (Beef Noodle)*. In France, for years Ferrero utilized a Warholian image of Nutella created with a color solarization technique. Painters have always found food evocative. Just consider the fruit and vegetables that Italian Renaissance artist Giuseppe Arcimboldo used in the portraits he painted at the end of the sixteenth century, or the beautiful serving maid whom Jean-Étienne Liotard painted in 1744, a *trembleuse* of hot chocolate in one hand. Sometimes industries have relied directly on artists' contributions: during the 1930s Italian companies Campari and Aperol selected brilliant ideas put forth by futurist artists to create advertising for their products; in 1969 the Spanish surrealist genius Salvador Dalí drew the logo for Chupa-Chups lollipops.

In 1991, an art exhibition held at the Palazzo dei Diamanti in Ferrara, Italy, entitled *Mistiche Nutelle* (organized by a group of Italian painters influenced by pop art), attempted to represent "the mystical in art, united with a need to reconnect with childhood." But the first authentic celebration of Nutella took place in 1996 in Paris at the prestigious Carrousel du Louvre, where the exhibition *Génération Nutella* (organized to celebrate the cream's thirty-year anniversary in France) was held. The artwork, produced by a number of different thirty-something artists (Philippe Decouflé, Caro et Jeunet, Kristian Gavoille, and Frank Margerin, among others) included a *machine à tartiner*—a machine created to spread Nutella automatically on a slice of bread. The piece was interactive and fun, and kids loved it. The machine's creator, François de la Rozière, art director of the street theater company La Machine, managed to make his machine a peripatetic production, traveling around numerous cities across France on a twenty-year tour, from Nantes to Toulouse and Calais, and ultimately to the Grand Palais in Paris, inspiring young and old alike. Dancer Toni Vighetto performed an acrobatic dance piece atop an enormous croissant. And Patrice Ferrasse invented the wordplay via telephone "*Nu t'es là?*" ("Are you there naked?"). Within the prestigious underground gallery located alongside the famous Parisian museum, jewelry by Sonia Rykiel, lithographs by Niki de Saint Phalle, Ray-Ban sunglasses, clothing designed by Paco Rabanne, films by Pedro Almodóvar, songs by Charles Aznavour, and drawings by Wolinsky were all put on display as part of the event. Children were given a chance to use Ante Vojnovic's *Scarabée*, which invited them to create words and sentences using the seven letters in "Nutella."

To complete this initiative, among the most original ever created around Nutella, a survey was conducted by the organizers that aimed to discover the values, tastes, and passions of thirty-something French citizens within a test group of 608 French men and women aged thirty to forty. The main element to emerge from these interviews was a *joie de vivre* that characterized this generation, particularly when it came to family: 67 percent of those interviewed were convinced that theirs was the most wonderful age of life. The people who conducted the survey also noticed that thirty-somethings who liked Nutella were on average more enthusiastic (69 percent of those interviewed) about life than those who didn't like it. Everybody wants to stay young: "happiness, delicious meals, and enthusiasm" were the values they took away from their childhoods. The pamphlet that accompanied the exhibition concluded: "The Nutella generation are comfortable being themselves. They see themselves in a family of like-minded folks, one that maintains the best parts of childhood, and at the same time they are preparing to have children of their own, a goal available to everyone. Most of these thirty-something people ate Nutella when they were young, and all of them remember wonderful times, pleasure, good flavors, vitality, and youthfulness connected with this 'modern-day Proustian madeleine.' This memory connection is so strong that it is rendered concrete today with a generational shift: these people are in turn giving Nutella to their own children. The brand has accompanied them in daily life across several generations: people in the 1970s, the 'liberation' years; those concentrating on careers in the 1980s; and those who've experienced the 'crisis' of the 1990s. Nutella first arrived in France in 1966, and has sold more than 600 million jars since it was launched. But today's generation of thirty-somethings stands alone. Now they've gotten their lives underway, despite difficult economic times, and have managed to escape the general unhappiness thanks to something they've been able to maintain, and which in turn maintains them: a sort of escape route, a safety valve. They've kept a 'little child' alive and thriving inside themselves. This childlike component, fundamentally happy, colorful, playful and healthy, has been expressed through the creativity of artists in their generation, no matter what their chosen expressive method may be."

CELEBRATED IN THE *NEW YORKER*

What may well be the most surprising article was published in the March 6, 1995, issue of the *New Yorker*, a sophisticated literary weekly that chose to publish a piece telling Americans about a product venerated by Italians. In the prestigious pages of "The Talk of the Town," writer Andrea Lee—who lives in Italy and is the author of a well-reviewed book of short stories, *Interesting Women* (2002)—dedicated an ironic article to the Italian cream, entitled "Guilt, Politics, and Eros in a Jar," in which she advised her compatriots to try Nutella because it would help them free themselves from their inferiority complex toward the Mediterranean diet. Lee wrote: ". . . defining Nutella—pronounced 'noo-tella'—as a gooey hazelnut-and-chocolate spread that comes in a jar is a bit like describing the David of Michelangelo as a large carved piece of marble. Like any inspired creation, Nutella has an animating spirit that takes it beyond its physical components. Shamelessly sweet but not too sweet, more unctuous than peanut butter but with the same curiously sexy capacity for gluing the jaws together, and intensely chocolate-flavored but with a peculiar pillowy mildness that appeals to regressive urges, it is made to be spread on bread but more often ends up being eaten in hasty spoonfuls, straight from the jar."

Citing melodic Italian singer-songwriter Gianni Morandi,

the first Nutella Party held by Silvio Berlusconi's political party, and books by Cassini, the author reminds her readers that "the increasing national love for Nutella kept pace with Italy's four-decade journey from poverty to world industrial power. Everybody under fifty seems to have childhood Nutella memories of blissful afterschool snacks, of midnight raids on the kitchen nooks where Mamma hid the jar." The article closes with the following invitation to all Americans: "Some jars have been sighted in supermarkets across the country, but not nearly enough for these unsettled times. There is no reason that New World citizens should not look to the Old World for solutions. After all, it was a proto-Italian commentator who came up with one of the earliest and best suggestions for keeping a nation happy. Instead of bread and circuses, we can easily make do with bread and chocolate." Twenty years later, the sleek jar of spreadable cream would win the hearts of consumers lined up at the checkouts in Walmart and supermarkets across America, changing the habits of people who were mostly accustomed to spreading peanut butter.

CONTENT GENERATED BY INSPIRATIONAL CONSUMERS

Tim Sanders, an executive at Yahoo!, once said, "For the company, they become the buzz marketing arm." These are "inspirational consumers," in other words "people who turn others on to your service [or product] and recommend it highly," according to the definition Kevin Roberts provides in *Lovemarks*. They are the protagonists of Nutella's transformation from foodstuff to icon, autonomously generating "veneration" content for their favorite brand. Prior to the digital era, they weren't easy to calculate, and could only be traced through spontaneous endorsements published in newspapers, books, theater pieces, or art shows. Once the web era began, these forms of communication were given a precise name: UGC, or User-Generated Content. In order for something to be considered UGC, it is important that it demonstrate several characteristics outlined by the OECD (Organization for Economic Cooperation and Development): they have to be published on a website or social network; they must be the product of real and true creative effort; and they must be created outside the routines or practices of a professional environment.

The real digital boom came with the celebration of Nutella's fiftieth anniversary, thanks to the website www.nutellastories. com, where memories provided by fans from all over the world were gathered together to create the first truly global communications campaign. Marketers wooed the interest of inspired consumers: "Waking up together around the breakfast table, birthdays with friends, special events . . . In the end everybody has a special Nutella memory!" And in just a few months' time a deluge of "love testimonies" flooded in for the brand: almost eighty thousand personal stories including drawings, videos, photographs, poetry, and short stories (discussed further in chapter 11 dedicated to the fiftieth anniversary). Dozens and dozens of celebrities (see the playlist on page 259) continue to declare themselves fans of Nutella without being official spokespersons selected by Ferrero. The latest and speediest of social networks, Twitter, generates viral phenomena not so much when it speaks directly about the brand, but when the brand becomes the object of its conversations. For example, a tweet posted by Lady Gaga on January 26, 2011: "Ok. Firstly, yes I love Nutella (with Banana+Wonderbread) who doesn't. Secondly, I can't believe 'Edge of Glory' was trending, sneakymonsters!" Stefani Germanotta, aka New York singer Lady Gaga, has more than 41 million followers, and is among the top ten most-followed Twitter accounts in the world, together with pop stars Katy Perry, Justin Bieber, and President Barack Obama.

And the Internet is only one side of fans' appreciation. Starting in the 1990s, they began organizing and conducting thousands of Nutella Parties all over Italy. Every year since 2000 in the small town of Alba, thousands of young people gather in the main piazza to celebrate the New Year with their beloved Nutella. Little by little the web has helped this local celebration go global. The idea was the brainchild of Sara Rosso, an Italian-American digital strategist who lives in Milan, together with her friend Michelle Fabio, an Italian-American lawyer who became a freelance writer and editor. Since 2007 they have organized World Nutella Day, held every February 5. The date has nothing to do with the history of Ferrero's product, but was in part inspired by the French holiday La Chandeleur, or Candlemas, which is held around the same time, and which is celebrated with crêpes, many of which include a Nutella filling. In just a few years the popularity of Nutella has grown to the point where it is rare to find a restaurant, bakery, or pastry shop in large American cities that doesn't offer some specialty inspired by the famous hazelnut cream. The World Nutella Day Facebook page now has 46,000 subscribers, and Sara Rosso shared her story on Ferrero's website as part of Nutella's fiftieth anniversary celebrations, thereby moving beyond a misunderstanding that had arisen between the blogger and Ferrero's legal offices, which had asked her to stop using the brand name unduly. An official company press release ended the disagreement once and for all: "Ferrero considers itself fortunate to have Nutella fans as devoted and loyal as Sara Rosso."

And what's more important than a book? After the Italian satire created with *Nutella nutellae*, there have been dozens of volumes (especially recipe books) dedicated to the jar of spreadable cream. In Italy and France there are some forty-odd books published on the subject in each country. Germany has around twenty books, while America's Library of Congress hosts a dozen different titles "*alla* Nutella" in its stacks. The authors are important chefs, recipe writers, bloggers, and pastry chefs who have created unusual specialties based on Nutella.

And where haute cuisine takes an interest in Nutella, could fashion be far behind? In 2006, the Gilli Nutella Cube was created based on a design by the Sciolla Company. Described as the "most delicious handbag in the world," one hundred limited-edition versions of the brown-and-white leather bag were produced, each sporting vertical stitching at the base of the handles designed to mimic the jar's lid. This fashion accessory debuted on the catwalk in the hands of professional tennis player Daniela Hantuchová and several different Italian actresses. Later, during First Ladies' day in Rome as part of the G8 convention held in Italy in July 2009, all the First Ladies attending received the Gilli handbag as a gift, including American First Lady Michelle Obama.

In the United States, after a long and somewhat "silent" presence on supermarket shelves, in recent years the hazelnut cream's popularity has soared. Just consider the long lines of eager consumers that formed outside the Nutella Bar in Eataly in Chicago and New York City. There have even been a few curious episodes, like the "theft" of jars of Nutella at Columbia University in New York City. This "scandal" started in February 2013 at the Ferris Booth Commons campus cafeteria, which serves meals to roughly three thousand students every day. When the cafeteria changed from providing Nutella spread on crêpes just on the weekends to offering Nutella on its daily menu, consumption of the cream exploded, reaching 45 kilograms (100 pounds) per day. Students were filling up teacups or stealing full jars and sneaking them up to their rooms, stocking up for midnight snacking or stress relief during exams.

What may well be the most surprising Nutella celebration took place in June 2014, in Seattle, at an event organized by the CEO and founder of Amazon, Jeff Bezos, to present his innovative Fire Phone: a smartphone featuring an incorporated camera and software designed to recognize and identify any object. The user need only aim the camera at something—a book, TV series, or music—in order to receive information about it and even buy the identified thing directly on Amazon. Firefly, the software, can identify up to a hundred million different objects quickly and effectively. During the press conference and demonstration, Bezos used the phone to identify a jar of Nutella: an iconic brand that everyone is familiar with, used as a paradigm of a fast-moving consumer product.

PART TWO
Nutella social

4

TV, sweet TV

Try doing this: just say the word Nutella to someone. You'll notice that his or her face will light up, a smile may appear, and they'll probably say something like, "Ah, Nutella . . ." What you're actually seeing is over fifty years of investment, money Ferrero has spent on a marketing mix made up of the "four Ps" proposed by McCarthy and Kotler: setting up an effective *promotion*; maintaining a convenient *price* with respect to the quality offered; taking care of the relationship with *place* (in other words, distribution and sales points); and remaining loyal to the *product* through three unshakeable certainties. For Nutella, these certainties are:

1. *taste and creamy texture*, thanks to an *original recipe* based on seven simple ingredients, blended together with *expertise from decades of craftsmanship*, the *"never-ending pursuit of quality"* (as Ferrero company documents attest);

2. the Pelikan-shaped glass jar (a nod to the distinctive Pelikan ink bottle), designed in the 1960s and capped with its *golden foil* seal, which guarantees and protects the integrity of the cream inside the jar; and

3. the brand's logo set against a white background, accompa-

nied by the image of a *knife spreading* Nutella on bread, with hazelnuts and a glass of milk to one side.

For decades, Nutella has always remained the same. This is the first secret of its success: its DNA has never changed, even when everything else has, and society has become liquid, voluble, and unstable. Even a drop in consumption failed to create any problems for the brand. Despite the widespread crisis that has enveloped the global economy since 2008, Nutella has maintained its market position, even registering some increases in sales. In the United States alone, if all the jars sold daily were stacked one on top of the other, their height would reach three times that of the Empire State Building.

This kind of global success can only be explained through the eternal youth of this spreadable hazelnut cream born in a small town in northern Italy in 1964: its popularity has never waned because the product lifecycle has been replaced by a promotion lifecycle. Nutella is the David Copperfield of sweets— the Houdini of mass-market delectability. But the company's main objective for Nutella has remained unchanged, and is the same for all the company's specialties: to make sure their products aren't restricted to seasonal sales, as is often the case for certain types of chocolate, *panettone* (Christmas cake), and chocolate Easter eggs. When Supercrema hit shelves in Italian *drogherie* (delicatessens), Tartinoise in French *supermarchés* (supermarkets), and Nusscreme in *Lebensmittelgeschäft* (grocery stores) across Germany, Ferrero's ad emphasized the cream's energy value. A few years later Nutella left its "predecessor" behind, and spread to food stores all over Europe, introduced to consumers as delicious food that could be eaten for breakfast as well as an outstanding source of energy for children. And so Nutella made its way onto shopping lists in many different countries. This had several consequences for marketing: careful management of product quality and freshness; constant attention paid to sales points through promotions, showcasing, and formats; and the need to continuously renew and refresh people's consideration of the brand.

This careful strategy was the only way Nutella could conquer an unshakeable market share among clients (all the more rare for a foodstuff). In a presentation of novel Apple products, Steve Jobs emphasized that in its own small way, his company was working to make the world a better place. His products were viewed as a way to remain constantly connected to friends and the information world, even before they were seen as status symbols. The vision of Pietro Ferrero and his successors, his son Michele and grandsons Pietro and Giovanni, has always been the same: talking to consumers through products and products alone, distributing—spreading, even—a little happiness around the world. One of the first TV commercials for Supercrema in Italy, broadcast at the beginning of the 1960s, ended with a rhythmic, rhyming song:

Ferrero
davvero davvero
la nostra vita
più dolce fa.

("Ferrero
truly, truly
makes our world
a sweeter place.")

ABOVE AND BELOW THE LINE

When Michele Ferrero, barely thirty years old, found himself running the company that had been founded by his father, all of the business that was done was guided by one simple key word: sell, sell, sell. People weren't aware of the sophisticated marketing techniques we're familiar with today. The world of poster advertising had just been left behind: a new advertising era had arrived, and television was ready to take the lead. Investing in TV became a priority for Ferrero right from the start. Michele oversaw ad campaigns personally, just as he had the packaging and naming of Nutella. During the 1970s in Pino Torinese—a small hilltop town located outside Turin where the company's headquarters were established, while production facilities were left in Alba—he founded the company agency Pubbliregia, which enabled him to maintain close, personal control of the entire advertising cycle, from creation to promotion: he wanted to keep the launch of new products a closely kept secret. Right from the start, Ferrero's advertising agency was the most international of its kind in Italy, boasting professionals from all over the world. These included Ernest Dichter, an Austrian-American psychologist considered by many to be the father of motivational research, responsible for inventing focus groups designed to understand and interpret consumer needs.

Back then brands still controlled the media. Up until the advent of the digital era, company investments were conventionally classified with one of two acronyms: ATL (Above the Line) or BTL (Below the Line). The definitions were derived from the world of accounting: "above the line" expenses were those included in the capital account and put into the budget; while those "below the line" were current expenses and considerably lower. There is also another acronym, TTL (Through the Line), used when agencies and their clients adopt an integrated communications program. In other words, while ATL is used to indicate media destined for a large, nonspecific mass public (i.e. radio, television, cinema, newspapers, billboards, and, ultimately, even the Internet), BTL is used to indicate niche marketing aimed at specific targets (i.e. sponsorships, public relations, direct marketing, direct promotions within sales points).

But today, in the digital era, marketing has been divided into four separate categories: paid, owned, earned, and shared.

- *Paid media* are classic advertising spaces, including commercials, newspaper ads, and billboards. They're something the company "pays for" in order to familiarize people with its brand, and are considered a valid means of reaching a desired target, due to the work that the people running the given vehicle (TV, newspaper, etc.) have already conducted.

- *Owned media* are just that: media the company "owns" in its own right and over which it exercises direct control. These can be websites or blogs, print publications, or even accounts on social networks like YouTube or Facebook. In other words, media that make it possible for the company to keep the brand's authoritativeness intact.

- *Earned media* are "earned" channels, or, in other words, what is generated in the media through public relations efforts, including articles, critiques, or reviews that offer outside endorsement or support.

- *Shared media* are social networks through which the brand "distributes" its content, like Facebook or Twitter accounts, or videos broadcast on YouTube. The company can decide content, but the platform's player can change the rules and functions; they add value precisely because they get the consumer directly involved. These media were originally called "word of mouth"; today they're known as *buzz marketing*.

Ferrero's marketing genius has been to find ways to use all four of these channels. In the beginning, investment was put in ATL, a tack that was used until the 1990s. Then funds were channeled to BTL through sports sponsorships in basketball and soccer, the Champions League, and deals with national sports teams in Italy, France, and Germany.

BRAND CONTENT

Many experts are convinced that the brand is a medium, insofar as it is a "socializing agent." But exactly what content does it convey? Today Nutella does not limit itself to satisfying nutritional needs or particular sensorial demands; it generates sensations and feelings in the consumer, establishing a sort of mutual understanding. During the 1970s, however, it was important to familiarize parents with the product's nutritional qualities through a top-down communications model.

The first rules for determining an ad campaign tend to be identifying both product positioning and the potential target consumers, as accurately as possible. The concept of product positioning didn't become part of marketing lingo until the 1980s, when it began to be used to indicate "that which the brand represents in the mind of both current and potential consumers, in terms of benefits and promise, including in relation to a competitive market," according to a definition provided by Lynn Upshaw, a professor at Berkeley, in *Building Brand Identity* (1995).

When the hazelnut cream first appeared in the 1960s in Europe, introducing a new merchandise category, it was deliberately presented as a modern, innovative specialty that could substitute jams and jellies or honey, considered to be something that belonged to the past. Nutella was positioned as a new, healthy, nutritional product made with natural ingredients. Therefore it became a "nutritional classic," with educational images detailing how it could be consumed. In ad campaigns, instead of targeting children, Ferrero focused on the parents doing the grocery shopping: for a number of years advertisements only showed mothers spreading the hazelnut cream on slices of bread for their kids. Then, during the 1980s, the focus shifted away from the mom and toward the child, who was pictured from close-up eating breakfast on their own, using a knife to spread the cream. In another series of commercials from that same period, young kids were replaced by teenagers, which marked the appearance of another very important theme in the brand's value: sociability.

Over the years, Nutella has consolidated a precise brand identity through brand signifiers that interact with one another over time:

- bread, highlighted in the first commercials together with the tag line, as well as a wooden cutting board hosting a loaf of bread, slices, a knife, two ears of wheat, and three cut daisies;

- family and children;

- hazelnuts and cocoa, presented as distinctive ingredients that characterize the product's flavor;

- breakfast and snack time are considered to be meals, just like lunch and dinner;

- the product's uniqueness, the fact that it is unlike any other product;

- the ritual of consumption, from twisting the jar open and peeling back the golden foil, to spreading the cream;

- an optimistic vision of a life nurtured with Nutella.

Even from the point of view of images, language, and the techniques employed, Nutella upheld several key rules:

- a limited use of famous movies or TV actors as spokespeople, because the brand had to be stronger than any individual;

- the use of sports champions, the category of spokespeople that well represented the world of Nutella. In Germany these included tennis player Boris Becker, skier Martina Ertl, windsurfing champ Björn Dunkerbeck, and soccer players (defined as *jungen Wilden*, or "wild youth") from Deutscher Fussball-Bund; in France, soccer player Youri Djorkaeff; in Spain, motorcycle racer Valentino Rossi; Brazilian national soccer player Kaká; and even the cook of Italy's national soccer team, Claudio Silvestri, together with national team former coach Cesare Prandelli;

- the use of cartoon heroes, both in TV commercials and in promotion campaigns conducted at sales points, as well as for a series of special glasses filled with Nutella: Disney characters; characters from Asterix stories; and Looney Tunes from Warner Bros.;

- a clear, straightforward message that eschewed special effects often used today in ad campaigns to sell cars or cell phones.

TV COMMERCIALS PART 1: EUROPE

Though it might at first seem like a handicap, Nutella was actually fortunate that it had to be introduced in each country as a new product, through a "pedagogical" communications program. According to Professor David A. Aaker of the University of California, Berkeley, this approach offered a unique advantage: "The brand relevance strategy is to create offerings so innovative that new categories and subcategories will be formed." In his book *Brand Relevance* (2010), Aaker goes so far as to cite

Sun Tzu, the great Chinese military strategist: "The way is to avoid what is strong and to strike at what is weak." This is because the brand has to know how to create a "competitive arena in which your competitors are at a decided disadvantage." Was this really how things were for Nutella? Before it could become a lovemark, an icon brand recognized and appreciated the world over, the first thing the company had to do was familiarize people with the product, make them aware that it could be spread on bread, that it was versatile and could be eaten along with fruit or other typical breakfast foods. Basically, Nutella had to clamber up onto what was already a crowded stage (rife with jams and jellies, honey, peanut butter, yeast extracts, cheese, cookies, and so on) and say to the consumer, "I'm here too, and I can give you more than all these other folks!"

This was the first step in Nutella's television advertising, created in the studios of Pubbliregia with contributions from individual "business units" (as they are referred to today) in each different country in order to help this new product "conquer" the masses. It was a media assault elaborated through numerous phases that changed according to continent, consumer habits, and competitors' reactions.

Nutella produced hundreds of TV commercials in some twenty-odd nations. These were a joyful procession of hazelnut cream spread on bread (as well as on waffles, pancakes, pita bread, and more); of children enjoying breakfast with their parents; of athletes confessing their passion for Nutella, and not devoid of a little entertaining irony. Over fifty years both the techniques used to tell the story and the quality of images have changed, but the product's DNA appears to be relatively unaltered. Nutella got its start in Italy, France, and Germany, then reached out to spread across the globe. Simply put, TV advertising tries to get consumers involved through the use of two different stimuli: emotion and rationality. When a TV commercial emphasizes emotional content, it attempts to inspire an impulsive, immediate purchase, without considering the characteristics of the product in question. When it emphasizes rationality, however, it draws out the intrinsic qualities of the product being sold: how useful it can be and the advantages it offers the person purchasing it.

Italy, France, Germany: 1964–73

British fashion designer Mary Quant invented the miniskirt, shocking respectable Brits across the nation. Songs by The Beatles and the Rolling Stones flooded the airwaves, while hippie protests flourished across the United States. On July 20, 1969, Neil Armstrong became the first man to set foot on the moon. Those were the magnificent 1960s, and the ad campaigns of that period adopted an educational, functional language that somehow clashed with the cultural revolution that was also taking place. Nutella had to adapt to the times as well. During this decade, Ferrero's communications focused on a straightforward objective: to win mothers over and convince them to let their children try Nutella for breakfast or lunch. The first TV commercials only ran in Italy, France, and Germany. All the commercials were set up the same way, but content varied from one country to the next depending on conditions in the local TV market. Black-and-white images of the product's debut gave way to tennis players on grassy courts, swimmers, and kids, all singing, "All for one, Nutella for all," playing on the famous battle cry of Alexandre Dumas's three musketeers. Some of the ads, for instance in France, were funny. In one of them, viewers watched a ramshackle road race, during which a race car driver suddenly rushed off the track to go stick his spoon in a jar of Ferrero's cream. In another commercial from 1971, a professor is trying to hold a "Nutella conference," only to be attacked by a swarm of rubber sucker-tipped arrows. Dejected, the professor stops lecturing and simply says, "When talk turns to Nutella, you can't control them anymore!" The payoff was straightforward: "*Délicieux entremet à la noisette, dessert savoureux*" ("A delicious hazelnut treat, a savory dessert").

In Germany the company set breakfast in its sights right from the start, in keeping with local consumer habits. In 1965, the first short TV commercial ran "Nutella for breakfast, Nutella on bread," because *mutti* (mom) knows what her kids like. The pairing "*aufs Brot*" ("on bread") even appeared on the labels of the first German Pelikan-shaped jars. The TV commercial informed viewers that Nutella was a *nuss-nougat creme* made with "only the best hazelnuts," while a stream of perfect hazelnuts, still in their shells, poured down from the "soft, round hills of the Langhe."

The situation was different in Italy. The country was just heading into an economic boom after the hardship of World War II. There were only two channels on TV, and Italians would gather in front of their sets at nine o'clock every evening to watch comedy sketches on the variety show *Carosello*—a window into nascent Italian consumerism, featuring ads for everything from washing machines to nylons and detergent. The program was created as a vehicle for advertising, and ran from 1951 to 1971 in accordance with rigid rules dictated by the Italian government through RAI, the national television network: two minutes to present a story, never once naming the product directly, and then a thirty-second "coda" that included advertisements. Ferrero hired only the best directors and actors in public television, and ended its sketch with a rather traditional tag line: "*In ogni famiglia la festa di tutti i giorni è con Nutella*" ("In every family, there's a party every day with Nutella") (1964–66); "*Ferrero, il mondo semplice e naturale della famiglia italiana*" ("Ferrero, the simple, natural Italian family life") (1967); "*Ferrero, la più grande industria dolciaria italiana e dell'Europa conti-*

nentale" ("Ferrero, the biggest confectionary company in Italy and continental Europe") (1969). These were followed by *Gigante amico* (Giant friend), an animated cartoon series (1971–76) that became an unforgettable childhood experience for millions of Italians.

"But I don't want to eat iron": 1974–83

Nixon resigned as president of the United States, Mao Zedong died in China, and Margaret Thatcher rose to power in Great Britain. Movies like *Star Wars* and *Saturday Night Fever* became blockbusters, and young people grooved to the sound of disco music. In the 1970s, Nutella hadn't become an iconic brand yet. But then again, in those days, food products were advertised based on their nutritional characteristics or ingredients. In Italy, in 1973 the slogan "A food classic" introduced Nutella as a "healthy daily treat": the product's good taste, explained the commercial, was the result of its simple ingredients. This was the time for the tag line "Nature calls nature." It was a rational approach, and played on an emotional chord through the use of entertaining, enjoyable cartoon animals. Then, up until 1988, ads began to focus instead on childhood memories. In one TV commercial, a mother remembers when, as a little girl, her own mother would give her bread and Nutella: the same slogan would be repeated for thirteen years: "Mamma, nobody knows better than you—Nutella is good for your kids, just as it was for you back then."

Around the same time, a smiling blond boy appeared in the pages of French magazines, holding a ball in one hand, and a slice of bread spread with the hazelnut cream in the other. The slogan read: *"pain et Nutella, l'union fait la force"* ("bread and Nutella, strength in unity"). This took place between 1973 and 1974. During those same years, in the United States, Nestlé presented its instant chocolate drink Quik (which would later become Nesquik), showing a glass of milk on a table while a voice offscreen invites you to drink it because it contains vitamins A, B, B12, C . . . Calcium . . . But the glass just sits there, that is, until the same voice adds that it can also contain two spoonfuls of Quik, and we see a hand reaching out and grabbing the glass. Another ad is set on a baseball field. In it, a rabbit (later to become the official animated mascot Quik Bunny) hops over to help a kid who seems to be too tired to throw the ball. But after drinking the rabbit's "magic potion" of milk and powdered chocolate, he wins the game. In keeping with the spirit of the times, Nutella broadcast an entertaining family saga on German and French screens. The scene takes place during breakfast. We see a young boy listlessly resting his head on the kitchen table. Then we hear a mother's voice from offscreen, saying "If you want to be big and strong when you grow up . . ." Annoyed, the boy interrupts her: "But I don't want to grow up!" ". . . you'll have to eat your protein, vitamins, calcium, and iron," continues the mother. "But I don't want to eat iron!" the boy insists stubbornly. "Then what *do* you want?" asks the mother. We see her spreading a slice of bread with the magical cream, and the child, who is finally happy, exclaims, "Nutella!" In 1982 German television broadcast a little scene that would make today's viewers smile: a "nutritional scientist" wearing a white lab coat holds up a jar of Nutella that he's taken down from a shelf that hosts a series of other jars of unrecognizable competitors' *nuss-nougat creme*. We then see the scientist using a few colored wooden blocks to assemble an imitation Pelikan-shaped jar as though he were playing with Lego bricks. Each of the blocks has "iron, calcium, protein" written on it. An offscreen voice says, "Vital pieces of everyday life." The payoff was: "*Nutella, Lebensbausteine für jeden Tag,*" ("Nutella, building blocks for everyday life"). During those years Nutella also had to defend itself from attacks by imitators, spreadable creams created by "private labels." In 1983, a campaign got underway in France that included full-page ads boasting the slogan, "*20 ans d'experience feront toujours la différence*" ("Twenty years of experience always make a difference"). Meanwhile in Germany, TV channels hosted another little sketch in which an interviewer gave a child two different kinds of hazelnut cream to spread on bread. The little girl recognizes Nutella immediately. Why? "Because it tastes better, so it has to be Nutella." The payoff became an instant hit: "*Man schmeckt, was alles in Nutella steckt,*" or, in other words, "You can taste everything that's in Nutella." But the same slogan could also translate as "You'll like everything that's in Nutella," because the word *schmecken* means both tasting and recognizing a flavor, as well as enjoying that flavor, creating a play on words that became impressed upon Germans' collective memory.

Energy on full: 1984–92

The scene changed: with the end of the baby boom and a drop in growth rates, Europeans were now having fewer children, which meant a smaller core target for Nutella. These were the hedonistic 1980s, a decade that encouraged everyone to be energetic and performance oriented. The first home computers produced by IBM and Apple made their way into homes, and New Wave music blasted over the airwaves. Thanks to Gorbachev's rise in Moscow, the world was about to witness the fall of the Soviet Empire. Ferrero set two distinct objectives for itself: to expand its potential consumer base by introducing young adults into its advertising, and to extrapolate the energy ready in every jar of the product from its inherent nutritional qualities. TV commercials began to feature adolescents as well as little children. Final slogans changed as well: in Italy it became "*pane e Nutella, energia per fare e per pensare*" ("bread and Nutella, energy for doing and thinking"); in Germany it became "*die Leistungszulage zum Fruehstueck*," ("Added energy for breakfast"). The associated imagery was both entertaining and witty: people who didn't eat Nutella at breakfast fell into an "eleven o'clock hole," as exhaustion sucked students (at what looked like a university) down underneath their desks. There were more peaceful scenes too, with kids playing basketball or sitting in front of their computers, and in France the payoff was "*énergie pour penser et se dépenser*" ("energy for thinking and doing your best"). This was a period during which Ferrero relied relatively little on emotional content, placing as much emphasis as possible on rational information.

Celebrating a legend: 1994–2007
As the Cold War ended, tragic ethnic conflicts began to erupt all over the world. Nelson Mandela was released from prison and rose to power in South Africa. Computer-animated films like *Toy Story* (1995) invaded the movie theaters, while *The Simpsons* debuted on TV and Madonna became the world's pre-eminent pop diva. Top models like Claudia Schiffer and Naomi Campbell paraded down fashion's catwalks, and the world discovered a need for new icons, celebrities they could focus on now that all the ideological reference points had fallen.

In Europe, halfway through the 1990s Nutella began to move toward icon brand status. It all began with the legendary line, "*Che mondo sarebbe senza Nutella?*" ("What would the world be like without Nutella?"), an Italian slogan that became gospel for many generations, and was suggested to the ad exec who came up with it, Fulvio Nardi, by a twelve-year-old boy. A period of advertising that was more emotion-oriented began in France and Germany as well. The painter Paul Klee claimed that "art does not reproduce the visible; rather, it makes visible." Perhaps this is the secret of advertising. While Nutella Parties were becoming all the rage in Italy, the creativity of ad execs and film directors was being expressed through engaging, amusing commercials: a surprise birthday party with lit candles added to a baguette smothered in Nutella (1994), created by American director Jack Piccolo; a father and son who meet up in the kitchen late at night to "steal" a little Nutella from the pantry (1996, "Intergenerazionale," also shot by an American director, Mike Cuesta); the beautiful ad "Vicina," starring a pretty neighbor from upstairs who, after running out of Nutella during a party, knocks on the door downstairs and asks a little kid, "Do you have any left?" (1997, directed by Riccardo Milano, Nanni Moretti's assistant director). The saga was broadcast in France in 1999–2000, with the commercial "L'anniversaire," dedicated to a surprise Nutella birthday party that ends with a slogan that stuck with viewers: "*Nutella, chaque jour, c'est du bonheur à tartines*" ("Spread a little happiness every day").

During those years, Ferrero Deutschland began to experiment with more emotion-oriented communications as well. Abandoning a rigorous list of ingredients and emphasizing emotional content, they relied on important spokespersons like tennis player Boris Becker, who was at the height of his career. Viewers saw him running through fields of lavender, while the sweet notes of "Cantilena," composed by Karl Jenkins, play in the background. Offscreen, the German champ says, "To tell you the truth, my personal philosophy is to work for life, and here pleasure comes first, starting with a daily breakfast. I grew up with Nutella, and I've been eating it for years. I love it spread on tasty bread. At Wimbledon, Nutella always gave me a helping hand. My son has started eating it now, and he always says, 'Dad, Dad, eat some Nutella!' It's funny, because I can remember when I first started eating Nutella at the same age . . ." The commercial ends with a shot of Becker licking the knife he just used to spread Nutella on a slice of bread while he winks at the camera. Although the gesture aroused the criticism of some

German parents, the message was clear: the hazelnut cream invented in Alba and produced in Allendorf is not merely a blend of protein and vitamins, but a childhood experience to think back on fondly and enjoy anew every day.

German soccer players and a saga: 2003–14

Nutella puts a smile on your face whenever you sit down for breakfast. This message was drilled into Germans' heads from 2003 to 2011 through a long sequence of TV commercials starring young soccer players from the German national team, nicknamed "*die jungen Wilden.*" Ferrero identified young, promising players, champions who would become famous in later years and emerge victorious from the European and World Cup championships like Mesut Özil, Mats Hummels, Benedikt Höwedes, Arne Friedrich, and Manuel Neuer, the World Cup champion goalkeeper at Brazil 2014. A player would show up at practice late, and tell one of his teammates, "Okay, now we can go grab a snack . . ." while his face betrays a Nutella "moustache." Neuer dreams of saving a penalty kick, but a Pelikan-shaped jar has replaced the soccer ball. "Manuel," say the other players, "you're a great keeper!" and Neuer reminds them all, "I have my mother to thank for that," dreaming of how he used to have to protect his jar of hazelnut cream from his friends when he was a kid. The entire ad campaign was an enormous success, even though it put breakfast in the backseat in favor of an almost subliminal message: "Even champions eat bread and Nutella." A different message was broadcast in Italy, where a TV commercial starred the real-life cook of the Italian national soccer team as its spokesperson and breakfast remained the ad's primary focus. Most importantly, in Germany the payoff—"*Hast du's drauf?*"—became quite famous. Literally, the words mean "Do you feel it?," but they could also be interpreted as "Are you ready?" This connected with another slogan from 1994, which went *"Nutella aufs Brot. Da hast du was drauf!,"* which could be translated as "Bread and Nutella, that's something worth the effort!"

Once the series of commercials starring soccer players was finished, Ferrero's creative team turned its attention to the average family. In the wake of the Lehman Brothers crisis and global uncertainty following 9/11, the zeitgeist had changed: families returned to being a reassuring value. In 2012–13 the claim *"der Morgen macht den tag"* ("the morning makes the day") began to appear as part of a sort of sitcom featuring a typical German family. A couple with two growing kids, struggling with everything from girlfriends to drowsy morning shuffling around that only a jar of Nutella can awaken, and jokes between the husband and wife as they share a slice of bread spread with the hazelnut cream.

Taking on Marmite in the UK: 2007–14

In Great Britain, Nutella first went on sale back in 1966, but it had been forced to reckon with Marmite since the day it appeared on British shop shelves. Marmite is a spreadable, salty yeast-based cream created in 1902. In England, and in South Africa as well, people traditionally spread it on toast. It's an acquired taste and one that would be dismissed by many people elsewhere in the world, although it is quite popular in Australia as well, where there's a similar product called Vegemite. Then there was Great Britain's traditional British marmalade, an equally tough opponent. For these reasons, Nutella got off to a slow start in the UK. Ferrero thus decided to win over consumers with other products, especially with its Rocher chocolate treats, which were enormously successful, in part thanks to a savvy ad campaign about an embassy reception. Then the rollout for Nutella arrived in 2007, with strong Above the Line investments. In actual fact, its TV debut had already taken place in 2003, when a short commercial with the tag line "spread the happiness" was aired. But the product's biggest campaign came during the 2008–9 season, with a short entertaining clip starring a slice of bread that pops out of a toaster at the same time in six different apartments in the same building, viewed in cross section, like a traditional British doll house. The aim was to convey energy, *joie de vivre*, and optimism, and the tag line "wake up to Nutella" summed it all up. In 2013–14 the slogan remained unchanged, but the video had a very "British" ring to it, and it focused on the versatility of this spreadable cream. Nutella was presented "subjectively," with a close-up that started inside the jar and moved to "spread" itself over a piece of toast enriched with bits of banana and strawberry, then dove into a bowl of porridge, or sidled up alongside a delicious-looking pancake. While it clearly focused on the product's functionality, the imagery gave it a fair amount of emotional content as well.

TV COMMERCIALS PART 2: OUTSIDE EUROPE

Ferrero's global expansion philosophy has never changed: first export the product, then, if it begins to sell, evaluate the possibility of opening up a local production line. Last but not least, once production is sufficient to satisfy demand, start broadcasting better targeted ad campaigns. With the new millennium, once Nutella had already established a stronghold in Europe, a new era of "overseas" investments in advertising communications, as they were called within Ferrero, had begun. This meant that the company started the twenty-first century operating on two separate paths: a decidedly "lovemark" language for mature markets, and more "pedagogical" advertising in markets that had yet to be conquered. For a number of years, the TV commercial style adopted in America, Australia, Great Britain, and Asia continued to be based on rational messages linked to why the product should be consumed: even as they became more creative and modern, such spots were basically designed to illustrate Nutella's characteristics and ingredients. Meanwhile, back in Europe, advertising aimed to get the consumer emotionally involved, by adopting evocative images, music with a powerful impact, and memorable tag lines. But starting in 2012, the strategies in Australia, the UK, and Canada changed: videos like "Breakfast loves Nutella" in Canada or "Morning Time" in Australia did not much differ from Italian commercials in which Pavarotti was singing or that showed idyllic images of French children running along the beach.

Spread happiness in the United States: 2009–14

Nutella has been sold in the United States since 1983. At first it was imported, but twelve years later the company inaugurated its first US-based production line, set in a small facility located in Somerset, New Jersey, just an hour away from Manhattan by train. While Tic Tac had taken over America, the hazelnut cream had a harder time making headway there than it had in Europe: maple syrup was the most typical pancake topping for American tables. Nutella got its true start there in 2009. Something that had been a niche product for years, available only in a few specialty stores in New York and popular with college students or soldiers coming home from Europe, became a widespread product and among the most popular in the vast area of FMCGs (Fast Moving Consumer Goods). The first commercial was aimed specifically at American mothers, who often grapple with the problem of getting their kids to eat breakfast before leaving the house for the day. It showed a mother who pulls a jar of Nutella out of the pantry (teaching viewers that it shouldn't be kept in the refrigerator), explaining, "As a mom, I'm a great believer in Nutella," adding that it can be spread on "healthy foods" like "multigrain toast." That affirmation—even though it was not directly connected to the ingredients and nutritional quality of Nutella—inspired a deceptive advertising lawsuit brought against Ferrero by a California parent. The lawsuit was eventually resolved through a class-action settlement.

In 2010 the narrative continued along the lines of a veritable "breakfast battle." What can this brand do for me? Thanks to its delightful flavor, it can convince children to eat breakfast at home. A typical American mom emphasized the message in a television commercial: "Breakfast? In this house? In the morning, I can use all the help I can get. That's why I love Nutella, a delicious hazelnut spread that's perfect on multigrain toast and even whole wheat waffles. It's a quick and easy way to give my family a breakfast they'll want to eat. And Nutella is made with simple, quality ingredients like hazelnuts, skim milk, and a hint of cocoa. They love the taste, and I feel good that they're ready to tackle the day. Nutella—breakfast never tasted this good."

Last but not least, and with a decidedly lovemark-worthy take, on the occasion of Nutella's fiftieth anniversary in 2014, the company adopted an entirely different style. Two TV commercials with engaging music hit the air. The first, "Fall for You," was sung by a young Nashville singer, Holley Maher; the second, "Happy Place," was performed by Oh, Hush! and featured Hanna Ashbrook. In the commercials, a jar of Nutella moves from the pantry to the breakfast table, from a street-food vendor's truck to a plate of waffles in San Francisco, from two young people out camping to a manager sitting in an office. The slogan is "spread the happy," at once simple and effective and accompanied by a stab at the competition: "the original hazelnut spread." This approach had become necessary precisely because Nutella's success had attracted the attention of a few extremely well-prepared competitors, including Hershey and Jif, the peanut butter giant.

Canada, from energy to love: 2000–14

The first jar of Nutella appeared in Canada in 1974. In 2006 a production facility was inaugurated in Brantford, Ontario, roughly an hour and a half from Toronto. Today it is Ferrero's most important production plant in the entire North American Free Trade Agreement (NAFTA) area. Its two production lines Nutella and Nutella & Go supply supermarkets all over North America, including in the United States. Fans of the hazelnut cream have since learned to eat it at breakfast instead of maple syrup, but things were very different fifteen years ago. Back then, Ferrero had to introduce people to a "brand-new" product. In the beginning, the values the brand expressed were the same ones transmitted in Europe by the "energy" campaigns of the 1980s and 1990s: in 2002–3 the tag line "Nutella helps provide energy to think and to do" appeared again. The language was somewhat refined between 2005 and 2007, when a young blonde woman who introduces herself as "a mother and a teacher" appears in a house pantry to share the slogan "spread some energy." She goes on to underline that the product has no "trans fats, preservatives, or artificial colors," all characteristics that most European mothers were well aware of, but which still needed to be emphasized for Canadians. A short commercial entitled "Spin," still focused on ingredients, ran between 2008 and 2010. In it a mother is surrounded by children, then the focus turns to hazelnuts, a cup of milk, and the words, "hint of delicious cocoa," "vitamin E," and "rich in antioxidants" (along with almonds, hazelnuts are particularly rich in vitamin E). The commercial ended with the slogan "spread some energy." During the 2010–12 season the company continued to insist on the same concept, employing the tag line "fuel the day," although the ads became more humorous and creative, and centered on three different sketches: a talented boy dancing in a "Ballroom" (Ferrero's title for the commercial); a gifted child who builds a huge "Castle" at home; and a child gymnast who scrambles up the "Rope" in a gym. Appearing at the end of these achievements is the line "You can tell who's had Nutella." This campaign continued until 2013–14, when the commercials began to explain that breakfast itself has fallen in love with Nutella. Viewers are shown just how many mixes and blends are possible, outlined by a warm voice offscreen: "Brown bread, white bread, dark and light bread, all-grain, multigrain, bagels, strawberries, kiwis, blueberries, apples, bananas, blackberries, muffins, pancakes, waffles, and crêpes . . ." And all to be enjoyed with a "knife, a spoon," and even one's "fingers." The commercial ends with the line, "Breakfast loves Nutella." It was a simple, effective message that stimulated the appetite and invited viewers to start the day off right.

"As mom and teacher" in Australia: 2001–14

Nutella began to be produced in Australia in 1979, one year after the first jars went on sale in stores. A Ferrero facility was established in Lithgow, in New South Wales, roughly ninety miles west of Sydney. One of the first ad campaigns to use a local spokesperson ran in 2001–2. Ferrero hired marathon athlete Heather Turland, famous for the gold medal she had won at the 1998 Commonwealth Games. The company highlighted the "competitive advantages" Nutella provides over other competitors in the children's breakfast market, insofar as it has "about 40 percent less fat than most peanut butters" and "about 10 percent less sugar than many jams." From 2003 to 2009 Australian airwaves were home to Fiona, who introduced herself as "a mom and teacher," explaining Nutella's nutritional makeup: protein, calcium, iron. The tag line came as children swam around in a pool: "energy to live and learn." The concept was the same as the one that was being used in North American commercials: rational information and a focus on the ingredients. From 2009 to 2012 the children running around on a beach from the series created in Europe reappeared, with an initial script that read, "Kids do a lot of living in a day," along with the payoff, "It takes a lot of energy to be a kid." But everything changed in 2012 thanks to a very evocative commercial. The atmosphere of the clip was unquestionably Australian: viewers saw kids sitting outside, spreading Nutella on bread; a mother bringing snacks to her kids in the warm light of a sunset; exchanging kisses and "toasting" each other with slices of bread covered with Nutella. The guitar notes of an English folk rock band play in the background, and a particular tag line emphasizes sunny optimism with the words of "Rise & Shine".

New markets: 2009–14

In Singapore and Southeast Asia, television commercials show Asian children starting their days eating bread and Nutella, "the tasty way to start a day." In Dubai, Nutella is spread on pita bread, while a mother says, "With a breakfast with Nutella I'm sure I'm giving my kids a delicious start for a day full of activity. Good morning, Nutella." In South Africa, the tag line is the same as in Asia, and the images show kids dressed in the uniforms of a local boarding school. In Russia, ad campaigns from the "energy" series began to run in 2009 on local TV stations in Moscow and Saint Petersburg, followed by other cities. That same year the company opened a large Ferrero facility to produce Nutella in Vladimir. In 2012 *un día en la vida de Jorge* ("a day in Jorge's life") ran in Mexico, showing a young drummer struggling to perform during an extremely important tryout. His dream is to join a band and become a successful musician. The ad doesn't show the outcome of his attempt to achieve his dreams, from working on math homework to playing music in a garage with his friends, because what really counts is his passion, his energy for life. The closing question is "*¿Qué desayunaste?*" ("What did you have for breakfast?"). That same year Ferrero made its first investments in Nutella TV commercials in Colombia and Brazil. One very successful commercial featured breakfast in the home of famous Brazilian soccer player Kaká, together with friends of his son Luca. At the end of the commercial, a slice of bread with the emoticon :-) written in Nutella appears on the table accompanied by an optimistic message: "*sorria & bom dia*" ("smile and good morning"). Creativity and innovative language continue to be leitmotifs in countries where Nutella is beginning yet another successful climb up mountains of market share.

WHEN MUSIC TAKES THE LEAD

Jingles were the heart and soul of sound in advertising during the 1970s and 1980s. But even when jingles fell out of fashion, the importance of music in commercials didn't diminish; in fact, it is often the first true problem creative ad execs face: everyone is always looking for a "striking" sound—as communications experts have defined it. This sound can be derived from a preexisting song, but must connect the commercial's script with a narrative or specific declaration. For television commercials, careful contemplation of the soundtrack has been a constant throughout Ferrero's history.

The first example may date to an ad campaign realized at the end of 2003 by the Parisian company Providence, directed by

Michel Guimbard, a specialist in refined advertising. The film created a new musical identity, one that was adjusted in different ways depending on the different countries in which it was broadcast. Entitled "Life Energy" ("*Énergie de vie*" in French), it starred children and ended with the tag line "It takes a lot of energy to be a kid." The children run around in the sunlight, smiles on their faces, engaging in the experiences typical of their age: launching a model airplane, doing classwork on the blackboard, running around with a ball on a green field, all the way up to an example of first love. This is pure emotion, designed to touch the hearts of adult viewers. "*C'è tanta voglia di fare nella vita di un bambino / così tanta energia da spendere / per giocare / per sognare / per concentrarsi / tanta energia per provare, riprovare, per imparare, per crescere / e scoprire il mondo*" ("Kids want to do a lot in life / So much energy to spend / to play / to dream / to concentrate / lots of energy to try and try again, to learn, to grow / and discover the world"). The music is the engaging and evocative song "Glorious," released in 1999 by Swedish singer Andreas Johnson. After debuting in France, the campaign would continue to run for years in a number of different markets, both in Europe (Great Britain, Holland, Belgium) and in Australia (2009–12). The same commercial was set to different music in Italy and Spain, where the soundtrack became the famous song "Que Será, Será" by Jay Livingston and Ray Evans, a piece that dates all the way back to 1956, when it was originally sung by Doris Day in Alfred Hitchcock's *The Man Who Knew Too Much*.

A similar operation was undertaken in 2012 in Italy. A flock of pigeons fly up into the air above a city, a café opens, window shutters roll up: elegant black-and-white images illustrate the dawn of a new day. Then the video turns to Technicolor and Nutella appears: a grandmother offers it to her granddaughter and a young woman spreads it on bread while her companion gives her a hug. Nobody says a word; all we hear is the optimistic-sounding song "Buongiorno a te," "Good morning to you," written in 2003 by Michele Centonze and sung by Luciano Pavarotti. The payoff is: "*Un buongiorno con Nutella fa più buona la vita*" ("A good morning with Nutella makes life better"). In Australia the same commercial used two songs from the past, both of which were quite successful: in 2009–11 the song for the commercial was "I Say a Little Prayer," written by composers Burt Bacharach and Hal David in 1967 and sung by Aretha Franklin; while in 2013 the video "Rise & Shine" was made magical by a folk song by an English group, Martin Stephenson and the Daintees, with their happy tune "Morning Time," released on the album *Salutation Road* in 1990.

Last but not least, in September 2013 in France and Belgium Nutella served a "waking up enthusiasm" (*réveille notre enthousiasme*) message in an attempt to get lovers of the cream involved in a heartwarming family dance that unfolds upon a very particular stage: an enormous white cap from a Nutella jar, illuminated in Charlie Chaplin "limelight" style. Music was key to the commercial's success, and its creators chose the Jackson 5's iconic 1970s song "I Want You Back," one of the group's most famous tunes.

* * *

If a brand wants to stay alive, it has to breathe, speak, smile, and know how to evolve while remaining true to itself. This is the secret of Nutella's success. The brand's television commercials have always managed to adapt to local culture. It's what Douglas B. Holt, a professor at Oxford University, identifies as "cultural branding" in his book *How Brands Become Icons* (2004). "Cultural branding applies particularly to categories in which people tend to value product as means of self-expression," writes Holt, "such as clothing, home decor, beauty, leisure, entertainment, automotive, food, and beverage." Even though it uses different stories and languages and is present in countries with different, even contrasting habits, Nutella has always found a way to extend a shared vision, bringing its consumers (and now fans of the brand) both rational and emotional benefits. The stories its creative thinkers invent for the cream convince you you'll start the day with a smile. In an engaging ad campaign that ran in Spain, the scene develops, as usual, during breakfast. Outside it's pouring rain, but inside the children are optimistically looking forward to their day, reciting a poem about how a sudden rainstorm washes their faces and the earth beneath their feet. As a result their father, when he leaves the house for work, folds his umbrella unexpectedly, smiles and lets the raindrops splash down on his face. "What can we learn from children? Enthusiasm. All you have to do is reawaken it." The payoff is "Nutella reawakens enthusiasm."

YOUR NAME ON THE JAR

Nutella has always brought people back to their childhood: it creates a personal memory in each and every one of us. This is what has defended the product from the risk of decline. It is a sweet Peter Pan, one that manages to take advantage of emerging strategies, adapting to changes in society.

In recent years a tendency toward self-celebration has emerged thanks to modern media, social media, selfies, and the human urge to share unfiltered versions of individual experience. The trend has moved towards individualism, but one that can only find its way in relation to others. Within this new sensitivity brands risk being forgotten because they can no longer communicate effectively. But nothing attracts an individual's attention more than hearing or reading his or her personal name. With this in mind, in September 2011 a "great idea" was hatched in Australia that managed to skyrocket consumption of Coca-Cola during the summer and focus attention on the brand. The labels for plastic bottles of the product were printed with 150 of the most common Australian names, inviting purchasers to "share a Coke with a friend." The aim of the campaign was twofold: to increase consumption of the most famous drink in the world and to get people talking about Coke again. The initiative was wildly successful, even beyond the company's expectations, and it was soon repeated in fifty additional countries.

In this case, the brand sought individual communication that centered on each individual consumer. But Coca-Cola wasn't the first to pull this kind of stunt. In the summer of 2008 small, colorful chocolate candies beloved by kids everywhere—M&M's—launched a "Faces" campaign on the dedicated website www.mymms.com in order to provide a special service that continues to operate today: a person could order a bag of M&M's produced with the image of her/his own face or name on each piece of candy. In France, on August 26, 2013, Milka launched a promotion entitled "*Le dernier carré*" ("The last square"): the company sold perfectly normal, impeccably packaged chocolate bars that had just one square removed. Online, purchasers could fill out a form and have Milka send the missing *carré* to a friend.

In Italy, it should be noted that Nutella has been engaged in relationship marketing since as far back as March 2003, when the company began creating personalized glasses. Ninety-six different names were printed on glasses that could hold 200 grams (7 ounces) of cream, each accompanied by a description of the name's etymological meaning. Ten years later Ferrero decided to try again, this time with a promotion held online in Belgium in February 2013. It all started with two twenty-second videos realized by Providence Belgium and created by artistic directors Christophe Delarsille and Alexandre Guenet, entitled "Casanova" and "Papa maman." In the first video a young boy sits in his bedroom, gluing a new label on a jar of Nutella. The label has the same lettering as the original, but reads "Julie." He takes the jar to Julie's house, rings the doorbell, and when Julie answers, she's obviously surprised and happy. She accepts the jar and gives him a kiss on the cheek in return. As the song "Glorious" plays, we return to the boy's bedroom, where we see our young "Casanova" now hard at work on the rest of his project. His desk is covered with lots of other labels: Emma, Alice, Elise, Nathalie, Sarah, Marie, Nina . . . A voice offscreen says, "Now, you too can personalize your Nutella jar." The second video stars a ponytailed girl who dedicates her jar to *maman* and takes it to her. The father is caught slightly off-guard, but smiles all the same. The happy ending comes when the jar is turned, and we see *papa* written on the other side. The two films went online in February 2013 on Nutella Belgium's Facebook page, as well as on lots of news websites as part of a preroll for media content. It created an enormous buzz, and quickly went viral. The company registered requests for one hundred thousand personalized labels, with an exponential increase in people signing up as fans of the Facebook page and on the company website. Nutella's marketing team was a little stunned: the success extended well beyond their most optimistic hopes, even though Nutella has been sold in Belgium for fifty years and is purchased by one out of every two families.

Following the extraordinary success of this first endeavor, the company tried the same promotion in Spain, which ran from April to December 2013. For years the Spanish market was the province of a spreadable cream called Nocilla, first created in 1967 by Italian food company Star as an imitation of Ferrero's product and released in Spain before Nutella could debut there (although today Nutella has almost drawn even with its would-be competitor). Nutella Ibérica has a penetration index that is barely a third of that of its Belgian counterpart, but despite this difference, the promotion was overwhelmingly successful in Spain as well. Even though the brand had a much shorter and more recent history on the Iberian Peninsula, this attempt to move closer to the consumer through the creation of personalized labels accelerated Nutella's transformation into a lovemark.

From this moment forward, Ferrero decided to extend the initiative into areas where Nutella already enjoyed significant market penetration. On June 17 and July 14, 2013, the French campaign got underway, and in autumn 2013 the company perfected its strategy in Italy as well, using various platforms simultaneously: a TV commercial, posters, websites, and social media. Millions of personalized labels were printed and provided for free in supermarkets around the country. The slogan was "*Nutella sei tu*" ("You are Nutella"), designed to accentuate the idea of a shared experience with the consumer as much as it possibly could. "*Da sempre c'è un po' di Nutella nella tua vita e un po' della tua vita in Nutella*" ("There's always been a little Nutella in your life, and a little of your life in Nutella"). The accompanying communications campaign involved famous Italian television hosts and radio deejays whom Italians knew by their stage names, displaying large ads with jars boasting their real names on the labels. The promotion also ran at the same time in Holland, Portugal, and in Turkey at the end of the year.

Wherever a big idea has worked, the reward has been a significant increase in sales, inspiring an ironic, self-deprecating video on the Italian YouTube channel that shows Ferrero's marketing people gluing labels on their product day and night, ultimately keeling over and falling fast asleep. In Italy, Spain, and Turkey videos were broadcast showing bakers who turn on their ovens late at night to bake bread, surprised to receive free, personalized jars of Nutella from a company representative as gifts. Agustín, Rafa, José Luis, Mehmet, Ali, Hasan all say, "Bread is love, continuing for generations." There's even the story of Hüseyin, who has been waking up every day at five o'clock in the morning for thirty-two years to bring his clients *simit*, a circular Turkish bread similar to a bagel, and who is moved to tears when he sees a jar with his name on it.

This award-winning campaign became the object of study at management schools. In Turin, Italy, it was the focus of a student questionnaire that was part of a course taught by professor and researcher Cecilia Casalegno. According to Casalegno, the Coca-Cola campaign and the Nutella campaign had significant differences, some of which showed up in students' focus groups. In "Share a Coke" the famous logo on the label is substituted by personal names, essentially generic first names that are widespread and popular, in order to create a bottle that someone can share with a friend. The Ferrero campaign, on the other hand, was designed to tell consumers their own individual stories; personalization of the label focused attention on the childhood and individual growth of each single member of the target market. "I asked the students to think like marketing experts and provide an answer that analyzed the two promotions as deeply as possible: just 10 percent of the students believed there were close analogies between the two campaigns." This led to a questionnaire that gathered together the opinions of 262 students in a more scientific approach. Nutella's brand longevity is considered a normal fact, precisely because of its uniqueness, or because it has become a lovemark. Six students out of ten were convinced that it was an "essential product," like Parmigiano-Reggiano cheese or a vegetable protected under a European DOP label (*Denominazione di Origine Protetta*, or "controlled designation of origin," connected with the territory in which it is produced, and subject to rigorous standards). The questionnaire also contained another surprising result: two-thirds of those interviewed were convinced that Nutella was a "new" product, despite the fact that it had just turned fifty, because it is an "evergreen" product—firmly rooted in Italian tradition—and a "versatile" one.

Although limited, this academic study illustrates how Nutella's marketing team choice of personalized labels is perfectly suited to our day and age. The results of the campaign speak for themselves: during the various promotions, sales of Nutella increased by between 10 percent and 40 percent, depending on the country. It's a kind of marketing mix that will no doubt continue to be a part of the company's strategy. People are increasingly interested in taking part in the life of a product they love, and by now Nutella doesn't belong just to the company that created it, but to its consumers around the world as well.

5

Spread the Web

My grandfather used to bring it from Italy when I was a child [and] now it's included in my breakfast with chocolate chip pancakes or fruit—delicious!

> Rosanna, Huntington Beach, California, USA, 2014
> (Nutella USA Facebook page)

Nutella gives me a little bit of happiness every day.

> Marine, Perpignan, France, 2013
> (Nutella France Facebook page)

I'm dropping everything, I'm having Nutella for breakfast, lunch & dinner today.

> Lea, Kingscliff, New South Wales, Australia, 2011
> (Nutella Australia & New Zealand Facebook page)

I can't live without it, it's like oxygen.

> Sandro, Pisa, Italy, 2003
> (mynutella.it website, now closed)

Nutella puts you in a good mood—it chases the blues away. It's the sweetest, creamiest escape from reality.

> Marta, near Milan, Italy, 2003
> (mynutella.it website, now closed)

What would life be like without Nutella? A window into dreams; a long, warm breath; a gust of wind . . . Ah yes, yes. Nutella, you are a companion through sad days and happy days, forever adding color . . .

Giorgia, 1998
(fan-driven blog *NutellaFans.it*).

Press "send" on a smartphone, click a computer mouse, enter a few lines on a tablet touch screen, and the love of Nutella by its countless fans is instantly spread across the web. This has been going on ever since the Internet became a mass phenomenon. After years of TV ads, at the dawn of the twenty-first century, Nutella realized just how important the Internet is, as an on-line presence for web "surfers" the world over. For a long time the company watched, while spontaneous citations and references to Nutella sprang up in fan clubs, blogs, and websites. Although the references did increase brand awareness, they were also potentially counterproductive because of the tone people used, and the way they sometimes related the product to excessive or uncontrolled consumption.

After an initially cautious approach to the Internet, Ferrero slowly got more and more involved, first by inaugurating a showcase website that went online in the United States in 1999 at the domain www.nutellausa.com then, later that year, the company registered a website in Italy, although it only went "live" in September 2001, overseen by the agency Inferentia DNM. Today the digital era has completely transformed the marketing panorama. If you Google the word "Nutella," you'll receive between sixty and eighty million hits, which include videos, blogs, photographs, and drawings posted online by the product's fans. In 2011 Jim Lecinski, vice president of Americas Customer Solutions for Google, created the acronym "ZMOT," a further challenge for professional marketers. ZMOT stands for "zero moment of truth," which, in Lecinski's words, refers to "that moment when you grab your laptop, mobile phone, or some other wired device and start learning about a product or service." It's a fleeting moment during which an aspiring consumer looks for information about the product he or she is interested in. According to Google's studies, more than 80 percent of all moms "say they do online research after seeing TV commercials for products that interest them." The 2011 research study was conducted on US consumers, but in an article published on the website www.thinkwithgoogle.com in August 2014, Lecinski wrote that "we've seen the boundaries of ZMOT extend to every corner of the connected world, and not just for high-ticket items. In our latest study, Winning the Zero Moment of Truth in Asia, we saw that 78 percent of Asian women use search as a vital part of their decision process for consumer-packaged goods (CPG) brands."

Today, execs handling digital marketing for products are doing everything they can to improve their SEO, or search engine optimization. In 2014 Nutella's global digital marketing strategy was based in Luxembourg. In each individual country, local managers glean guidelines from headquarters and adapt them to ad campaigns currently underway, promotion events going on at sales points, and the local national culture at large. But even for the web, the guiding principle remains "think global, act local." Today, anyone who visits www.nutella.com will open a global webpage linked to each individual national domain. But in 1999, when American journalist Tamara Ikenberg advised her readers in the *Wichita Eagle* in Kansas to go through their preferred search engine and look for the brand "Ferrero" if they wanted to find "the gospel of Nutella," the results were quite different. Google had only just been created and wasn't popular yet, and back then, the search engine Altavista provided a mere 3,500 hits; Yahoo! barely 1,600.

Before omnipresent social media such as Facebook and

Twitter had been created, Ferrero was asking itself how it could communicate with consumers over the Internet, applying its own editorial tools rather than giving too much leeway to the independent fan clubs that had sprung up all around the world, and that were using the brand name in an unsupervised manner.

It took a long time to make this happen, but after a cautious Internet debut, the company succeeded in remaining one step ahead of other major food companies. The same year Ferrero debuted the site in Italy, it also opened an institutional brand website in Germany, as well as in 2002 in France and Austria. Today there are thirty-eight Nutella websites online across all five continents: twenty-five in Europe, five in America, three in the CIS (Commonwealth of Independent States, which includes Russia and several other ex-Soviet countries), one in Africa, two in the Middle East, and two in Oceania. As you can see in the table below, these sites serve people in twenty-nine different countries. In some cases there are multiple sites dedicated to Nutella, in addition to the "institutional" website, and they are usually connected to a specific campaign or promotion. There are also dozens of websites for each Ferrero product. Today, the confectionary company can boast around three hundred websites related to institutional profiles in a given country or for a specific product, including Tic Tac, Kinder, Ferrero Rocher, and more.

Nutella websites

Europe	North America	CIS (Russia & Ex-USSR)	Africa	Middle East	Oceania
25 websites	5 websites	3 websites	1 website	2 websites	2 websites
14 countries	2 countries	2 countries	5 countries	4 countries	2 countries

Source: Ferrero, August 2014

According to the ITU (International Telecommunication Union, the United Nations' specialized agency for ICTs, which allocates global radio spectrums and satellite orbits and analyzes global digital activity on an annual basis), there are roughly 2.9 billion people connected to the Internet (2014 estimates) out of a total global population of roughly 7 billion. These include 1,942 million in developed countries and 981 million in developing countries, in other words roughly 40.4 percent of the total global population. Percentages change according to geographic area: the highest penetration index (74.8 percent) can be found in Europe, followed by the Americas (65.5 percent) and the CIS area (55.9 percent). Perhaps the most surprising fact to emerge is that mobile telephone users worldwide are "approaching the number of people on earth," as Brahima Sanou, director of the ITU's Telecommunication Development Bureau, has noted.

Mobile Internet has radically changed the way brands communicate. Suffice it to consider the fact that adult smartphone owners use their devices for an average of two hours per day (data provided by the analysis agency GlobalWebIndex). Of course this data changes according to age. Ninety-four percent of young people between sixteen and twenty-four connect to the Internet everyday, compared to 51 percent of consumers between fifty-five and sixty-four. In 2014 the blog run by the same agency noted that 59 percent of Internet users "are reviewing brands and products"—in other words, a potential audience of 1.5 billion people around the world.

Therefore it makes sense that, over the past decade, Nutella's true lovemark phase has developed over the Internet: love for the brand, born of spontaneous sentiment, as turned into a full-fledged brand management strategy. The idea at the heart of all the web-based initiatives Ferrero has conducted for its brands, but with the company's hazelnut cream as the trailblazer (www.nutella.it made it to the Web well before Ferrero.it) has been to transform passion for the product into a reason to meet and learn more about it. It is a sort of protected community within which the company can communicate with its clients.

George Bernard Shaw once wrote that "there is no love sincerer than the love of food." This may help explain why the relationship that links individuals to a specific brand often resembles a bond of love. As American marketing experts Larry Weber and Lisa Leslie Henderson explain in their 2014 book *The Digital Marketer*, "whether in New York or Nairobi, today customers are connected, informed, and more vocal than they have been in the past."

A BRAND COMMUNITY

Within the digital context, the post-purchase engagement the brand establishes with consumers plays a key role. Brand communications must constantly be kept "alive" and regenerated. The creation of a strong, long-lasting relationship with clients through forms of online dialogue and brand communities is crucial. This was the beginning of relationship marketing, which first developed at the very start of the twenty-first century. Two typologies were created: brand communities created *for* consumers (as was the case with Badedas or Pampers); and brand communities created *by* consumers (for example, Absolut Collectors, who search for the most recent bottle of the famous Swedish vodka; fans of the legendary Harley-Davidson; or owners of Swatch, the popular Swiss watch, thanks to the Swatch Club). Toward the late 1990s, the most important example of this kind of brand experience for "consumers" may well have been Club Nokia. The Finnish company, now owned by Microsoft, tried to make the tag line that had informed so many people about its product—"Connecting people"—a concrete reality. Members of the club were given access to a privileged help line for cell phones, as well as the chance to see popular movies at reduced prices and purchase music or concert tickets with a discount. This was recently repeated (through music) with Nokia Trends Lab. This helped the brand facilitate virtual encounters between people, providing opportunities for those who love the product to share experiences, images, and thoughts with one another. With this as a starting point, the first important web investment Ferrero made was tested in Italy, where Nutella enjoys stronger penetration, opening the www.mynutella.it website in April 2003. The site is an excellent example of a virtual community organized around a relationship brand, one that "connects people harmoniously." Powerhouse, an agency based in Conegliano Veneto, in northeastern Italy, was charged with organizing and managing the project. At the time, the agency was already handling other web communities, working, for example, for Henkel detergents, Aprilia scooters, and several furniture and interior design companies.

When the www.mynutella.it website went online, Harvard student Mark Zuckerberg hadn't yet written the code for his creation, Facebook, which now boasts 1.2 billion users around the world. Nor was there any concept of Web 2.0, which arose following the advent of social media. With this in mind, it's even more interesting to note the way the www.mynutella.it brand community was conceived and created, with characteristics so advanced that they in some ways anticipated modern-day social networks like MySpace, another site created in 2003 based on an idea by Tom Anderson, a student at Berkeley University in California.

Each person who signed up with www.mynutella.it (and

there were over 150,000) could manage his or her personal space, posting thoughts, photographs, and drawings inspired by Nutella. The result was a deluge of digital images, mouth-watering phrases, and random observations exchanged in messages. In them all, love of the legendary jar—up until that point a tale told only by writers, directors, and artists—became what bound the fans together and the focus of their shared passion. The company, for its part, responded with content marketing activities: brand values were communicated through short articles, easy recipes, and prize competitions reserved for community members. Hence, the company's brand communication became multidimensional, generated by a three-pronged system: brand, market, and consumer. Nutella was both the star and the focus of the flow of communication. The one-way advertising method was abandoned, especially in 2003–4, when the kind of consumer who used the Internet regularly could boast a certain level of cultural and technological savvy. Therefore the brand had to serve the consumer in order to obtain competitive advantages, with the aim of getting to know its client all the more closely and intimately. Of course the brand made its own decisions, but compared to earlier instances, it took the emotions and feelings gathered online much more to heart: if it hadn't, it would have risked ruining the very feeling it had labored so hard to create. At Powerhouse, people claimed that the information obtained through www.mynutella.it didn't make the company more powerful, but rather empowered each individual client. The then-president of the Veneto company, Michele Castorina, stated, "This way, consumers will become decision makers."

The website was divided into five different areas that users could only access after signing up:

- *My area*. This was similar to a modern-day social network account, with a brief biography to be shared with other users and the reason why each person had signed up.

- *Area magazine.* For the first time in Italy, the brand became a publisher, creating its own content thanks to an editorial staff that published news gathered from newspapers or directly from fans. For example: "The Gourmet Thief: Blinded by Nutella, a person can lose his head and forget to pay the bill. This is exactly what happened to a forty-five-year-old man from northern Italy who was beyond suspicion. Would you be able to resist a sudden and unexpected Nutella-attack?" This area of the website was one of the most popular, because it gave people the chance to leave comments, supervised by a moderator.

- *Personal sites.* These were self-managed personal spaces, similar to a blog or accounts on MySpace or Facebook, where each Nutella fan could post photographs, text, and personal observations. It was a way to share their Nutella experiences. Initially these were often dedicated to sports or passions for comic books or pets, but eventually they included humorous entries, childhood memories, and small daily pleasures.

- *Fan club sites.* The aim of this area was to create small leaders within the virtual space, identifying highly motivated people who were closely connected with the world of Nutella. The company thus inspired the birth of fan clubs that could organize their own parties and events, and not just online.

- *Nutella art.* For this area the website offered an impressive gallery of images posted by different people, including slices of bread smothered with the cream, as well as crêpes, and cakes.

Signing up with www.mynutella.it meant your email was automatically included in the mailing list for the company's monthly newsletter. The publication included five or six news items in each issue, along with trivia, news, and questionnaires that enabled the company to survey the mood of its most loyal clients directly, without setting up a specific focus group. For their part, fans sent countless emails to the company asking for news about the product, merchandise sporting the Nutella logo, and information about how to organize a Nutella Party, or where to find special three- and five-kilogram (11- and 13-pound) jars. Everything was regulated by a service known as "nutiquette"—netiquette adapted to the hazelnut cream's ethos— and included precise rules: no vulgar, aggressive, provocative, or discriminating language; no offensive or obscene material; no sharing third-party personal data (general info, addresses, telephone numbers, or similar information); a warning to share one's own personal data with discretion; no using www.mynutella.it services to promote economic activities or to advertise; no publishing nonoriginal material on the website; no sending or exchanging information that violates the rights of third parties.

WE ARE NUTELLA

A research study by Saatchi & Saatchi, the agency that created the term "lovemark," has shown that 61 percent of the people who have a lovemark want to interact with that brand by way of a community. Harley-Davidson owners can get together in exclusive clubs, excluding anyone who drives a different kind of motorcycle, but Nutella fan clubs are inclusive and social by definition. Ferrero discovered this when the company launched a photo competition related to Nutella, complete with merchandise and digital cameras as prizes. One of these initiatives led to the creation of a large-format book published in Italy in 2006 and called *Nutella siamo noi* (We are Nutella), edited by Giampaolo Fabris. The volume is an anthology of evocative images and quotes based on the great love of Nutella that all its authors share. It is filled not only with the customary images of children with Nutella moustaches, but also with a few smiling grandmothers caught with their hands in the Nutella jar. It's an imaginary zoo filled with cats, dogs, hippopotamuses, horses, bears, and birds, with the legendary jar rising above them all. Across the pages of that book, the brand first began to display its dreamlike aura, presenting a perennial message that extended beyond even the brightest hopes of its marketing execs.

From that moment onward, the people working in Ferrero realized they could move beyond www.mynutella.it. A marketing mix approach was used to open a new website for the community that was even more engaging, with an entire city spread with hazelnut cream: www.nutellaville.it. This virtual world drew inspiration from Second Life, a portal created in 2003 that had millions of users, each of which became a "resident" in the site, interacting through an online avatar.

In order to familiarize fans with this new development and show them how to migrate to the new platform, the company organized the first and only official Nutella Day (June 21, 2008) in Turin. Ferrero distributed a press release explaining that the date was chosen in order to usher in the summer, "celebrating the values of niceness, joy, and positive thinking." These were values Nutella embraced "because it has always embodied them; that's why nothing's more authentic than an invitation to spread joy and positivity." Several different sections of the city were involved, with picnic-perfect areas and tablecloths laid out on the green grass of the city's main piazza in order to host a metropolitan Nutella tasting. The party wasn't just for children, it was also for their parents who'd been raised on bread and Nutella. The website was also used to run a number of contests: in early 2009 participants could win T-shirts or a jar-shaped pouf simply by creating a fruit-like avatar. Each participant had to become a "citizen" of www.nutellaville.it and fill out a test form based on the best pairing of fruit and Nutella, taking part in a simple, intuitive game. It was a form of web marketing in which each person had to tell the company something about him- or herself. Some people described it as a form of tribal marketing.

However, www.nutellaville.it was short-lived. Perhaps the era of spaces "controlled" and directed from on high had come and gone. It was a well-designed and entertaining website, but it didn't leave enough room for individual creativity. It was the advent of the age of social networks: 2008 was the year Facebook registrations exploded in Italy. Ferrero realized it needed to change its game plan.

INTERNET SPONTANEITY

With the advent of the Internet, suddenly each individual could express his or her love for a brand. An awareness of this enormous new development conditioned Ferrero's extremely cautious approach to the web. This is typical of all companies that invest heavily in their own brands, constituting one of their main assets, also in terms of their economic value. Internally, many companies were beginning to debate whether or not to act on signals they were getting from society. Generally those in marketing and communication were in favor of acting on these signals, while others were more inclined to protect the brand. There arose a new need to find a balance between those who manage a brand, starting with its logo, and consumers who want to express all their affection for a lovemark, taking full advantage of their own expressive and creative capabilities.

Today people understand that digital communication is like a room in which everyone is talking at once. This means that when a company wants to make itself heard, drowning out the background noise, its actions have to be international. The brand has to transmit "meaning" that could be understood on a global scale. Some major multinational companies, for example Coca-Cola, Red Bull, and Starbucks, are already doing this. Coca-Cola has become a "happiness factory" for the world at large. The energy drink Red Bull "gives you wings," helping you overcome your natural limits. Nutella is beloved by everyone who wants to start the day off in a positive manner, with optimism and enthusiasm. At least that's the message that Nutella sends out to the world over the web in an attempt to stand out at sales points, especially compared to competitors who have brought imitation products into the fray. The brand, with what it makes available online, presents itself as a content provider on a par with other media—one that can take advantage of the viral nature of consumer-made contributions in order to increase its own brand equity.

However, the Internet is also a source of some conflict, because every company has the right to avoid the "vulgarization" of its own brand, keeping it from becoming a common term used to define an entire product category. It was relatively easy to intercept incorrect usage of the brand in a newspaper or dictionary, but once the Internet went mainstream this task grew a lot tougher. The first official case came in 2000: a program created in San Francisco to "spread" music content over the Internet from one user to another was named Gnutella and boasted a logo with the same lettering used by the hazelnut cream. Gnutella's website was very successful, but the legal team in Ferrero Germany was quick to act, getting them to change the graphics of their platform, though not the name, which is still used as a peer-to-peer software today.

On February 5, 2007, two Italian-American bloggers, digital strategist Sara Rosso and lawyer Michelle Fabio, launched World Nutella Day, gathering together spontaneous participation from fans (mostly in the United States) online. In order to boost visibility for the initiative they included an image that had went viral, the *Nutel Lisa* created by Turkish photographer and writer Cenk Sönmezsoy and posted on his cooking blog, *Cafe Fernando*. The image displays a new version of Botero's take on Leonardo da Vinci's Mona Lisa, in which she is clasping a jar of Nutella in her arms, and smiling, the telltale cream on her lips. Right from the start, the www.nutelladay.com homepage stated quite clearly, "World Nutella Day is an unofficial fan site for lovers of Nutella!! WND does not represent official views or opinions of Ferrero, S.p.A. (makers of Nutella)." Starting in 2007, the two entrepreneurial bloggers published recipes and news about the hazelnut cream without encountering any problems, regularly celebrating World Nutella Day every February 5. Then, probably due to some "automatism" in Ferrero's legal offices, a letter of warning was sent to them on May 25, 2013. After receiving it, the bloggers posted a note that shocked fans all over the world, turning the incident into a media event: "Good-bye to World Nutella Day?" It seemed as though the website had to be shut down.

A few days later Ferrero resolved the issue, proving that a discussion between people who want full expression on the Internet and those who support "absolute" defense of the brand can lead to a compromise satisfying to both parties. A company communiqué explained that "a positive, direct contact between Ferrero and Sara Rosso, owner of an unofficial Nutella fan page called World Nutella Day, has brought the case to a close. Ferrero wishes to express its sincere gratitude to Sara Rosso for her passion for Nutella, gratitude that the company extends to all fans of World Nutella Day" (tens of thousands by the last count). The website stayed alive and online, thanks in part to this elegant gloss: "Ferrero counts itself fortunate to have fans of Nutella as devoted and loyal as Sara Rosso." In 2014, during an interview that was published on Ferrero's website as part of the fiftieth anniversary of the legendary product, Sara stated: "I grew up in California. I spent a lot of time in the countryside of Gilroy, 'Garlic Capital of the World.' I think that the first time I saw Nutella was when I got to Italy, in 1994 . . . delicious. When I returned to the US, there wasn't any Nutella there. Now Nutella is so popular!"

6
Brand friendship on social media

Web 2.0 has changed communication strategies: brands can no longer express themselves solely through showcase websites like www.nutella.com. Nowadays they need to rely on listening and dialogue, creating spaces for conversation in areas of the Internet that are "alive," where people contact and converse with one another. Brands have entered a new, more social dimension. At a time when ideologies and grand narratives are waning, lovemarks have become a form of identity aggregation.

Consumers can even take part in defining a new visual identity, selecting advertising or product packaging. Thanks to the web, the individual consumer becomes a creative actor on the stage of consumerism, and can reinvent and distribute announcements, messages, and the brand's signs. Therefore the brand must offer informative, guiding, and entertaining content that will be welcomed as interesting while avoiding information overload, a bombardment of stimuli and news that detracts from the communication of a brand's intent or meaning.

Chris Anderson, editor in chief of the magazine *Wired* for over a decade, wrote: "The ants have megaphones." In other words, consumers can talk now, and companies would do well to listen. Ferrero learned how to do so through its brand community, and has continued to listen over recent years on various social media that have risen to the fore: first Facebook (created in 2004) and Twitter (2006), but also through sharing videos on YouTube (2005), and photographs via Flickr (2004), Instagram (2010), and Pinterest (2010).

In 2010, Nutella's marketing team began working within this "town square" to increase the sense of belonging and loyalty to the brand, sometimes engendering direct dialogue with consumers about promotions, the raw ingredients used, the shape of the various jars, and more. They also maintained close contacts between social media and the company's showcase websites, which were never abandoned, often creating new sites *ad hoc* for special events and ad campaigns. According to Weber and Henderson, in their book *The Digital Marketer*, it has become of crucial importance to "engage customers via social communities." Addressing company management, the two marketing experts note: "Through social networks we can successfully build awareness, encourage simple engagement, and garner feedback."

When Ferrero became aware of the need to change its digital strategy, opening official Nutella accounts on social networks (and not only in Italy), the company provided a very clear briefing: consolidate the brand's emotional capital and develop an increasingly intense relationship with fans in such a way as to augment the product's desirability as a breakfast item, which at that time continued to be the company's main objective.

The first move was to get onto Facebook. In February 2014, the platform created by Mark Zuckerberg celebrated its ten-year anniversary, accumulating a total of 1.2 billion users. In June of the same year—according to official data from Menlo Park, the social networking service's headquarters—that number increased to 1.32 billion, making it the world's most popular social network in terms of registered users, followed by the Chinese network Qzone, which has 623 million users (Facebook is outlawed in China), Google+ (300 million), Tencent Weibo (a Chinese microblogging service that has 220 million active members), and Twitter (271 million).

FACEBOOK STATISTICS

829 million daily active users on average in June 2014
654 million mobile daily active users on average in June 2014
1.32 billion monthly active users as of June 30, 2014
1.07 billion mobile monthly active users as of June 30, 2014
Approximately 81.7 percent of Facebook daily active users are outside the United States and Canada.
Source: www.newsroomfb.com, Facebook's official news website

Relationships between Facebook users are termed "friends," and no user is allowed more than five thousand friends per personal profile. Of course, they're not all "real" friendships. Social networks are the home of fluid friendships. It's also possible to develop another kind of contact thanks to people's interest in "pages," which are managed by individual brands and have no member limit. People can connect to these pages and receive updates and news by clicking Facebook's famous "like" symbol. This little blue thumbs-up is a viral icon—a symbol of ancient Rome, used by the emperor and the crowd at an arena to save a gladiator's life. Just like many other brands, Nutella chose to use Facebook as a way to manage communication with its fans through a structured page with precise editorial content.

Other sites Ferrero uses include Twitter, a fast-growing player in the world of social networks that can boast more well-to-do, younger, and technologically and culturally advanced user profiles than those who "live" on Zuckerberg's platform. Facebook is where people set up relationships and exchange content (photographs, video, personal notes, comments with no length limits), while Twitter is more unidirectional and instantaneous. Users are required to skillfully condense an idea, joke, link, online post, comment, TV program, event, or any other news worth sharing with others into a maximum 140-character mini-text. Twitter conversations can involve everyone, including brands. Its users mostly communicate via smartphone (78 percent on average) through hashtags (the pound sign: #). Unlike Facebook, which only allows people to see pages they are a fan or friend of, everyone can read tweets from any account. Every person who signs up for Twitter has a number of people, or followers, who connect to his or her account and who can read any and all tweets on that person's timeline.

TWITTER STATISTICS

271 million monthly active users
500 million tweets sent per day
78 percent of Twitter active users on mobile devices
77 percent of accounts outside the United States
Twitter supports thirty-five-plus languages.

Source: about.twitter.com, August 2014

These are the working rules for the main social media websites through which Nutella operates: an environment where the marketer's attention is aimed at three fundamental "Fs"—Friends, Fans, and Followers, i.e. the new dogma in branded content management lingo. If you want to increase your Fs, you have to supply the Internet with content that is no longer episodic but continuous.

The first objective is to achieve maximum visibility among fans and followers, in such a way as to obtain precise ROI (Return on Investment) metrics through Facebook Insights, Twitter analytics, and YouTube analytics.

Then the company has to evaluate the degree of engagement achieved based on responses to and interest in its page, which often vary depending on the algorithms the platform selects. In fact, the average flow ("reach" is the expression commonly used) of posts can vary a great deal: in recent years Facebook's management has been well aware that a great many brands are active on its platform, and has been trying to get them to invest in advertising. Careful analysis helped the company recognize the effectiveness of this marketing plan: Internet is in fact the easiest media to measure, but its indicators need to be used correctly if they are to encourage fans and followers to become satisfied consumers and, hopefully, loyal supporters of the brand.

FIRST PLACE ON FACEBOOK

"Welcome to Nutella's Italian fan page! A Facebook page that keeps you up-to-date on the most exclusive news from the world of Nutella, a place that's filled with new developments and surprises. Stay connected and experience the emotion along with us!" This was the first entry posted by Nutella Italia, on April 15, 2010. A few months later, on August 3, 2010, the international account (in English) was inaugurated: "Welcome to Nutella's new international Facebook page! We have 'combined' multiple Nutella Fan pages to create a closer community of Nutella Fans. As we are a very large community, tell us something about yourself so we can get to know each other better. Who are you? Where are you from?" This question garnered an unexpected deluge of responses, with thousands of "likes" and confessions of "loooooove . . ." Everyone was happy to have found a virtual space where they could share their passion with others. The user Yoyi wrote: "Wow, great to meet all [Nutella] lovers here. I am from Hong Kong and I am the first one [to] post from this place." Responses came in from all over the world, demonstrating the brand's global reach. User Birgit wrote: "I'm from Germany and grew up with Nutella. Now my 3 girls can't live without it!" Nick from Greece wrote: "Really amazing, Mr. Nutella." There were posts left by Silvana from Italy, Bella from Buenos Aires, Humberto from Mexico, Tamar from Lebanon, Thierry from Quebec, Sue from Lago Vista, Texas, and many more—all united by a single passion: their love of the famous hazelnut cream.

Nutella's third national account, inaugurated in November of the same year, was opened in Germany. Then, in October 2011, the company addressed Australia and New Zealand, asking consumers there, "What's your favorite thing about Nutella?" The responses were "the taste" (756) and "the way it spreads" (38). In Christmas 2011 the company reached out to fans in the United States: "We're thrilled to announce the launch of the Nutella USA Facebook page! Please visit the 'Guidelines' tab on the left to take a look at our page policies. We have many fun things in the works for the holiday season, so be sure to 'Share' this with your hazelnut-spread-loving friends!" (December 16, 2011). Last but not least, for Christmas 2012 the company put pages online for Belgium and France, announcing: *"Ouvrez l'œil et restez connectés, le compte-à-rebours jusqu'à Noël est lancé! Jusqu'au plus beau matin de l'année, nous allons vous offrir plein de contenus exclusifs à dévorer dès le petit-déjeuner."* ("Keep your eyes open and stay connected, the countdown to Christmas is on! Right up until the most beautiful morning of the year, we will offer you plenty of exclusive content to enjoy at breakfast and throughout the day.")

Month after month these accounts have multiplied, and now reach fifty-one countries in thirty different languages. The *lingua franca* is English. Beginning halfway through 2014, as part of the campaign celebrating Nutella's fiftieth anniversary, the company decided to create a single, unique Facebook account for the entire globe, one that is appropriate for the spread's status as a global lovemark. The page, titled simply "Nutella," allows users to change countries and languages by clicking on the Facebook menu in the window alongside the "share" buttons. If the user chooses not to modify these settings, the social network will automatically connect the user to the language he or she usually uses while surfing the web.

Ferrero conducted its first experiment using the planet's foremost social media in Italy, relying on the agency Neo Network (which became Zodiak Active in 2011 and continued to manage the site until February 2013). In just a few short months the page's "likes" reached a total of two million (on October 7, 2010). On November 15, 2013, the number of active fans reached five million, putting the page in first place in Italy among those managed by a brand. Nutella achieved the same position and success in France and Belgium, and remains among the top four in Germany.

In the standings for brand webpages presented on the website www.socialbakers.com—a company that monitors media, celebrities, politicians, sports champions, and more—Nutella stands in sixteenth place (data as of August 2014) with 29 million fans. The number one brand is still Coca-Cola with 87.5 million acolytes, followed by the Austrian energy drink Red Bull (44.4 million) and American sneakers company Converse (40.4 million).

Brands on Facebook

Brand	Fans (in millions)
1. Coca-Cola	87.5
2. Red Bull	44.4
3. Converse	40.4
4. Samsung Mobile	38.8
5. PlayStation	37.9
6. Nike Football	37.9
7. Oreo	37.3
8. Starbucks	37.3
9. Walmart	34.6
10. KFC	34.5
11. Pepsi	33.1
12. iTunes	32.3
13. McDonald's	31.9
14. Skype	30.7
15. BlackBerry	30.2
16. Nutella	29.0

Source: www.socialbakers.com, August 2014

Nutella's position in this ranking is surprisingly positive when we consider the fact that it's competing with brands that have longer histories and larger budgets. When the Ferrero brand competes "equally" with fast-moving consumer goods (FMCG) brands in Food (a category created by Socialbakers that excludes drinks), it achieves an honorable second place behind Oreo, the chocolate-and-cream sandwich cookies. Oreos have a much longer history, given that they were invented by Nabisco (part of the Kraft-Mondelez Group) in 1912, and millions of Americans have grown up eating them.

FMCG food brands on Facebook

Brand	Fans (in millions)
1. Oreo	37.3
2. Nutella	29.0
3. Pringles	27.4
4. Skittles	26.3
5. KitKat	24.1
6. Ferrero Rocher	19.2
7. Pizza Hut	15.3
8. Garoto	13.6
9. Trident	13.4
10. Tic Tac	12.9

Source: www.socialbakers.com, August 2014

Ferrero has used the same strategy for its other products as well: Kinder Chocolate, Ferrero Rocher, and Tic Tac. It's worthwhile noting that two other Ferrero brands show up among the top ten brands with the most fans on Facebook: Ferrero Rocher chocolate treats and Tic Tac. These both come in ahead of competing confectionary companies that boast a much higher turnover, like Nestlé and Mars. If we add together the fans of Ferrero's "grand brands," the total amounts to almost seventy million, so that it comes in second place right after Coca-Cola among global brands. In actual fact, the calculation isn't entirely accurate: a person who loves Nutella may have clicked "like" on the Tic Tac page or the Ferrero Rocher page. However, it is an interesting indication of the significant awareness these global products have achieved around the world. As for the distribution of Nutella fans in individual countries, the following table confirms expectations, with Italy in first place, followed by France. The fact that the United States is third comes as something of a surprise, and demonstrates the significant growth that the brand has enjoyed in this market over recent years.

Nutella fan distribution

Country	Local Fans (in Millions)	Percentage of Fan Base
1. Italy	4.5	15.7
2. France	3.3	11.6
3. United States	2.6	9.3
4. Brazil	2.5	9.0
5. Germany	1.9	6.8

Source: www.socialbakers.com, August 2014

A ROADMAP TO ENGAGEMENT

Convincing the people on Facebook to tell others about their love of the hazelnut cream is a case study in successful marketing: the 4.5 million fans of Nutella represent Italy's largest online community of brand lovers. Its implementation was presented in November 2012 at the third Social Case History Forum, held in Milan, Italy, and dedicated to marketing projects in social media. Davide Scodeggio, vice president of the Brands business unit at Zodiak Active, took the stage at #SCHF to explain: "If I have to talk to an audience made up of diehard fans of the hazelnut cream, probably most people listening expect me to tell them more about the legend of Nutella or how they might organize a Nutella Party. But if I start going on about the brand's nutritional properties, trying to explain just how good it is to eat at breakfast, most of them would probably stand up and walk out." It was clear that the company needed a model that could help it understand people's interest in

Nutella, based on active audience principles. Four different phases were laid out:

1. *Brand to many*: informational content and entertainment designed to reawaken the client's attention. During this phase, Nutella pages hosted articles about breakfast and the philosophy of "*buongiorno*" ("good morning"), as well as videos, games, and images that appealed to the emotions.

2. *Brand to one*: interactive tools, competitions, games designed to engage. The consumer is encouraged to share content and personal information. This approach was the goal of the Facebook application *Pane e Nutella* ("Bread and Nutella"), launched in June 2011: it allowed users to "spread" a name or message on a virtual slice of bread, providing a precursor to personalized labels.

3. *Many to brand*: dialogue and sharing within a community. This is the "authorization" phase, which consists of a larger fan participation, with the opportunity to share more extensive personal details, including by way of competition with awards and prizes.

4. *Many to many*: support for brand ambassadors, the brand's spontaneous "narrators" who serve to "evangelize" others through their experiences as enthusiastic consumers.

The real strategic and creative value of this project consisted in knowing how to direct the energy provided by people who love the brand, thereby transforming their ardor into "gas" to fuel a long-term relationship that is carefully shepherded so that it doesn't stray off course with respect to the brand and its positioning.

In the articulated analyses that marketing agencies dedicate to brands with Facebook pages, there is an engagement index (based on the number of posts read and relaunched, using complex algorithms) and the value of PTA, or "people talking about," which is provided by Facebook Insights and calculates the number of people who are "talking" with the page through interaction, connection, reading posts, and so forth. Obviously, the PTA can vary a great deal. Socialbakers, for example, underlined a peak of frenetic activity around the Nutella page between September and October 2013, when the personalized label promotion was launched: the page expanded from roughly ten thousand users to almost two hundred thousand.

Vincenzo Cosenza of Blogmeter explains: "Nutella is a highly visible brand, built up over time, that has know how to take advantage of the viral sharing mechanisms provided by Facebook. It found itself in fertile terrain, because it's a lovemark. But it's important to note that the number of fans isn't the only data required to evaluate how a brand is operating on this platform. You also have to measure engagement, or in other words, the propensity to interact with Nutella on a daily basis, after you've already left behind a 'like,' a comment, or a share."

Today's companies are finding it increasingly difficult to capture users' attention: the web has gotten crowded, and lots of companies have digital strategies. Online, consumers are bombarded with information, part of which now comes from traditional media, because newspapers and television stations have discovered Facebook can be an effective way to share news as well. The way each individual user connects to social media also counts, because people who interact via smartphone have markedly discontinuous reaction times and interest levels. But Nutella managed to earn an important recognition, already in 2011: the Italian e-business market research agency Demoskopea awarded Ferrero's brand a prize for Best Italian Social Page "for its ability to interact with the consumer."

ONLINE TALENT FOR YOUNG ARTISTS

Nutella's sleek Pelikan jar has been seducing designers since the 1960s. Its curved, iconic form has been the subject of a thousand reworkings and design projects, such as the refrigerator and chest of drawers called NutMobili ("NutFurniture"), presented in 2006 at the Salone del Mobile in Milan by three famous architects. Nutella's artistic side has been developed over the social media as well, where fans of the brand were given the opportunity to vote for their favorite Nutella-inspired artwork online. The company even took things a step further, giving consumers the chance to choose which line of glassware it would put into production.

In today's digital era, Web 2.0 undoubtedly influences companies. One striking example was the Winner Taco dessert created by Algida, which the multinational company Unilever, currently the owner of the brand, decided to reintroduce to the Italian market in January 2014, thirteen years after the product had disappeared from supermarket shelves. In Italy, thirty- and forty-something fans of this cream and caramel dessert, popular during the 1990s, had pushed for its reintroduction through a Facebook page group, insisting the company bring back their favorite childhood snack. In 2010 the American company Gap, a clothing colossus with three thousand stores around the world, had to rethink its decision to change its navy blue and white logo after its loyal fans rejected the idea. The longstanding concept that "the customer is always right" moves with lightning speed over the Internet. Another example was Cadbury's milk chocolate bar Wispa, famous for its "tiny but dense bubbles." Launched in Great Britain in 1983, the company retired the product in 2003. But in October 2008 it became available in stores again, put back into production after a massive online fan campaign supported by consumers all over the

UK. Cadbury explained the development to people on its company website: "But such was the popularity of this sumptuous milk chocolate, that the nation began an online campaign to bring it back. Cadbury was happy to oblige!"

In the May 2008 issue of the magazine *Bloomberg Businessweek*, Steve McKee wrote that these "friendships" are generated by the most important factor in branding: "relevance." "Brands that generate the strongest sense of tribal identity are so relevant to the wants and needs of their consumers that they generate a natural gravitational pull," wrote McKee. This "tribal identity" cannot be modified without incurring the tribe's wrath. Even a simple change in the recipe of a beloved product can be enough. This is what happened on April 23, 1985, when the then-CEO of Coca-Cola decided to change the formula for the most famous drink in the world in an attempt to compete more effectively with Pepsi. The company launched New Coke, a sweeter, less carbonated version of its soft drink. It was an epic fail. Indeed, it has been described in the United States as "the biggest marketing blunder of all time," and just three months later everything went back to the way it was. This is exactly why Nutella's flavor hasn't changed or been modified in fifty years. At most, some steps in the production process have been improved, along with the quality of raw ingredients.

Sometimes a change in communications can constitute a valid marketing tool, as Ferrero experienced with its packaging for the Kinder Chocolate bar. For three decades, starting with the product's debut in 1974, the image used in advertisements and on packaging remained unchanged: the face of a young, blond, blue-eyed German boy. In 2003 the original image was substituted with a new version, surprising loyal customers and causing a stir in the media. As a result, in 2009 Ferrero decided to take advantage of the attention people had paid their poster boy in order to hold a contest for parents everywhere: "If you have a child between three and ten, send us a picture. We might be able to put it on our new label." The company's Italian headquarters were soon flooded with photos.

That Italian experience inspired three new Nutella projects based on the television talent show model. Young artists selected competitively beforehand gave performances that were judged by fans on Facebook.

The first contest was entitled *"Un buongiorno a regola d'arte"* ("A classic good morning"), and invited participants to design new graphics for a limited-edition series of 200-gram (7-ounce) Nutella glasses. After the entries were reviewed, in April 2012 images of the four most interesting proposals were published on the social network so people could vote for them. The winning entry was designed by a student in Rome, whose series of colored glasses—entitled "Funny Morning"—won first prize and was produced by Ferrero. A few weeks later, in the summer of 2012, online voting began for the contest *"Il buongiorno si vede dal talento"* ("You can tell wether it's going to be a good morning from the talent"), which involved young, emerging opera professionals, in collaboration with the Pavarotti Foundation. It was a battle down to the last note, with Luciano Pavarotti singing the aria "Buongiorno a te" used for a moving commercial aired by Nutella in Italy that year. The third initiative was held as part of a self-produced design exhibition/marketplace held in Turin. In November 2012 two Nutella-inspired projects won prizes: "Super-nu," a desk and child's chair built of recycled cardboard; and the crêpière "Hold Me Tight," which featured graphics inspired by a famous painting by Magritte.

Similar experiences were organized in other countries. In Germany these included an exhibition held in Frankfurt for Nutella's fortieth anniversary that displayed drawings made by fans and gathered through a company website, as well as a competition held in 2009 to create limited-edition labels for the 2010 FIFA World Cup in South Africa. Five different labels were created, four of which were selected by a jury made up of Ferrero Marketing, Design Agency and the Museum für Angewandte Kunst Frankfurt. The fifth was selected through online voting. The same approach was used in France in summer 2014, with the concept "L'Atelier Nutella," which got 3.3 million fans involved through the company's Facebook page. Selection of all the new labels, to be applied to a collectable "pot," took place through "likes" registered on the social network: the finale held between the four different designs was a race to the last click, where the winner was selected by 43,000 fans and the runner-up came in a close second, with 41,000 votes. Ultimately the company's initiative was the real winner: 185,222 votes registered; 5.8 million contacts on Facebook; 535,000 people engaged (share, comments, one-click likes) for an overall engagement rate of 9.1 percent, compared to the Facebook average of 1 percent.

"You are what you like," some might say. There's even a research study conducted by the University of Cambridge on the "like" clicks in social media that analyzes this new tendency in human behavior. While online interaction can involve sensitive data, attracting calls for safeguarding privacy, Facebook "likes" are useful, traceable tools for companies that want to understand their brands' popularity.

LADY GAGA'S TWEET

The social web offers us a constant flow of information and comments. Every individual brand has to study how to join, and what kind of content to offer. As Weber and Henderson note, "social media can be enticing, but it can also be overwhelming." This is particularly true for Twitter, the fastest growing social network. "It is the fastest-growing player in the world in terms of active users: 21 percent of the world's Internet population uses Twitter every month."

Speed, creativity and "push" interaction—welcome to the world of Twitter, the latest social media company to enjoy success via the Internet. To be honest, Twitter has been a relatively tough nut for companies to crack, and they've only recently begun using it. Nutella has been tweeting in Italy since May 2010, and as of August 2014 the brand's account had 135,000 followers. In the United States, there's even a little bird that chirps: "Spreading the joy of Nutella one tweet at a time." There are also accounts in France, Turkey, and Mexico. But marketing strategists are convinced that what counts the most on this platform are endorsements from celebrities and opinion leaders. Twitter generates viral phenomena not so much when the brand does the talking as when it becomes the object of conversation for others. A perfect example is one of the most viral tweets ever produced, written by pop star Lady Gaga on January 26, 2011: "Ok. Firstly, yes I love Nutella (with Banana+Wonderbread) who doesn't? Secondly, I can't believe 'Edge of Glory' was trending, sneakymonsters!" Native New Yorker Stefani Germanotta, aka Lady Gaga, boasts 42 million followers and is in sixth place on the list of the world's most followed accounts, behind such people as Katy Perry (56.0), Justin Bieber (53.9), and President Barack Obama (45.8). For Nutella, her spontaneous declaration of love was more important that any promotional campaign, especially coming at a time when Nutella-mania hadn't yet exploded in the States.

To be honest, traditional brands haven't had it easy on Twitter, judging from their rankings in terms of followers: Coca-Cola has "barely" 2.65 million fans (August 2014), while it boasts

87 million on Facebook. According to marketing expert Mark Fidelman, in order for a brand to be successful through Twitter it has to continue to respond to the questions people ask it, always and forever, and it must find a way to create interesting content. The mistake many brands make is to treat this social media merely as a broadcasting channel, using it as a one-way street. Companies working for brands have to listen around the clock to what's being tweeted, and remain ready to toss in a joke or quip based on the current buzz. During the 2014 World Cup, as they watched the match between Italy and Uruguay, many users commented on the bite Uruguayan attacker Luis Suarez inflicted on Italian defender Giorgio Chiellini's shoulder. Among brands, the fastest to make it online was a tweet from McDonald's Uruguay, which jokingly invited the attacker to have a hamburger the next time he was hungry: "*Hola @ luis16suarez, si te quedaste con hambre vení a darle un mordisco a una BigMac ;).*" Whole Foods Market, an American supermarket chain, added: "This can be your dinner . . . ITALIAN FLANK STEAK PINWHEELS #WFMdish." Snickers wasted no time inviting the Uruguayan champ to take a bite of their snack bar, insofar as it was "more satisfying than Italian." In the end, even the Italians laughed the incident off. The famous Italian food store Eataly cited a cover from the daily newspaper the *New York Post*, with an enormous "EATALY" splashed below a photo of the incident as it happened on the field. When Italy lost and exited the tournament early, Italian pasta company Barilla welcomed the Italian soccer team back home with two images launched online: a strainer filled with cooked pasta above a banner that read "*Ci hanno cotti in 90 minuti!*" ("They cooked us in 90 minutes!"); and an image of the Barilla logo on a blue background with eleven individual macaroni lined up, one of which had a bite taken out of it. It was a perfect example of instant marketing, something that requires quick reflexes, in-

telligence, and humor. Some companies, like Mars, have even set up a company newsroom that follows each of its brands, adhering to an appropriate editorial framework. Nutella is taking its first baby steps in this arena, and for now it mainly distributes pictorial content online that fans can share with one another. But plans are in the works for digital development on Twitter as well.

Millions of daily tweets offer an extraordinary opportunity to interpret the company's brand reputation live. In the past, companies needed telephone interviews, specific surveys, and focus groups in order to listen to loyal consumers. With the advent of the Big Data technique, which gathers together large quantities of tweets during a limited time period so that they can be studied, companies can now conduct emotive analysis as well, interpreting the Internet's natural lingo. This happens thanks to the rules of Twitter: its content is open to everyone who is signed up for the service. Therefore monitoring tweets makes it possible for people to garner extremely useful and interesting data on anything from individual brands to TV shows, politicians, and pop stars. In just one year (data from August 2013 to August 2014), Ferrero found that tweets launched online containing the word "Nutella" totaled 17 million, while 440,000 were launched with the hashtag #Nutella.

Sometimes a brand can find its way into a Big Data investigation by chance, as happened to Nutella with "*#italianelmondo, il Bel Paese visto con la lente dei 140 caratteri*" ("Italy in the world, the Bel Paese seen through a 140-letter lens"). The analysis was conducted by Almawave, an Italian business consulting company in the Almaviva Group, which studied the content of roughly 7.9 million tweets in six different languages (English, French, German, Spanish, Portuguese, and Italian) that focused on Italy. The study was conducted over a single month, focusing on tweets launched between September 24 and October 28, 2013, but is ongoing and has gathered (as of March 2014) no fewer than 31,076,637 tweets. The results were rather surprising: the subjects addressed most often included soccer player Balotelli, Capri, pizza . . . and Nutella. On Twitter, sports was the topic of choice (40 percent of the tweets), followed by tourism (15 percent), politics (8 percent), local events (6 percent), the economy (6 percent), and so on. It revealed a growing interest in Italian food and wine. Chianti topped the list among wines, while food products were in line with common stereotypes: pizza was number one (25 percent), followed by pasta (18 percent), and coffee (11 percent). Curiously, truffles and Nutella each earned a respectable 2 percent, tying for position. Once again the hazelnut cream proved that it's perceived as being a trademark of Italian living, capable of competing with more traditional specialties.

Valeria Sandei, the CEO of Almawave, had this to say: "Big Data analyses can constitute a valid tool for obtaining a snapshot of the current situation, because they tell us about the real world and offer unexpected keys to understanding things." The #italianelmondo project proved once again that advanced technologies are providing analyses that are useful to commercial brands. Almawave's staff emphasized that the results were obtained using the new, semantic-ontological platform Iride Customer Centric Suite, which can monitor even nonstructured Big Data such as the kind generated by social networks. Our digital words, jokes, quips, and sighs are turned into precious statistics and information for marketing departments. Is it a sort of Big Brother that controls everything? Not exactly, because individual users' privacy remains intact, and the inquiry is designed to sift through millions of tweets in search of trends and nothing else.

Big Data is most likely the future of marketing, because it makes predictive inquiries possible: through a "live" monitoring of tweets it can allow people to understand what kind of consensus a politician will have during elections; if the name of a new product will be accepted; if the packaging that boasts a new label will prove popular. The important thing is that the brand be able to offer its fans original content: this is the frontier of branded entertainment.

A survey conducted by Frank N. Magid Associates, an American consulting and research company, created an overall profile of Twitter users as they stood during the early months of 2014. It showed that Twitter users were thirty-four years old on average, and therefore younger than the average age (thirty-seven) of people using other social networks. Furthermore, 31 percent earned a salary of over $75,000 and spent a lot of money on high-tech items, and 19 percent more time tweeting than they did using other media. Teenagers proved to be the fastest-growing group of tweeters, with a 44 percent increase in 2013.

This audience has excellent economic potential, and therefore is extremely attractive to companies. Logically, investments in digital technology, even for "analogical-born" products like Nutella, can only go up. This has become a consolidated choice among major food companies, which today direct between 10 percent and 20 percent of their promotional budgets into the web.

Twitter and Facebook aren't the only social media, either. Sharing videos on YouTube has exploded in recent years. Today Nutella has fifteen channels on the website, the most popular of which is the Italian channel, with more than 11 million views. As of August 2014, Nutella had already opened its own dedicated Instagram accounts in Italy, the United States, the Middle East, Denmark, and Colombia, through which 4.5 million images have been shared, and the number is growing every day. The web is covered with "likes" for savory and flavorful photos and recipes with Nutella, as well as lots of news items dedicated to the hazelnut cream. Nutella has also opened Pinterest accounts in Italy, the United States, Australia, New Zealand, and the Netherlands.

In 1964 there were only TV commercials. Today Nutella is all grown up, and knows how to navigate the great seas of global communications, taking advantage of the most innovative technologies out there.

PART THREE
Nutella company

7

The Factory that planted trees

An inebriating aroma takes you back to when you were a child. When the wind blows down off the Alps and into Alba, the scent of roasted hazelnuts wends its way through red medieval towers, caressing the bas-reliefs of evangelists on the façade of the Alba cathedral and coasting across Piazza Savona, where locals gather to sip aperitifs outside. This pleasurable sort of hazelnut "pollution" from "Nutella City" was what the inhabitants of this small town where the spreadable cream was born became accustomed to. Sometimes the capital of the Langhe region—a hilly area in the south of Piedmont—is brushed by mint-flavored breezes, while other times they are chocolate-flavored, sharp and intense.

Between the Po River and the Ligurian Apennines, in northern Italy, in a landscape that UNESCO included among the fifty Italian World Heritage Sites in 2014, lie hills that have been shaped by centuries of two different agricultural traditions: at lower levels, wine growing and wine making; 500 meters (1,640 feet) above sea level and over, the cultivation and processing of hazelnuts. As UNESCO officials wrote in their explanation for awarding this prestigious global prize to the Langhe, the area is "an outstanding example of man's interaction with his natural environment." Today, thanks to Nutella and Ferrero Rocher, a hazelnut orchard can guarantee a decent profit. But when Pietro and Giovanni Ferrero first began collecting the hazelnut oilcake they used to create their *Giandujot*, hazelnut orchards were experiencing a crisis, and many farmers had decided to abandon them altogether. Proof of this can be found in *The Moon and the Bonfires*, the last novel written by Cesare Pavese, one of Italy's most important twentieth-century writers, published in 1950. The main character of the novel is an orphan, a farmer who wants to placate his "rage at not being anyone," because forty years earlier he had been forced to leave Italy and go seek his fortunes in America. After the war he returns to the hills of his homeland in Piedmont and says, "The other year, when I came back to the village for the first time, I came almost secretly to see the hazelnut trees again." For him, the greatest surprise is discovering that the trees of his childhood are no longer there. "But I had not expected not to find the hazelnut trees any longer. It meant that everything had come to an end." Without those trees, he believes everything is over for him, because for the Langhe region hazelnut trees do not just represent agriculture, but ancient culture as well.

Today Ferrero buys roughly half the hazelnut harvest in Piedmont, but given that there are now eleven "Nutella Cities" spread out across five continents, not even the entire Italian production of *Corylus avellana* (the scientific name for the hazelnut tree) would be enough to satisfy its demand.

For this reason, the hazelnuts also come from Turkey, the United States, Chile, and Georgia. The same happens with cocoa, milk, sugar, and other ingredients. For Ferrero, supplying the necessary raw ingredients has become a business worth billions of dollars per year: they're collecting everywhere, always searching for the best quality and freshness. Company experts follow the collection process step by step, and for the past few years have overseen the agricultural production of hazelnuts directly as well.

When it comes to ingredients and the company's specialties, Michele Ferrero never compromised. Undoubtedly, over the past thirty years, this company has done more than anyone else to safeguard and encourage hazelnut cultivation around the world, and one could easily compare Signor Michele and his collaborators to Elzéard Bouffier, the main character of the poetic tale *The Man Who Planted Trees*, published in 1953 by the French writer Jean Giono. Elzéard's story inspired dozens of "tree planters," and it is even believed to have pioneered ecologist culture. The tale details the story of the extraordinary life of a shepherd who lived in Provence, France, and who managed to create an entire forest by personally planting over one hundred thousand acorns, restoring a desolate valley to its ancient splendor.

There's no way of knowing whether Michele Ferrero had read Giono's book. However, in the late 1980s, encouraged by management personnel in German facilities, and by the difficulty the company was having purchasing hazelnuts on the global market, he had an innovative idea worthy of Bouffier. Why not plant hazelnut trees in the world's southern hemisphere, so that Ferrero would always have fresh nuts for its products, even out of season? The *Corylus avellana* only develops in temperate areas around the globe, between the 35th and 42nd parallels: in addition to Italy, the trees grow primarily in Turkey, Georgia, Spain, France, Azerbaijan, and the United States. Starting in 1991, Ferrero became "The Factory That Planted Trees." As of today, through agricultural companies it established in Chile, Argentina, Georgia, South Africa, and Australia, Ferrero has planted 6.6 million hazelnut trees, covering a total of 21,850 acres. And, thanks to its nursery of hazelnut suckers (plants that develop directly on the trunk or at the base of an existing tree, created in company greenhouses like the Chilean orchard in Temuco or the Georgian facility in Chitaskari), it will soon plant many more.

One could say that by planting and growing hazelnut trees, Nutella has helped reduce carbon dioxide around the world. AgriGeorgia, an orchard the company set up in 2007 in the former Soviet Union's Transcaucasian republic, has earned five hundred thousand "carbon credits" based on the CarbonFix Standard, with independent validation from TÜV SÜD, the German environmental certification multinational (one of the largest in the world), due to its "Afforestation with Hazelnut Plantations in Western Georgia" project.

In Luxembourg, the Ferrero headquarters hosts an HBD, or Hazelnut Business Development division. The division was set up to improve hazelnut cultivation techniques, provide consulting services to suppliers, and purchase large terrain properties around the world in order to create new agricultural businesses. Every year, the confectionary company purchases roughly 100,000 metric tons of shelled hazelnuts (110,200 tons), making it one of the world's primary users. In 2014, a year in which the harvest was scarce in Turkey due to adverse climatic conditions, Ferrero transformed roughly one-third of global production. When harvests are normal, production can go as high as roughly 400,000 metric tons (440,924 tons) of unshelled hazelnuts, which means that the percentage utilized by Ferrero drops to 25 percent. Turkey remains the number one hazelnut producing country, totaling between 600,000 and 650,000 metric tons (661,387-716,500 tons) of shelled hazelnuts per year, roughly 70 percent of the global total (international statistics are calculated in shelled fruit, which weigh roughly twice as much as unshelled fruit). Turkey is followed by Italy (roughly 13 percent, or 110,000 to 120,000 metric tons—121,000 to 132,270 tons), the United States (4 percent, or 34,000 metric tons—37,478 tons), and Spain, Georgia, and Azerbaijan (each of which produce 3 percent, or 25,000 to 30,000 metric tons—27,557 to 33,069 tons).

In Nutella's world, the agricultural companies Ferrero set up to cultivate hazelnuts—beginning in the 1990s and continuing today—are becoming increasingly important, currently numbering over one thousand employees. A development plan for the future calls for a significant increase in these activities. In Australia the company only recently began purchasing land, and the first harvest is expected between 2018 and 2020. In February 2014 the Group signed a memorandum in Serbia for the purchase of an additional 12,500 acres, establishing cooperation agreements with individual agricultural producers.

Ferrero agricultural companies

	Year established	Employees	Acres
AgriChile	1991	372	7,400
Ferrero Corilicola (Argentina)	1994	9	600
AgriGeorgia	2007	595	7,660
Agri SudAfrica	2009	34	800
Agri Australis	2011	2	4,950

Source: CSR Ferrero Report 2012

THE LARGEST HAZELNUT ORCHARD IN THE WORLD

Inside Ferrero operates a hazelnut "task force" with a precise goal: to achieve 100 percent traceability of the small fruits used to create the *manteca* (the hazelnut puree used in Nutella), the crushed bits (used, for example, to top Ferrero Rocher) or those used whole (inside pralines). The project, called Ferrero Farming Values, invests millions of euros in order to achieve certain objectives: guarantee the excellence of agricultural production; respect and make sure suppliers respect work conditions in compliance with the laws; avoid any kind of child labor; and set up and apply safe workplace practices. Many of them are young Italian, Turkish, or Chilean farmers who fly around the world, planting trees and teaching other farmers these modern agricultural practices. Here is a look at how they operate in different countries.

Turkey. In mid-August 2014, when hazelnut harvests in the primary producing countries were already underway, the global media focused its attention on this sector: "The cost of hazelnuts has soared by more than 60 percent over the past year, after crop-killing hailstorms and frost hit the world's biggest hazelnut producer, Turkey, which controls 70 percent of the global market. Even Canada's tiny homegrown supply is in jeopardy, devastated by a disease known as the Eastern Filbert Blight." (CBC News, Toronto). In the *New York Post*, journalist Sophia Rosenbaum added that it was: "Time to stock up! A Nutella shortage may be on the horizon thanks to a March frost in Turkey that wiped out about 70 percent of this year's hazelnut crop." Interviewed by Italian journalists about the matter, former ambassador Francesco Paolo Fulci, vice president of Ferrero International and president of Ferrero S.p.A., declared, "This type of harvest fluctuation has already occurred in the past. Consequently, for years now, commodity and raw material markets have grown accustomed to high price volatility. Ferrero is equally accustomed and can manage it adequately. The Group is confident and prepared for this situation and will continue to purchase hazelnuts, along with the other raw materials, at their usual high quality." To be truthful, this drop in production wasn't the first in the more than six centuries that hazelnuts have been cultivated, harvested, and exported from Turkey: others occurred as recently as 2005, 2008, and then in 2012. But alarm nonetheless spread among Nutella consumers by word of mouth over social networks; the ensuing race to buy up jars of the cream provided further proof of how much the product had become a lovemark. It may be the closest connection between product and raw material of its kind anywhere in the world.

In order to safeguard Nutella from geographical and meteorological risks, Ferrero has worked to diversify its supply, including a recent, extremely important acquisition. In July 2014 the company acquired 100 percent of the Oltan Group, a world leader in the production and commercialization of hazelnuts that boasts sales of over $500 million per year. This Turkish company is based in Trabzon, one of two hazelnut "paradises" on the Black Sea, near the border with Georgia and other cities like Samsu, Ordu, and Giresum: a green swathe of small farms, each cultivating between one and three or four acres at most. The other traditional area for *Corylus avellana* cultivation can be found in the Akçakoca basin, 260 kilometers (just over 160 miles) east of Istanbul. Beginning in 2013, these two areas have been overseen by a group of fifteen experts employed by Ferrero Farming Values, led by a young Turkish agronomist. They provide training courses, help mechanize agriculture techniques, control quality and collaborate with over 1,600 small farmers in Turkey. They have created thirty-five "modern farmers," who can act as models for others around them. Those who participated in the project received a card providing them with the opportunity to purchase agricultural products in partner stores and amass points worth 0.15 Turkish lira (about six cents) for every kilogram of guaranteed quality product they deliver. The project aims to achieve 355 modern farms by 2020, involving a total of ninety thousand farmers, and thereby convincing young

men and women to remain in the countryside, which is important given the fact that the average age of people cultivating hazelnuts in Turkey increases every year.

Chile. In Turkey Ferrero chose not to purchase and cultivate its own land, but in South America, to help small farmers
produce more effectively, the company exported a little of the
culture so dear to Cesare Pavese, buying four hazelnut plantations in Chile all the way back in 1991. The Group's company, AgriChile, is based in Curicó. Three of its properties are
located in the VII Maule Region, roughly a three-hour car ride
south of Santiago, with another in the XI La Araucanía Region. The Camarico farm—located in the VII Maule Region—
hosts the single largest hazelnut plantation in the world, which
became fully operational in 2003. This is a single 3,700-acre
plot spread out across lowlands, within a long, broad valley
that contains one million trees, all artificially irrigated. Here
a number of different cultivars were planted: 'Tonda Gentile
delle Langhe', 'Tonda di Giffoni', 'Barcelona', and others. Currently AgriChile owns 7,400 acres and supplies roughly three
thousand metric tons (3,306 tons) of hazelnuts per year, harvested fresh between February and April. But another thirty
thousand acres have been planted by independent farmers in
Chile, all of whom recognize the opportunity for profitable harvests in what is a new sector for their country. Usually farmers
don't like to take risks, preferring to wait and see how things
develop. But now they've seen that hazelnuts work. Chilean
newspapers have given ample coverage to the *"boom del cul-
tivo de avellanas,"* estimating potential revenues from the nut
at around five thousand dollars per year for every 2.4 planted
acres, and with additional growth opportunities for the future.
Before the advent of Ferrero in this country, hazelnut cultivation was all but unknown in Chile.

Argentina. The cultivation of *avellanas* began with the establishment of Ferrero Corilicola in 1994, whose offices are in Viedma, roughly 1,000 kilometers (a little over 621 miles) south of Buenos Aires. The orchards are located in Valle Inferior del Rio Negro (VIRN), where the confectionary company currently oversees around five hundred acres of hazelnut trees. Thanks to these orchards and the efforts of independent farmers, this territory already has a total of 1,400 acres of hazelnut trees. Local media have celebrated the opportunity this kind of cultivation offers, stressing the fact that while hazelnut trees require artificial irrigation in semiarid areas, they nevertheless adapt well to all kinds of terrain and resist sharp shifts in temperature throughout the year.

Georgia. In 2007 nearly 1,500 acres of hazelnuts were planted here. Today, that number has increased to 8,400. AgriGeorgia boasts one of Ferrero's largest plantations. The area is located near Zugdidi, a city with a population of one hundred thousand near the Black Sea, just 10 kilometers (6.21 miles) from the Russian border with the republic of Abkhazia. The Russians had initiated cultivation of tea shrubs in this part of Georgia in order to satisfy domestic demand, but with the fall of the Soviet Union and the birth of the republic of Georgia, these plantations were abandoned and quickly became bushy jungles. Together with a group that included two other "pioneers," later expanded to four, Ferrero created a model plantation that has earned a significant number of carbon credits and includes mechanized harvesting (just as in every Ferrero company around the globe) and 15-ton silos for drying the hazelnuts. In previous centuries at farmhouses in the Langhe region, hazelnuts were left to dry in the sunlight, and had to be covered with large canvases whenever it rained. As a result, the nuts risked developing mold and had final humidity levels higher than the optimal 6 percent. The cycle that the company's hazelnut taskforce has set in place for Nutella production is complete: "planting, harvesting, drying, cracking, processing." This was a "new job" even from an agronomic point of view, insofar as hazelnut orchards are normally spread out over plots ranging from two to twelve acres at most: "We had to reinvent everything, from harvesting machines to the silos where the nuts are housed and dried, our irrigation techniques and our relationships with suppliers," say experts inside the company. It wasn't easy, and included emotionally charged moments, like when Russian tanks rumbled through the property during the Russo-Georgian War in Ossetia in August 2008. Fortunately, all's well that ends well.

South Africa. This may well be the boldest endeavor Ferrero has undertaken in the southern hemisphere, one in which the company had to build up everything from scratch. In 1991 it established the first outpost for AgriSudafrica, an agricultural company that was developed near Kokstad, 1,350 kilometers (approximately 839 miles) east of Cape Town. The terrain is mountainous, running between 1,000 and 2,000 meters (3,280 and 6,560 feet) above sea level, and located south of the Kingdom of Lesotho, on the Drakensberg. The Kwazulu Natal area is famous for its fruit orchards, and was chosen based on a study that examined the land, climate, and availability of water resources in numerous trial sites all over the country. The plantation is scheduled to yield its first hazelnuts in 2015, and the South African government intends to promote the project in a way similar to what happened in South America. This hazelnut plantation is the first experimental attempt to cultivate hazelnuts on the entire African continent.

Australia. This country is home to Ferrero's most recent investment, enthusiastically welcomed by the local press and media, who are convinced that the 70 million Australian dollars (US$57 million) Ferrero has invested in the "youngest" continent of all will transform Riverina—a region located southwest of New South Wales—into "the hazelnut capital of Australia." During a ceremony held in May 2014 in Narrandera, a small town of three thousand inhabitants, NSW Minister for Primary Industries Katrina Hodgkinson stated, "Today's planting of the first of a one million hazelnut tree plantation marks a significant milestone for our primary industries sector and for the Riverina. The NSW Government has worked closely with Agri Australis to facilitate this investment. This investment will not only directly create up to fifty permanent jobs and more than fifty seasonal jobs; it will indirectly provide a welcome boost to the Narrandera economy." The first hazelnut harvests are tentatively scheduled between 2018 and 2020.

Only a family business can allow itself to make these kinds of long-term investments, displaying the farsightedness of an entity that isn't quoted on the stock exchange and doesn't have to respond to investors' demands. Hundreds of thousands of farmers in Turkey, Georgia, South America, and soon in Africa and Australia can harbor hope for a better future every time they look at a jar of Nutella. Those 6.6 million trees planted around the planet are a concrete contribution to the fight against carbon dioxide pollution. It is a small green revolution, led by the spread of this ancient plant into the planet's southern hemisphere, expanding what the ancient Romans considered a universal symbol of happiness all over the world.

ON NUTELLA ISLAND

Every day hundreds of freight trucks stop in piazzas around the Nutella City factory, in Alba, where they wait to deliver raw materials that, inside enormous warehouse facilities, four thousand men and women wearing white shirts and hats will transform into the flavorful specialty. In truth, machines and computers do most of the work: production line workers control, blend, press buttons, and read reports. Everything is automatic, aseptic, and hyper-technological. Today the industrial facility where everything first started in 1946 continues to produce not only Nutella (550,000 jars per day when it's running at full steam), but also 20 million Ferrero Rocher pralines (also per day!), Kinder chocolate bars, Estathé tea drinks, Tic Tac, and plenty of other products. In reality, Nutella City is a small town stretching out over 400,000 square meters (nearly 100 acres), more or less the size of Alba's historical center: it is the largest production site in Europe, and over the past fifty years it has grown and continued to expand on the exact location where Pietro Ferrero set up his first factory.

When visitors enter Nutella City, they too are required to wear white shirts and baker's caps, which might make them feel a little like Charlie Bucket, the young hero of Roald Dahl's 1964 novel for children *Charlie and the Chocolate Factory*: eyes glowing with joy, nostrils filled with rich, sweet odors, taste buds tingling . . . But no cameras or video, please! Here, every single machine is top secret, designed and revised by Ferrero Ingegneria, the engineering division. The company planned the birth of each individual product right from the start and step by step, from naming to packaging to marketing strategies.

Nutella Island, the heart of this Italian chocolate factory, is a two-floor building: the ground floor hosts the enormous batches in which hazelnuts, cocoa, sugar, and powdered milk are blended together. The mix is then directed into a sort of cylindrical roller—the refiner—which chops this sweet "flour" into the finest powder. One of the secrets of Nutella, its inimitable texture, is achieved thanks to this step, during which the mixture is reduced to grains just a few microns thick: the human palate would perceive a mixture any higher or lower than this "perfect" value as a different taste. Then a white treadmill ribbon, covered with piles of Nutella flour, carries the whole enticing mixture inside an enormous hot basin, similar to those used for conching chocolate. Here vegetable oil is added and blended for two hours by large moving blades: this is where the magical, alchemical transformation takes place, producing a glossy, seductive cream that is almost ready to be eaten. This is when the "Nutelloduct" takes over: double-layered tubes heated by hot water move the blend upstairs to the top floor, all the way to the packaging line. This is the part that's pure ecstasy for every Nutella fan: containers filled with the warm cream, equipped with a merry-go-round of dispensers that fill jar after jar, are overseen by expert technicians who ensure that all defective packages are discarded. The machines produce hundreds of filled jars per minute. No detail is left to chance. Empty jars are checked one by one by an optical scanner, and there are tens of different check and control points set up along the assembly line in order to closely monitor every step. The hazelnut cream is dispensed at a specific temperature, and the glass jars are brought to the dispensers at room temperature, neither too hot nor too cold.

Particular attention is paid to the hermetic gold foil seal. The consumer has to be guaranteed that the Nutella seal hasn't been broken before it reaches the table: the jar has to make its characteristic "cracking" sound when it's opened.

The circle of paperboard beneath the cap and the gold foil are interconnected, only separating once the cap is unscrewed. At the end of this cycle, glasses and jars filled with Nutella are chilled and kept at low temperatures for two days in order to stabilize the product and help the cream crystallize. Finally, they're carried from this cold "cantina" to a refrigerated warehouse built specially for finished merchandise, set on pallets, shrink-wrapped in cellophane and ready to be sent out to supermarkets. This warehouse is yet another of the company's technological marvels: ten stories high and over three hundred feet long, the building is completely automatized and allows the company's logistics branch to maintain perfect control over distribution.

Even English writer Joanne Harris, the author of *Chocolat* (1999), is a fan of Nutella and made the trip to visit the facility in Alba, publishing an article about it in a women's weekly magazine. "There's something magical about a chocolate factory," she wrote, "as generations of Roald Dahl readers already know—and the child in me is fascinated by the size and scale of the place, the intricacy of the machinery, the precision, the noise, the movement, the smells of the entire process. [. . .] My guides have been more than generous with their time. My hour is long elapsed. And yet, they offer to show me one last wing of the factory; the place where Nutella—my favourite—is made. By now, night has fallen. We walk down a road in which mysterious underground vents give out a chocolate-scented steam towards the Nutella factory. My sense of smell is in overload. It's like being trapped in a giant jar filled with the scent of my childhood. I remember those jars now; suddenly, for the first time in forty years; the jars, which, when empty, could thriftily be reused as drinking glasses, inscribed with cheery cartoon characters; creatures from fairy tales; animals; birds. 300 tons of Nutella every day are produced in Alba alone—even the statistics have a kind of magic now, as if we are discussing the transformation of hay into gold."

NUTELLA'S FIRST SECRET: THE *MANTECA*

What's the recipe for Nutella? If you ask Ferrero, they'll tell you it's written right on the label. Sugar, palm oil, hazelnuts (13 percent), cocoa (7.4 percent), skim milk (6.6 percent), reduced mineral whey (from milk), soy lecithin as an emulsifier, and vanillin, an artificial flavor. That's it. Needless to say, there are a few secrets: secrets that have to do with the way these ingredients are processed and blended together. Which is the mantra of cult merchandise: never change, and leave a magic, inviolable halo of mystery around the product.

Elizabeth Candler, the great-great-granddaughter of the founder of the Coca-Cola company (acquired in turn from the pharmacist Pemberton), says as much in her 1994 cookbook *Classic Cooking with Coca-Cola*. In it she explains that when the Candler family sold control of the drink company in the 1920s, they most likely kept a copy of the original recipe, which contains a secret ingredient denominated "7X." Today people say that formula is kept under lock and key in a safe inside the multinational company headquarters in Atlanta. At heart, it's quite a paradox: millions of consumers "happily drink can after can," notes Elizabeth Candler in her book, "full of unidentified ingredients." And Nutella? In Alba they swear that there are no secret ingredients in their hazelnut cream.

As a company, Ferrero is reserved, speaking only through its products. Neither its managers nor the Ferrero family like to give interviews, but when it comes to ingredients and the production line they've become relatively transparent. All you need to do is read their official documents online, or reports detailing the company's social responsibilities.

Let's start with the hazelnut, the foundation for Nutella. The heart of the recipe is a *manteca*—a term used in cooking to indicate a "mixture of soft or fat substances with a creamy consistency"—or, in other words a hazelnut puree (as the www.nutella.fr website explains) that is toasted using special devices. The process is similar to the one used for cocoa beans. Ferrero applies a selection protocol based on the size of the fruit once they are shelled and skinned: only hazelnuts measuring a diameter between 13 and 18 millimeters (0.51 and 0.71 inches) will have the privilege of making it into the jar. In the same manner, each different size has different processing times in the large toasters. The extraordinary aroma released when someone opens a jar of Nutella is precisely due to the relatively lengthy toasting process the company employs, which helps enhance the fruit's aromas. Hazelnuts are purchased whole, then shelled, skinned, and subjected to a number of different analyses: size measurements, visual controls, laboratory tests on random samples, and tasting by special experts.

But most important are the criteria established by the company's HBD division for the hazelnut's value chain. The *manteca* is produced immediately after the nuts have been toasted, using the freshest fruit available at that time in each of the company's eleven factories around the world: that's the real secret of Nutella.

THE SECOND SECRET: CERTIFIED COCOA

Loved by nobility and kings, frowned upon by popes and theologians, the muse of artists, and a wonderfully useful ingredient for chefs and pastry makers the world over, chocolate remains a magical and satisfying substance: few foods excite people's passions the way chocolate can. It is synonymous with intense pleasure, and can vaunt a decidedly romantic image. But, as Carol Off writes in her 2008 book *Bitter Chocolate*, there is also an unfortunate dark side to the world's most seductive sweet, since an enormous divide exists between European and American children who enjoy a snack made with "the food of the gods" and their peers in Africa, who are forced to gather cocoa under inhumane conditions in plantations in the southern hemisphere. Cultivation of this tropical plant is widespread only in a narrow zone set between the parallels at 20° north and south of the equator. As with vineyards and wine, the position of terrain and the quality of the bean are both crucial to obtaining good chocolate. The entire Ferrero Group utilizes slightly more cocoa beans—which are toasted directly in house— than it does hazelnuts: a total of 120,000 metric tons (132,277 tons) per year. Ferrero chose to use African cocoa from Ghana, the Ivory Coast, and Nigeria, enriched by a percentage of aromatic cocoa from Ecuador, a country where the company has been collaborating with the Fundación MCCH (Maquita Cushunchic Comercializando como Hermanos) since 1998, a foundation run by Father Graziano Mason, a priest of Italian origins who has been working together with small farm communities for over thirty years. Cocoa certification is also important: the beans must be traceable and there cannot be any cases of child labor or forced labor anywhere along the supply chain. The company relies on UTZ and Rainforest Alliance certification, among others, as well as models designed to help farmers like the MCCH in Ecuador, in order to mantain standards. For Ferrero, the percentage of cocoa cultivated via sustainable agricultural practices has increased from 15 percent in 2010–11 to 40 percent in 2012–13, while the company's CSR (Corporate Social Responsibility) report indicates that Ferrero is aiming for 100 percent sustainability by 2020.

And that's not all. Ferrero has also initiated specific collaboration projects with cooperatives and agricultural associations in several African countries. The company will work with the Coopérative Anonklon de Bianouan in the Ivory Coast to build a school for two hundred students in order to educate farmers' children; and in Ghana and Nigeria it is working together with Source Trust to set up a project to encourage good farming practices. Last but not least, in Ghana and the Ivory Coast the company has started the Ferrero Cocoa Community Commitment (F3C) project as part of a "Framework of Action" originally set up by the US Department of Labor. The program involves 8,800 cocoa cultivation families in Africa, affecting a total of 26,000 children. Their production reaches a total of between five thousand and seven thousand metric tons (5,500-7,700 tons) of certified cocoa, and the program is providing training courses to help improve cultivation quality.

Roughly five million farmers around the world rely on the "food of the gods" for their survival, and large companies turn mainly to Africa to gather the ingredient (where 80 percent of global production is concentrated), often in countries in which certification is difficult. Small farmers with family-run businesses find themselves facing serious problems including vegetal pathologies, aging plants, and a lack of appropriate professional skills. This means that it's important to support families and provide technical support in order to slow emigration from rural areas into cities. The efforts of organizations that Ferrero is a part of—like the World Cocoa Foundation, which has over one hundred affiliated companies active in the chocolate supply chain; and the International Cocoa Initiative—is aimed at improving quality of life for people who work the land so that fortunate children in other parts of the world can consume chocolate that has been obtained ethically. The truth is, there are some small, specialized artisanal manufacturers that sell bars of chocolate bearing these brand names, but these are more of a flagship presence in the growing field of global chocolate commerce. It is important to note that large multinationals are behind the drive to increase the sustainability of their production lines.

Ferrero's Code of Business Conduct is based on principles drawn up by the International Labour Organization, and already in 2012–13 company CSR could guarantee that the volume of "sustainable" cocoa the company purchases corresponds to the amount necessary "for the production of Nutella and Ferrero Rocher, two of our most popular products." When talk inside the company turns to these farmers forced to work within difficult areas around the world, people often say that Ferrero likes to work with people who have decided to stay and work the land by choice, not out of necessity.

THE THIRD SECRET: A SHORT SUPPLY CHAIN FOR MILK

This may well be Ferrero's most surprising secret: the ingredients used to make Nutella include milk that's locally produced, such as the kind that's advertised by artisanal companies supported by Slow Food, or the cheese sold at the Union Square Greenmarket in Manhattan. In Italy, milk produced daily by Tamara, Reggina, Mafalda, and other Piedmont cows that graze the Padania plains between Cuneo and Turin all flows into a 35-meter-tall (nearly 115 feet) tower located in Moretta, a small town less than fifty kilometers (31 miles) from the Ferrero facility. The tower is the only one of its kind in Italy, and was built in 2010 by Inalpi, a company that collaborates with no fewer than five hundred dairy farms. It can produce powdered skim or whole milk using a "spray dryer" drying and atomizing technology, first invented by the Swedish company Tetra Pak. In 2013 this tower produced fifty metric tons (55 tons) of milk powder per day, 80 percent of which was delivered to Ferrero, as well as sixty metric tons (66 tons) of raw cream destined to be used in butter and other dairy specialties produced by Inalpi.

Part of the agreement set up by Inalpi along with Coldiretti, Italy's largest agricultural association, created and managed by the Università di Piacenza, in Emilia-Romagna, is an innovative price indexing system for the milk guaranteed by dairy farmers: a one-of-a-kind formula that manages to establish a truly synergetic cycle between producer, transformer, and final user, providing rewards based on the quality of the milk produced. Local milk is used not only in Italy, but also in the "Nutella Cities" located in other countries as well. In Australia Ferrero uses only Australian milk; in Canada, milk from Canadian and American cows; and the same deliberate localization also applies to Turkey, Mexico, and Brazil. In Germany the company uses more than 80 percent German milk, while in France that percentage increases to almost 100 percent. As the company's CSR notes, the Ferrero Group aims to create a "short, controlled and sustainable supply chain" for milk, and plans to have it fully in place by 2015. Animal health is part of the protocol for sustainability.

THE FOURTH SECRET: SUSTAINABLE PALM OIL

It all began in France in November 2012 with the advent of what newspapers called the "Nutella tax." The French government wanted to focus on palm oil, one of the raw ingredients imported by Ferrero France, increasing the tax by 300 percent. But the law didn't pass. For years, several environmental organizations had put the finger on that very ingredient, maintaining that it was partially to blame for deforestation in several areas of Indonesia, Malaysia, and Papua New Guinea (the countries where most palm oil is produced). According to the experts who drew up the law, the tax was not designed to punish consumers, but to send a strong signal to agribusiness, pressuring big companies to take the planet's health into greater consideration. Like olive oil, palm oil is extracted from the plant's fruit. First the fruit is pressed, then the resulting liquid is selected through a particular fractioning technique. Ferrero, which consumes roughly 150,000 metric tons (165,000 tons) of palm oil per year, responded with a press campaign in French newspapers and a website dedicated to the ingredients it uses called nutellaparlonsen.fr ("Let's talk about it"). "Today Nutella is being unfairly dragged into a debate over palm oil," read the double page spread. "We believe it is important to make several things clear. [. . .] For over forty years this product has been necessary in order to guarantee the creaminess and stability of our recipe, because it allows us to achieve the desired consistency without having to hydrogenize fats."

Ferrero's response went even further in setting up a plan for the selection of certified suppliers. The heart of the ecologists' accusation was a critique of agricultural practices that don't respect the natural environment. It was important to be able to demonstrate environmental propriety in the supply chain for each raw ingredient. The company joined the Roundtable on Sustainable Palm Oil (RSPO) program, an organization created in 2004 in order to help make palm oil harvesting sustainable in Malaysia and other countries, right from its inception. Other major industrial businesses participated as well, including Nestlé and Johnson & Johnson. According to Ferrero's French website: "Today 100 percent of our Nutella production facilities use 'segregated' RSPO-certified sustainable palm oil, the highest level of product available in terms of certification and traceability."

Ferrero also adopted a rigorous Code of Business Conduct for its palm oil, one that aims to achieve "excellence in quality and respect for human rights and sustainability." The company's managers have planned precise targets in order to achieve total traceability for its milk, eggs, coffee, cocoa, hazelnuts, and vegetal oils by 2020. It is an important step for a company that packages more than 1.1 million metric tons (1,212,000 tons) of products per year, from Nutella to Tic Tac, pralines and snacks, filling up 27,000 trucks that, if placed in a continuous line, would form a route 280 miles long, roughly the distance from Chicago to Detroit.

When it came to ingredients, Michele Ferrero was always demanding. A number of years ago in the company's laboratories in Alba, his son Pietro, who earned a degree in biology and passed away prematurely in 2011, introduced the use of an instrument designed to discover any genetically modified contamination in raw ingredients, making it possible to identify and discard them. Ferrero was the first Italian company to conduct these kinds of analyses, a practice it considered a given and never publicized. Production controls are continuous throughout all twenty Ferrero factories, and the company is now beginning to realize that the fact that it has set up five hundred different "attention points" might well be worth sharing with the consumer. Naturally the men and women in the company's marketing department need to highlight the care and attention Ferrero spends on its products through an effective communications campaign. It must become what's known as a USP, a unique selling proposition: that unique, powerful benefit for the client that none of the competition can offer, and which will help provide further proof that Ferrero products are worth purchasing.

8

Ferrero-ness

A statue of the Blessed Virgin Mary stands in the courtyard of the company's facilities in Alba. The Ferrero family is particularly devoted to Our Lady of Lourdes: an initial effigy was set among the warehouses, on the banks of the Tanaro River, following a pilgrimage to the French sanctuary in the Pyrenees, as a way of saying thanks for having escaped much of the devastation wrought by the floods of 1948. In December 1996, at a convention organized to celebrate the company's fiftieth anniversary, Michele Ferrero gave a short interview to the Italian newspaper *La Stampa*. "The secret of our success?" he said, "Our Lady of Lourdes. Without her, we wouldn't be able to accomplish much." "He's not kidding," explained his wife Maria Franca. "My husband is a man of faith. And faith doesn't take anything away from you; actually, it enriches you." German sociologist Max Weber related the Protestant ethos to the advent of capitalism. Perhaps it's not too much to relate Christian faith to the values intrinsic to Ferrero's business culture, which was born in the 1950s and 1960s in an area of Italy permeated with rural and Catholic traditions. At the same time, it would be a mistake to dismiss Ferrero's entrepreneurial philosophy as something folksy or old-fashioned. This confectionary company remains a family business, even today, led by a family who lives for its products and who identifies completely with the company. It's the kind of attitude typical of many who work in artisanal companies, and it is a particularly positive value in light of the unethical behavior evinced in the financial world in recent years.

Ferrero enjoys a sterling reputation, as confirmed by the ranking it achieved in 2009—coming in ahead of Ikea and Johnson & Johnson—on the Global Rep Trak Pulse, a list produced by the Reputation Institute of New York. According to a June 2013 ranking of "Italy's most attractive employers" compiled by the employer branding company Universum, based on preferences expressed by more than twenty thousand students at thirty-nine Italian universities and business schools, Ferrero is everyone's dream company, even coming in ahead of Google. The company's original character has evolved through a fortunate process of internationalization, even as it has preserved its original roots. In Alba, Ferrero has built housing near its factories, as well as nurseries, sports facilities, and clubhouses. While some may view this kind of "welfare" as paternalistic, it has nevertheless helped grow—amid Kinder eggs, spreadable creams, and pralines—a sort of "family" that's thirty thousand people strong (it includes Ferrero's farming companies and businesses in developing countries). These individuals all enjoy shared values, and every business in the Ferrero Group has to follow the same code of ethics, which guides the way the company behaves and their relationships with clients, local communities, employees and all the stakeholders.

While during the same years, in Ivrea, a small town near Turin, Adriano Olivetti was preaching (and practicing) a balance between social solidarity and entrepreneurial profit, the original Ferrero in Alba was already applying these principles.

Olivetti had only just passed away when the first Ferrero-sponsored convention for social initiatives was held, in 1961, entitled "Man's Adaptation to Industrial Labor." The company published journals filled with sociological analyses, and Michele Ferrero set up a "suggestion box" inside his factory in order to "offer employees an easier way to help improve and empower the company." One of Ferrero's inspirations was the 1961 "social" encyclical *Mater et Magistra*, promulgated by Pope John XXIII, who invited entrepreneurs to avoid transforming their collaborators into "silent executors."

When, in November 1994, the facilities in Alba were overwhelmed by a river of mud from heavy rains and flooding that caused deaths and damage across the Piedmont region, a thousand employees showed up unbidden, shovels in hand, in order to dig out from underneath the mire and clean the damaged and dirtied areas so that the factory could open up again as soon as possible. One month later, Michele Ferrero wrote an open letter thanking his employees: "We're the victims of a cruel destiny, one that has brought shock and desperation. Viewing all this devastation, which has erased decades of hard work, commitment, and sacrifice, has provoked a deep sense of disorientation and a distressing sense of irreparable loss. But it was precisely in that moment, at the deepest depths of profound desolation, that I felt all around me the old Ferrero 'heart' that has always, in the past, in the most difficult moments, expressed itself with full dignity and grandeur."

That "heart" is still at the center of company philosophy. Confirmation of this came from Michele's son, the current CEO, Giovanni Ferrero, during an interview given to the Italian newspaper *Corriere della Sera* in October 2011: "The sense of belonging and historical roots cannot be severed. They're being reinforced in light of new challenges. The more the world becomes global, the more we need strong identities."

THE MEN WITH MONKEY WRENCHES

"Loving your work (unfortunately the province of only a priv-ileged few) represents the best, most concrete approximation of happiness on earth," wrote Italian chemist and writer Pri-mo Levi in his collection of thoughts and essays *The Monkey's Wrench* (published in English in 1986), in which he detailed a series of adventures and experiences in the life of an Italian master rigger, Tino Faussone, who travels around the world putting up oil derricks and working on bridges. In Ferrero there are lots of "men with monkey wrenches," who have traveled around the world in order to set up the Group's facilities in countries across five continents.

Today there are twenty Ferrero factories around the world, eleven of which produce Nutella. After the first three large in-dustrial facilities—in Italy, France, and Germany—that the company built during the 1940s and 1950s, expansion to enable it to produce more hazelnut cream was undertaken in Austra-lia, Poland, Brazil, Canada, Russia, Mexico, and Turkey. When domestic demand rises above a certain level in a given country, the company begins to consider building a new production fa-cility in order to supply that market with fresh product made locally, as opposed to imported product.

It's important to carefully evaluate which site is best for the facility. Almost all of Ferrero's factories are in small towns that seem like copies of Alba, the company's Italian hometown: the company's localization experts avoid large, polluted cities or anywhere that has chemical or metalworking industries, which could damage Ferrero's confectionary products. Inside the company people say, "Every new facility is like a pastry shop." Furthermore, the location has to be near areas where the com-pany can get the raw ingredients it needs: near Manisa, in Tur-key, where the most recent factory was built over the span of

The twenty Ferrero facilities around the world

Country	Location	Year it became operational
Italy	*Alba*	1946
Germany	*Allendorf*	1956
France	*Villers-Ecalles*	1960
Italy	Pozzuolo Martesana	1965
Australia	*Lithgow*	1974
Ireland	Cork	1975
Ecuador	Quito	1978
Italy	Balvano	1985
Italy	*Sant'Angelo dei Lombardi*	1985
Belgium	Arlon	1989
Brazil	*Poços de Caldas*	1994
Argentina	La Pastora	1996
Poland	*Belsk*	1997
Canada	*Brantford*	2006
Cameroon	Yaoundé*	2006
India	Baramati*	2007
South Africa	Johannesburg*	2007
Russia	*Vladimir*	2009
Mexico	*San José Iturbide, Guanajuato*	2013
Turkey	*Manisa*	2013

* Ferrero Social Enterprise

Facilities written in italics produce Nutella.

two years, there are plenty of cows to provide one of the main ingredients in Nutella, as well as in snacks like the Kinder Pinguí, part of Ferrero's refrigerated snacks line. Hazelnuts are cultivated not far from Brantford, in Canada, Ontario. Even water is important: it must be readily available and devoid of pollution or heavy metals.

Once the choice has been made, people from Ferrero's technical division—a team of Italian and German experts who travel the world between eighty and two hundred days each year, bringing the know-how necessary to make sure the facility runs well—go to the location. A member of this team says, "We feel like we're 'missionaries,' not 'mercenaries,' in a foreign land." This may seem like company rhetoric, but when you meet these men and women face-to-face and hear them tell their stories, you soon realize that they mean every word.

"The smell of home is everywhere." Attilio Barra, who has been working at Ferrero since 1988, currently lives in Brantford, where he works as a process technologist. "My career at Ferrero began in Alba, where I worked for the first five years. Then I moved to our facility in Sant'Angelo dei Lombardi, located in southern Italy near Naples. Then I spent three years in Brazil; then another five in Ecuador; then I spent some more time in Italy; and finally in 2009 I moved here to work in the company's Canadian factory. In Poços de Caldas, in the state of Minas Gerais in Brazil, we were four hours north of São Paulo. The location was a nice city with a population of 150,000, set 1,200 meters (4,000 feet) above sea level and blessed with a nice climate and even thermal baths. We lived well and I went back later to add some improvements for the Nutella line. I've gained a lot of experience outside Italy, but I've always lived well, because every single one of our factories has the same smell: the aroma of Ferrero. When I move to a new country, it just seems like I've changed departments or gotten a new office. If anything, our families may encounter a few difficulties. They have to be motivated and be able to integrate into the new culture. I've been lucky, because my family has always traveled with me and been enthusiastic about the transfers, overcoming minor difficulties successfully. I'm living in Canada now and happy to be here, and I owe a large part of that to my wife and daughters. My eldest daughter graduated from school here, and I'm very proud of that. My second daughter, who is thirteen, was born in Quito, in Ecuador, and is happy to be living with us in Brantford.

"While our job is to set up production facilities, what we are actually doing is exporting our vision of food production and the concept of product quality out to the world. For me, this company is like a second family. Better yet, it's a family within the family. Every Ferrero expat carries a little of the company's culture with him out into the world. First and foremost, we've spread hazelnut culture. I was moved to see the plantations in Chile, and very happy to see fresh hazelnuts arrive here in Canada, in Brantford, for the production of our spreadable cream. One of my jobs is to taste the product, picking up samples all along the line. My role as technologist is an interface between quality and production in order to oversee and optimize the entire industrial process.

"I know that the way we work, with continuous exchanges inside our team—where everyone knows everyone else—was the deliberate desire of Signor Michele. Nowadays there are lots of courses in 'Ferrero-ness,' but in the past there was only one way to acquire these values: working inside the company. This 'soul' is in our blood, we bring it with us out into the world, and we share it with the people who work with us. We work side by side with people, whether they're in Italy, Brazil, Ecuador, or Canada. When people see that their supervisors are ready to roll up their sleeves and get to work when things get difficult, they're inspired to do the same: these supervisors automatically earn the trust of the people around them with a positive, can-do attitude. But beyond all that, every time we move somewhere new we feel a strong sense of responsibility for furthering the good name and reputation of Ferrero and Italy out in the world. And whenever the time comes to leave and go home, the smiles and tears we leave behind accompany us, helping us remember that we've done our jobs and achieved our objectives."

"That smile at the customs office." Maurizio Chimenti has been working at Ferrero since 1989 as a technician in Ferrero DSTI. "I worked for the Ferrero Group's mechanical workshop in Canale d'Alba, where I've been building systems for over twenty years, and where we design and produce the complicated packaging machinery we use for our products. Right from the beginning, my work at Ferrero has almost always been conducted abroad, where I've worked in almost every facility the Group owns. Recently I moved to DSTI, where I joined a team of technicians who oversee the Group's systems all over the globe. My first worksite was in Belgium, in Arlon, where I went not long after the facility was inaugurated. The factory is located about twenty kilometers (12.4 miles) from the border with Luxembourg. Then, one day they told me I had to leave for Poland, in order to 'baptize' a Nutella production line in Belsk Duży, in the Grójec district: a small, rural town with a population of six thousand located about an hour south of Warsaw. I left Alba together with two other mechanics and an electrician, and then a software expert joined us there. We set up the Nutella line. The dosage dispenser is the heart of that packaging system, and usually has several dozen dispenser "heads." These lines are made up of relatively delicate and complex machinery and instruments, and occupy a surface area inside the facility that is a number of yards wide. They can produce several hundred tons of Nutella per shift: it's impressive. . . The lines have been designed to work twenty-four hours a day during peak production periods, except for Saturday afternoons and Sundays, when they're closed for maintenance. Fortunately I made it to Poland during the spring and the weather was nice. The country was very different from Italy, but people there were friendly and nice to us. It took us three or four weeks to set everything up, working together with the local personnel. Then we had to conduct all the start-up tests to make sure the facility was working properly, and that took another two or three months.

"I had a great time in Canada too. I went to Ontario, out onto that strip of land between Lake Erie and Lake Ontario: an hour and a half from the US border and halfway between Buffalo, New York; Detroit, Michigan; and Toronto, Canada. Brantford is an industrial city with a population of almost one hundred thousand, and our facility there was expanded quite a bit. From 2011 to 2014 I was involved with designing and implementing two Nutella lines and two Nutella & Go lines, both very successful in the United States. In Canada the winters are harsh, with polar temperatures of between −5° and −25° Celsius (23° and −13° Fahrenheit). But we did all right, and life outside work was plenty of fun, a lot like it is in Europe.

"Of course the weather was a lot nicer in Mexico, in San José Iturbide, a small city with a population of twenty-four thousand, located 250 kilometers (155 miles) north of Ciudad del Mexico. The city sits 2,000 meters (6,560 feet) above sea level, and between 2013 and 2014 I traveled back and forth there from Italy five different times. It's a very different reality, of course. We enjoyed life in Mexico, and in terms of work everything went well. I was able to follow the entire project, working as the manager. You always need to know how to adapt to local needs and realities.

"Nutella opens a lot of doors. I remember once, traveling with some colleagues, we were stopped at an airport customs office because we had some tools and other devices in our luggage. They asked us what we had come there to do, and who we were working for. We showed them the invitations we'd received, which explained how the machines we had to test were built in Europe and needed Italian technicians for assistance. But most importantly, as soon as I said we were coming into their country for a Nutella project, they smiled from ear to ear and started telling us how much their kids loved the cream. Then they let us through right away, without any further delays.

"The fact that, in addition to dealing with the everyday business, the company also requires me to talk things over with my colleagues in other countries as well as come to terms with situations that exist there, has helped me to greatly expand my horizons, both professionally and personally. During the time I've spent in this company I've had the good fortune to meet Signor Michele personally, when he came to visit a facility we were about to inaugurate. It was a great personal pleasure to meet him face-to-face."

"Like one big family." Giuseppe Francone, a retired technician, worked in Ferrero from 1973 to 2001. "I got my start at Ferrero as a simple employee, working on a temporary contract. Then they hired me full time. In 1981 I started overseeing 'my' machine on the production line: I wanted to understand everything about how it worked, improve it, and do everything I could to make sure it was as synchronized as possible so that we could use it to make the product even more perfect. Whenever a specialty is successful, we build more production lines around the world. In 1997 they asked me to go to Brazil and help set up a new system. I was there for four months, and the factory had just begun production. I had an amazing experience there, and later I was sent to Belgium and Canada too. We went there to teach people, to share our experience. Some of the local workers asked me, 'Right now you guys are opening this factory, but you'll close it in a year or two, the way foreigners always do. . .' I told them, 'Wherever Ferrero opens a new factory, it doesn't close. If you work here, you'll be working for your own future.' I went to help out in Canada too, as a consultant, when I'd already retired. When Ferrero calls, I answer. For me Ferrero is like a big family. There's always been a strong bond between colleagues here, between bosses and employees. Everybody pitches in and lends a hand. And today I'm proud to be part of the Anziani ("Elderly") Group, people who have worked for the company for at least twenty-five years, and can take advantage of the services provided by Ferrero Foundation."

"Starting up a factory is like watching a baby being born." Michele Di Capua has been working at Ferrero since 1988, and is a quality manager at San Angelo dei Lombardi in Italy. "I'm one of the technicians charged with tasting Nutella every day, more than once a day. I have to admit it's not a bad job. . . My mission is to oversee Nutella quality. In addition to the sensory analyses we have to conduct with professional operators, it's also important for us to check how the beginning of production goes each morning: the taste tests give us a macroscopic indicator of perceived quality. We pay extremely close attention to the freshness of our hazelnuts. Right now I work in the Ferrero facility in southern Italy, one hundred kilometers (62 miles) outside Naples, in the Irpinia region, which was hit by a devastating earthquake in 1980, and where Ferrero decided to invest in this factory. But I've also traveled around the world for the company, first in Australia, then in Russia. In the first case, my experiences abroad were aimed at quality and technological oversight in a facility that was already up and running. In the second country I had to oversee the inauguration and start-up of a new factory. In both situations my work was especially aimed at safeguarding and improving the quality of the product, in particular Nutella, Tic Tac, and Raffaello.

"I spent five years in Lithgow, Australia, from 1992 to 1997. That was the first time I worked abroad for Ferrero, and back then I still felt like a pioneer. Nutella still hadn't fully penetrated the Australian market, so it was hard for local consumers to think of a hazelnut and chocolate cream as something to spread on bread. In the Anglo-Saxon tradition, chocolate is something you bite into, not something you spread. At best they had Vegemite or peanut butter. For a number of years Nutella had trouble advancing in the Australian market. Today Nutella is a leading product, recognizable and sought after. I'd say we had to wait through this physiological phase, a sort of generational shift, and Ferrero knew how to make the right investments in that market.

"Lithgow is a mining city set in the Blue Mountains, about two hours by car from Sydney. The area is a tourist attraction and there's a large forest nearby. This was Ferrero's first overseas experience, and there were only two Italians there: the director of the facility and me. The locals welcomed us; they didn't think of us as 'colonizers' because we had a different approach. Italians are oriented more on interaction than toward taking charge and giving orders.

"My experience in Vladimir, Russia, was considerably different. That was a start-up operation, conducted in 2009, and was a lot like watching a baby being born. It was a unique experience. We started with the cement, and had to build an extremely large facility. I stayed there for a little over two years, overseeing the start-up of Nutella lines, as well as lines for

Raffaello and Kinder Chocolate. I also followed the implementation of quality-control laboratories, as well as selection and
training for local resources. Vladimir is a historical Russian
town, part of the 'golden ring': it was the first capital of the
empire, from 1169 to 1238, and remained so until the Mon-
gol invasion. Today it has a population of 350,000. My encounters with the local population were a positive surprise. I didn't
know their culture very well, and my head was full of stereotypes. Instead I found myself surrounded by sensitive people,
and was able to build some really nice relationships. As a hob-
by I spent my free time working in theater as a director, so I
used this pastime to interact with people outside the facility:
these people are natural artists, and during that two-year stay
I was able to found an acting school there. We performed Ni-
kolai Gogol's *The Inspector General*, as well as *Bene mio core
mio* (*My Heart, My Treasure*) by the Neapolitan actor and play-
wright Eduardo De Filippo. My cast was made up of Russians,
and this gave me the chance to gain a clearer understanding
of their personalities. This helped us build a bridge between
two cultures, and Ferrero supported the initiative. It was also
a useful experience from a work point of view, although only
one of the actors was employed at the factory, because we built
friendships and earned one another's respect that lasted over
the years. Relationships need attention over time; they can't
be built on just one episode or event."

THE FIVE PILLARS OF FERRERO'S
ENTREPRENEURIAL PHILOSOPHY

The stories told by technicians "with monkey wrenches" highlight Ferrero's company culture. But today there also exists a
theory and a training program that have been prepared by the

Ferrero Geie Learning Lab. Whenever a new factory is built and production equipment is modernized, the company also follows a program for new hires, including training for young people who have just earned their degrees. These young men and women spend five weeks taking courses in the classrooms of a building that has become the company's corporate university, in Alba. The building is an old spinning mill located near the original factory that has been restored and repurposed, and now hosts a team of Ferrero managers who act as teachers. Then the new hires spend another two weeks on an internship, in close contact with experimental products, and then a final week working in one of the company's factories. This kind of institutional training is defined as "Ferrero-ness." It's a sort of added value, and normal procedure for every single person who works for the company: they learn how to join and take part in the "Ferrero family." This concept of "Ferrero-ness" can be summed up in the company's "five pillars of entrepreneurial philosophy."

1. **Consumers:** Ferrero aims for consumer satisfaction through an extremely high-quality product. The goal is to follow evolving consumer tastes in order to satisfy even latent desires. To cite one of the most recurrent messages broadcast by Ferrero's ownership: the consumer is the company's true CEO.

2. **Employees:** Attention to individuals is evident every day through the creation of a positive work environment, within which each individual can develop his or her capabilities and skills with humility and perseverance—traits that all Ferrero employees share. Every Ferrero facility has services dedicated to the people working for the company and their families. Ferrero Foundation takes care of the company's "old-timers," focusing on the interests of retirees and providing a wealth of values, experience, wisdom and humanity.

The Foundation also uses its spaces and resources to provide opportunities for people who have retired from the company, helping them pursue a growth path even after they've stopped working for the company.

3. **Products:** The product is the company's epicenter; everything else is derived from and revolves around it. Products are born as high-quality specialties, always fresh and boasting unique characteristics. "Our products speak on our behalf," is a phrase often overheard inside Ferrero, and constitutes the heart of the Ferrero Group's communications strategies.

4. **Environmental and Social Commitments:** Social responsibility is in the company's DNA, and was already a part of Ferrero back when no one had ever heard of CSR (corporate social responsibility). During the years following World War II, Ferrero set up a special bus service that picked up farmers out in the countryside throughout the Langhe region, bringing them to the factory so that they could work, and taking them back home at the end of the day. This allowed people to stay connected with the land and agriculture, and the company organized work in its factories so that they could continue to farm seasonally. This service is still functioning today. Ferrero invests in less fortunate countries around the world (Cameroon, South Africa, and India) through its *Imprese Sociali* ("Social Enterprises") model, bringing work to indigenous peoples and directing part of the resources generated in the field to the health and education of local children. From an environmental point of view, the company makes important investments both in local initiatives designed to foster energy savings, and in the supply of raw ingredients and packaging it uses in order to guarantee that the company remains socially responsible.

5. **Innovation:** The foundation of innovation lies in a willingness to creatively develop products with a strong, exclusive USP (unique selling proposition). In other words, products capable of creating brand new categories. Innovation is considered the primary source of competitive advantage, and is experienced transversally not only in the product, but also in packaging, the selection and treatment of raw ingredients, advertising, distribution, and the company's production processes.

This framework might lead one to think of Ferrero as a sort of layperson's "religion." In truth, some scholars underline the "religiousness" of certain large companies. One oft-cited example can be found in the famous text "Our Credo" published by American multinational Johnson & Johnson, edited by Robert Wood Johnson II (1893–1968). Robert Wood Johnson ran the company from 1932 to 1963, transforming it into one of the most important industrial realities in the United States. A study conducted by Stanford University during the 1990s and run by Jim Collins together with professor Jerry I. Porras analyzed eighteen famous companies in order to try and understand the reasons behind their long histories of success. The study resulted in a book that has sold millions of copies (*Built to Last: Successful Habits of Visionary Companies* [1994]), and highlighted several criteria that can be used to identify "visionary companies" and are a perfect fit for Ferrero: "Premier institution in its industry; widely admired by knowledgeable businesspeople; made an indelible imprint on the world we live in; had multiple generations of chief executives; been through multiple product (or service) life cycles; founded before 1950."

In less grandiloquent terms, this can be defined as "company vision." It's precisely what Bill Gates had when he believed he could install a computer with his software program on every desk in the world. Or what Steve Jobs, the co-founder of Apple, was thinking of when he advised students to follow their hearts and intuition. In his introduction to the book *Lavorare Creare Donare* ("Work Create Give"), published to celebrate the twentieth anniversary of Ferrero Foundation, Italian sociologist Francesco Alberoni wrote that "nowhere in the world has there ever been a food company and food entrepreneur that have invented, created, realized, and promulgated such a high number of original products. No one else has had such extraordinary gifts as an inventor—like Meucci, Ford, Marconi—and combined them with an amazing ability to understand needs that have not yet been expressed, that are underlying and waiting to be born in consumers in countless countries around the globe."

PERMANENT TRAINING

The Ferrero Group is a multinational company, and this is reflected in its employees, who come from ninety-seven different nations. Italians account for 32 percent of the company's workforce (8,152), followed by 3,869 Germans, 2,118 Indians, 1,763 French, and 1,414 Polish (as of August 31, 2012), as well as Brazilians, Russians, Georgians, Ecuadorians, Argentines, Canadians, Chinese, South Africans, Belgians, and others. The company is a Babel of languages and cultures that isn't always easy to govern. New employees sign a thirty-five-page code of conduct when they join the company, distinguished by this opening phrase: "Ferrero has always embodied two souls: creating value for the community; creating value for the company." This is followed by chapters dedicated to consumers, human resources, the environment, raw ingredients, the market, company partners, institutions, local control and oversight agencies, local community, and finally a list of procedural regulations and controls.

Personnel policies are oriented first and foremost on teamwork; in other words, the ability to interact with others within a given team. Every Ferrero facility hosts training packages that include technical content for workers. When a new facility is inaugurated abroad, a number of local workers are trained in advance in other facilities around the world so that they will be professionally ready when the factory opens. One important example of this involved the facility in Turkey, the most recent addition to the Ferrero family. Lots of workers and technicians in Ferrero's Allendorf facility are of Turkish descent, so the company asked twenty-odd employees to handle training for around thirty of their fellow Turks, who were flown in from Manisa, where the new facility would open. Subsequently, the instructors were flown down to Turkey in order to finish training the company's newest employees and expand their job knowledge. As the chief of the Manisa project noted, "This way the new hires learned their way around the machinery, how to maintain instruments, our tasting techniques and quality control processes. And once the production line was underway, they played an active role in fine-tuning it, first without any product and then with the raw ingredients added too. Usually, at a certain point there's a sort of 'rejection' phase, when the teachers begin to be a little less welcome. It's a good thing: it means that the local resources are mature and ready to work on their own." The company also addresses the theme of diversity management, using different tools in order to integrate people from different cultures, ethnicities, religions or generations.

The intangible patrimony of every company includes a hidden reservoir of knowledge. Ferrero has its own professional academies dedicated to the product, raw ingredients, production technologies, sales, and marketing. Each of these areas can rely on significant planning conducted with experts both inside and outside the company: this way people build paths that are coherent with the company's values; that make it possible to integrate people from different countries, who don't know one another and who sometimes grew up professionally in a culture organized around a functional hierarchy, while at Ferrero they need to get used to an organization based on process. Individual qualities Ferrero looks for in hires include enthusiasm, the ability to work in a group, and the courage to think outside the box. In other words, the company wants people who are unafraid to share their own ideas, rather than those who bend to fit whatever the boss has to say next.

CORPORATE SOCIAL RESPONSIBILITY

Stock market companies are required to draw up a social statement. Ferrero is not publicly traded, and therefore doesn't have this obligation. But in 2009 the company presented its first CSR (corporate social responsibility) report, which ran the following premise: "As the social responsibility statement for the Group, we intend this report to confirm the Group's ethical vision and express its business principles clearly, sharing them in a transparent, coherent manner." Michele Ferrero also outlined the principles that have allowed his company to continue to prosper: "the strength of its products and the spirit that unites all of its collaborators." The first lines of the report stress the fact that Ferrero "is a family story" based on values like "loyalty and trust," "respect and responsibility," and "integrity and sobriety," as well as a "passion for research and innovation" that privileges "the ethics of doing over the practice of appearing."

For the first time, in 2009, a great deal of information about the Group was collected in a hundred-page folder, available to everyone because it was also published online. That first report was followed by others published yearly, in which the Ferrero model of social responsibility is described, based on four pillars: "Our products," made with the utmost attention to the needs of the consumers and their safety, by way of continuous innovation, quality excellence, original preparations, freshness and appeal; "the Ferrero Foundation," which takes care of former Ferrero workers and promotes cultural and artistic initiatives; "Ferrero Social Enterprises" in India, South Africa and Cameroon that seek to create new jobs and implement projects and events for children's education and health at a local level; "Kinder + Sport," an educational program aimed at facilitating and encouraging physical exercise among young children and adolescents. In the report attention is paid to product quality and nutritional problems. In particular, "Ferrero does not use hydrogenated fats, and therefore its products do not contain the transfat acids (TFA) that derive from them." In line with this rationale, the company presented its "Kinder + Sport" project, created in 2006. Through the project, Ferrero helps support youth sports "in order to motivate younger generations to adopt active lifestyles, the true antidote to obesity." The Kinder + Sport program encourages and facilitates "the spread of physical activities among kids all over the world, in order to inspire them to join the culture of movement." During 2013, activities for the Kinder + Sport project involved twelve million kids in twenty different countries in the practice of twelve different athletic disciplines, and boasted the participation of twenty national federations and twelve Olympic committees. Ferrero's goal is to "make the program a global point of reference in order to motivate physical activity among the highest number of children possible all around the world." Today this program is—after the company's products,

Foundation and Social Enterprises—the "fourth pillar" of the Group's social responsibility.

The most "pleasurable" profession for people working inside Ferrero may well be tasting: there are 1,700 expert tasters working for the company, and the CSR report revealed a little bit about their activities. Even the management takes part in tasting, and was often joined by Michele Ferrero himself. Together with a few close collaborators, Signor Michele loved to browse through supermarkets around the Côte d'Azur, where he lived for a number of years, and test his competitors' products. A special test known as the "Spider Web" has been created for tasters to evaluate eight key factors, the key criteria for Nutella: luster, the presence of foreign flavors and scents, hazelnut aroma, hazelnut taste, consistency, "swallowability," cocoa aroma, and cocoa taste.

"Standard" spider web sensorial profile for Nutella

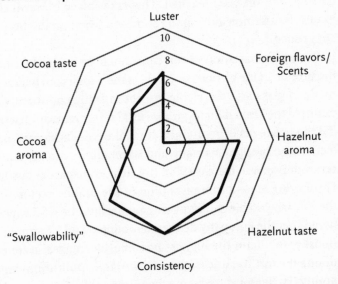

This test, created by a group of experts, is capable of offering a deep, far-reaching sensorial profile that can substitute for judgments like "excellent," "good," and "okay." In the diagram the result of the tasting is illustrated in the shape of a spider web, joining the points relative to the average for each evaluation. Ferrero conducts roughly 510 analyses on its products per year, with an average of ten tasters participating in each facility. Every year the Group conducts over four hundred tastings for an average of 33,900 tests per month and a panel.

As the CSR report outlines, the company is equipped with "rigorous internal systems and procedures designed to protect our consumers and employees from health problems connected to allergens and gluten intolerance." Ferrero also conducts "constant monitoring of resellers," and buys back "products that do not present the best tactile, visual and olfactory conditions at market price, even when the expiration date has not yet been reached. This takes place in warm climates, for example during the summer, when production is suspended."

Packaging has always been considered an integral part of the product. One obvious example is the Nutella jar, which is made of glass and recyclable (except in some countries, for example the United States, where local safety regulations forbid the use of glass in products for children). Packaging protects every company specialty, and is sometimes a key product reminder, as was the case with the clear, transparent box for Ferrero Rocher—a true revolution in the praline sector—or the Tic Tac container. For packaging design, the CSR report noted that the company deliberately adopted a "5R strategy" in order to obtain the highest possible advantages in terms of quality and freshness, minimizing the amount of waste produced: Removal (reducing the number of elements in the packaging); Reduction (lowering weight by as much as 40 percent, as happened with Kinder Country); Recyclability (substituting coupled materials wherever possible with mono-materials, which are easier to differentiate during the waste and recycling process); Reuse (the philosophy applied to Nutella glasses or recycled papers); and Renewability (with the use of materials deriving from resources that can be reintegrated).

Last but not least, there is a chapter dedicated to environmental impact and energy production. This constitutes a reality few people are familiar with: Ferrero produces electric energy for its facilities from both renewable sources and cogeneration. The factory in the Langhe region employs an Alba Power system for heating that provides both drive and electricity for the production lines, as well as heat for the city of Alba itself: 820 buildings in Alba are connected to it via roughly 30 kilometers (18.6 miles) of tubing.

FERRERO FOUNDATION

How much culture does a single jar of Nutella contain? A great deal, judging from the intense activity that the Piera, Pietro and Giovanni Ferrero Foundation, the foundation the company dedicated to its founders, has been conducting for over twenty years. The foundation's headquarters in Alba are grouped in a modern building located not far from the factory. Ferrero Foundation was the brainchild of Michele Ferrero, who wanted to provide a "home" for people retiring from the company; a place where former employees could meet, enjoy recreational activities, take courses, and be guaranteed health care. Founded in 1983 as a social enterprise, it became a foundation in 1991, run by Maria Franca Ferrero, Michele's wife, who continues to oversee the foundation today. She explained the reasoning behind her activities in the book *Trent'anni di Fondazione Ferrero* (Thirty Years of Ferrero Foundation, edited by Caterina Ginzburg), published for the 2013 anniversary. "In 1983," writes Ferrero, "when my husband decided to create a space that could host former employees, he expressed his idea by saying, 'I want the people who have helped us develop innovative products and take them all over the world, and who were therefore always stimulating their own creativity, to have a physical space made available to them, as well as human and financial resources, so that they can continue to learn new things, with the only caveat being that the product of what they learn be given back to the territory.' Only in recent years did we realize that the foundation is actually a shining example, because an analysis of the most recent scientific literature combined with considerations expressed by important scholars made it clear that creative, recreational, and social activities undertaken for one's self and for others, combined with a proper lifestyle, actually helps enhance active and successful aging."

The foundation's most recent creation is "the Nursery," which hosts children aged three months to three years old, both the children of employees and those sent by the Alba municipality. The objective of the Nursery is to create a "family space" where people can cultivate connections and relationships. In her introduction to the book, President Maria Franca Ferrero adds, "Thanks to their strong emotional and educational core, relationships between grandparents and grandchildren can make a powerful contribution to the growth and development of young kids."

The foundation, which has honored its motto *Lavorare Creare Donare* ("Work Create Give") for over thirty years, has now initiated activities in Villers-Ecalles, France, as well. In Alba, starting in 1996, the foundation began an intense series of cultural activities, including conferences and major exhibitions, attracting thousands of visitors to admire Leonardo da Vinci's machines; the work of Alba-born painter Pinot Gallizio; the architect-poet Bruno Munari; Renaissance artist Macrino d'Alba; and the writer Beppe Fenoglio; as well as the retrospective *Carlo Carrà 1881–1966*. The exhibition was free to the general public and attracted seventy thousand visitors.

Every summer since the 1970s, Ferrero has hosted the Festa degli Anziani Ferrero ("Festival for Elderly Ferrero Employees"), which the Ferrero family participates in directly. Michele Ferrero would also attend and it was not unusual for him to spend time with his collaborators, even floor workers, and recognize them by name. The company's reputation has in part been built through the attention it has always paid to its personnel. People say that Signora Piera used to get up an hour early in order to make coffee for the workers who were coming in to start their shifts. But before long, and perhaps against Signora Piera's wishes, automatic coffee machines took over. In Germany, many people remember the activities provided by "Villa Piera" in Allendorf, which during the 1960s gave a home to young women from southern Italy who had moved to the Hesse in order to work on the Nutella production lines. Today the villa has been transformed into a social enterprise, and falls under the aegis of the foundation. Some 430 retired employees spend time there, sometimes meeting up with young apprentices who have recently been hired at the nearby factory, thanks to the project "A Bridge between Generations." Referring to all of these activities during the Festival of Elderly Employees in 1989, Michele Ferrero noted that they have "become a sort of ritual that has become part of our tradition, an expression of our way of living, of the way we conceive of the ethical sense of life and work, permeating our consciousness and becoming an integral part of our daily lives."

SOCIAL ENTERPRISES

Cameroon. Laure Ingrid Matouomkam, thirty-three, says: "I've been working at Ferrero since 2005; I was one of the first people to be hired, so I've worked here since the very day it opened for business. Now I'm in charge of organization and packaging. It's an important position. Back then I didn't have a real job, so I tried to get by doing odd jobs. During a difficult period in my life I had the good fortune to meet Sister Angélique [. . .] I went to the Marie Dominique Salesian Institute and they told me there was an Italian company looking to hire people. That's how I got my start."

India. Pushpa Deokar, thirty-five, shift head of the Kinder Surprise department: "I've been working at Ferrero since May 1, 2007: I remember my first day clearly, because not only was it my first day of my first job; it was also the first day the company opened! [. . .] To tell you the truth, in the beginning I did a little bit of everything: stock, merchandise, sales . . . sometimes I even took care of cleaning. It was exhausting and demanding, but my hard work paid off: today I have an important position. [. . .] First and foremost, working at Ferrero has given me the proud feeling of watching a company grow, of helping to move it forward thanks to my own efforts, my own commitment."

South Africa. Carlene Dyosiba, thirty-two, works on the production line: "I've been working at Ferrero since 2006, when the factory was still in Alrode [a town in the Alberton region, located roughly 30 kilometers (18.6 miles) from the current location in Walkerville]. I was one of the first people hired. There were about thirty of us, divided into two different spaces: one for filling Kinder Joys, another for product packaging. I was a housewife, but when my son was born I realized that it was time for me to get a job. [. . .] Ferrero helps us deal with transportation costs: every month they give us a sum of money to use for the group taxis that bring us all to work."

These are just three of the many stories gathered together and published in the photographic volume *Imprese Sociali Ferrero* (Ferrero Social Enterprises), edited by Caterina Ginzburg. As of 2013, there are more than 2,700 persons spread out across factories in Yaoundé, Cameroon; Baramati, India (where the company's largest facility is located); and in Midvaal, South Africa. These production sites operate according to a "social spirit" not only because they are designed to create jobs in less fortunate areas of emerging nations, but also because they are connected with humanitarian initiatives that aim to improve healthcare and education for children, under the banner "United Kinder of the World."

The technology that social enterprises adopt in their production centers is innovative and automatized for the food production section (such as Kinder Joy), and manual for the creation of "surprises" inserted into the products, so that the facility can offer jobs to the highest number of people possible. In India and South Africa, Tic Tac are produced with Ferrero technology, while some of the packaging is semi-manual.

People working in Ferrero's social enterprises

	2009	2012	2013
Yaoundé—Cameroon	90	191	177
Baramati/Pune, Maharashtra—India	650	1,886	2,155
Midvaal, Gauteng—South Africa	185	358	407

Source: The 2013 Ferrero CSR Report

Alongside the social enterprises, the company has also implemented a number of charity projects near its factories: in 2012 in South Africa Ferrero restored the Japie Greyling school in Daleside, where today 1,400 students attend classes. In India, the company supports the program "Un toit à Bombay," as well as the Don Bosco home. In Cameroon, it provides assistance to the pediatric ward of St. Martin De Porres hospital.

In May 2013, writing in the company's CSR report, Giovanni Ferrero noted, "Our Group's long-term success is anchored in the ethical values that guide us. Everybody talks about the social responsibilities of business: Ferrero has those responsibilities in its blood. We fulfill them on a daily basis with respect for the people who work for us, in the way we scrupulously safeguard the environments we work in; in the responsibility with which we manage our relationship with civil society; and especially through the relationship we establish between consumers and our brands, taking care of quality, communications and value. Our social enterprise initiatives are the highest and most concrete expressions of these values, inspired not by charity, but by illuminated entrepreneurship."

9

The United Nations of sweetness

THE FRENCH ARE . . .

The French consume more Nutella than anyone else. Every year, thanks in part to their national passion for crêpes, they empty a one-kilogram (2.2-pound) jar per person. France is the country with the world's highest pro capita spread, followed by Italy, Germany, and Belgium, where people eat on average 900 grams (31 ounces) of Nutella per year. Europe remains Ferrero's core business area for the hazelnut cream: 20 percent of the Group's consolidated revenue comes from Italy; 59 percent from Europe; and 21 percent from the rest of the world. However, the markets in the United States, Russia, India, and Asia are in continuous expansion, especially for Nutella: while based on quantity sold, Germany, France, and Italy occupy the top three positions, the United States is Nutella's fourth-largest market, followed by Middle Eastern countries, North Africa, and Turkey.

The economic crises that have struck many markets around the world haven't slowed the sale of Nutella. In fact, just the opposite has happened. Why? Perhaps diminished salaries, uncertainty about the future, and general employment problems have driven people to look for some kind of consolation for their daily anxieties, something to help them forget their fears for a while. Based on surveys, Ferrero's managers are convinced that the real reason is far more rational: an unbeatable quality/price relationship. Not even the private labels—products produced and packaged by third parties with a label bearing the supermarket's name—have managed to unseat Nutella: in the end, all you need is a little pocket change in order to purchase your own spread of happiness. Gourmet chocolate, a bottle of fine wine, even pizzas cost more and are small pleasures that aren't too hard to give up. Nutella, on the other hand, fits on a shopping list alongside bread, milk, coffee, olive oil, and pasta. Even in European countries in which the economic crisis has hit consumer purchasing power the hardest—for example, Greece, Spain, and Portugal—sales volumes continue to increase.

Fifty years after it first appeared on supermarket shelves, Nutella has proven it is an increasingly global product, part of a melting pot. It's also an object of study for one of the world's most prestigious economic institutions, the OECD (Organisation for Economic Co-operation and Development), which is based in Paris and can boast thirty-four developed countries among its members. According to *Mapping Global Value Chains*, a report published by Koen De Backer and Sébastien Miroudot in December 2013, Nutella is defined as an example of ethical globalization, a paradigm for the agro-food sector.

The study was part of an evaluation of the "value chain" generated by Nutella: this concept includes a range of activities that the company and its employees engage in to bring Nutella to its end use. Nowadays global value chains (which the economists shorten to GVCs) have become the object of study insofar as today's companies operate on a global scale, influencing economies in various different countries. GVCs generate relatively simple effects, for example the advantages derived from foreign direct investment (when the Group opens a factory in a nation other than the one hosting its general headquarters); or other benefits that are more difficult to calculate, for example, the relationships between factories in different nations that compete to produce the same item, transforming raw ingredients arriving from other areas around the world. The GVC study analyzes relationships between rich and poor countries in order to establish where the value the company generates ends up.

The De Backer–Miroudot report highlights several sectors: agri-food, chemical, electronic, automotive, and financial and commercial services. The OECD has underlined that the agri-food business has been profoundly transformed in recent years, both in the role it has taken on in large distribution chains and because now "a relatively small number of companies organize the global supply of food, connecting small producers in developed or developing countries with consumers all over the globe."

The two economists offered a detailed analysis of a successful case: "Nutella is a famous hazelnut and cocoa spread sold in more than one hundred countries. About 350,000 tons of Nutella are produced each year. Nutella is representative of agri-food value chains. The food processing company Ferrero International SA is based in Luxembourg and currently has ten factories producing Nutella: five are located in the European Union, one in Russia, one in Turkey, one in North America, one in South America, and one in Australia. Some inputs are mainly locally supplied, for example, the packaging or some of the ingredients like skimmed milk. There are, however, ingredients that are globally supplied: hazelnuts come mainly from Turkey, palm oil from Malaysia, Papua New Guinea and Brazil, cocoa mainly from Ivory Coast, Ghana, Nigeria, and Ecuador, sugar mainly from Europe, and the vanilla flavor from the United States and Europe. Nutella is then sold around the world through sales offices. Nutella is a registered trademark used for Spread Containing Cocoa and Other Ingredients and owned by Ferrero. The location of production is close to final markets where Nutella is in high demand (Europe, North America, South America, and Oceania). There is no factory in central and east Asia so far because the product is less popular (another Ferrero delicacy, the Ferrero Rocher, is however more popular in Asia). In agri-food business value chains, there are more developing and emerging economies involved, as can be seen with countries in Latin America and Africa in the case of Nutella."

In her best seller *No Logo* (1999), Naomi Klein maintains that the triumph of economic globalization has driven many organizations to investigate multinationals to uncover unethical behavior in their production facilities, especially with regards to child labor in emerging countries and the acquisition of raw ingredients without respect for sustainability. The OECD's economic investigation of Nutella's GVC—reported in the media with titles like "The OECD Likes Nutella" and "A Positive Example of Globalization"—has "absolved" Nutella.

The company's CSR report, certified by independent agencies, has further consolidated the Group's positive reputation. This may be part of the reason why Nutella has never been exposed to attacks like those waged against other global brands in the agri-food sector, including Coca-Cola, Nestlé, and McDonald's. Even though it is a global product, the same all over the world, Nutella maintains its connection with its ingredients and the land where it was first created. The study conducted by two economists from an independent organization sheds light on the reasons for its enviable relationship with consumers.

A PRODUCT-BUSINESS

After half a century, is it unreasonable to suggest that Nutella is a mature brand, on the verge of decline and forced to follow the same economic reasoning that concerns all industrial products: introduction, expansion, maturity, and decline? The truth is that Nutella has become a global longseller, one that creates a market wherever it appears. It has an advantage: when it was created, Nutella took its place alongside a specialty that had until then been the joy of a privileged few— chocolate. And it didn't introduce itself as chocolate's "poor cousin," but as the ambassador of a new, different category of merchandise: the spreadable hazelnut cream.

Nutella's longevity is the result of two characteristics: an ability to innovate (which it then transferred to communications); and the business decisions made by Michele Ferrero. These characteristics have made Nutella a sort of company all its own, with its own governance and autonomous from the rest of the Group.

This is Nutella's primary "competitive advantage," to use the language of economist Michael Porter. It remains one of the few examples of "important innovation" that has emerged from Italy following World War II, according to a 2002 research study conducted by the company Evidenze. In an article published in the Italian financial newspaper *Il Sole 24 Ore* on July 29, 2003, Professor Carlo Maria Guerci (then teaching economics at the University of Milan), wrote: "The result (of the study) was that Italians were unable to achieve more than fifteen innovations: they were completely different products and services, from polypropylene to the Vespa to Nutella, Getter, prepaid credit cards, tire production, and the Common Rail engine. But we could have learned a great deal from these experiences. Some of these innovations were achieved inside large companies, but weren't fully taken advantage of (polypropylene and the common rail), while others made it possible for small- and medium-sized companies to grow and become giants (Nutella, Vespa, Getter). Overall, their number is truly irrelevant when viewed in light of the potential and industrial ambitions of Italy at large."

From an organizational standpoint, Ferrero considers each of its products to be an independent business, one capable of regenerating itself, adapting to the needs inherent to new consumer habits or emerging markets. Global sales of Nutella alone total roughly $2 billion (1.6 million euros). From the consumer's point of view, Nutella, Tic Tac, Kinder Chocolate, and Ferrero Rocher each have the characteristics of an independent brand. Often the person spreading Nutella on a slice of bread in the United States or Turkey has no idea that the same company also produces Tic Tac mints or milk chocolate bars.

The autonomy given to this product-company requires a rather long test phase, especially in today's hypercompetitive marketplace: it has to have what it takes so that it can achieve high sales volumes and justify costly investments in facilities and a far-reaching ad campaign. This means that Ferrero is not an "umbrella brand" that can provide guarantees for all the company's products. A diametrically opposite approach can be seen in a brand like Hello Kitty, which celebrated its fortieth anniversary in October 2014 at the Museum of Contemporary Art in Los Angeles. Owned by Sanrio, a Japanese multinational specializing in toys and comic books, today the character Hello Kitty (essentially a cute anthropomorphized white kitten) is a logo impressed upon roughly twenty-two thousand products sold in forty different countries, generating an annual business volume of $1.3 billion (1 billion euros).

Making a unique product-business successful means relying on unconventional business organization. In general, business organization is defined as a "matrix," and has three hierarchy levels: top management, administrative management (with product managers on a horizontal line), and business units. This is more or less the model adopted by Procter & Gamble, an American business giant that oversees more than one hundred brands including Tide, Gillette, Duracell, and Pampers, and is currently the world's number one advertiser with a budget of roughly $8.2 billion invested in advertising annually.

Since only a few product-businesses are destined to withstand the test of time, Ferrero has relatively few points of reference when compared with other confectionary companies, which usually sell lots of specialties but remain "small" in terms of overall sales. This is why Ferrero has no more than a dozen "big brands," with considerable production volumes (see table).

As the data shows, every year a mountain of products wind up on family tables in more than one hundred countries around

Volumes sold per year (2012–13)
(Measurements in thousands of quintals)

Nutella	3,650
Kinder Chocolate and Kinder Maxi	850
Ferrero Rocher	650
Kinder Bueno	570
Kinder Surprise and Kinder Joy	385
Kinder milk-slice	350
Kinder Pinguí	290
Raffaello	260
Kinder Délice	260
Tic Tac	240

Note: 1 quintal =100 kg (220,46 lb.)

the world: it's a sort of "United Nations of Sweetness," backed up by a set of curious data that make the numbers even more interesting:

- Set side by side, the line of Nutella jars produced in a single year would measure 1.7 times the earth's circumference.

- The amount of Ferrero Rocher packaged in just a little over two days would be enough to completely cover the Great Pyramid of Cheops in Egypt.

- The amount of Kinder Chocolate produced in six weeks weighs the same as the Eiffel Tower in Paris.

- Set end to end, the line of Tic Tac produced by Ferrero's factory in a single year would measure 1.4 times the distance from the earth to the moon.

- The number of Kinder Surprise sold in the international market in just one month would be enough to pave Tiananmen Square in Beijing.

Ferrero is the undisputed leader of the global praline market, where it enjoys a 19 percent share. Ferrero Rocher is the most popular chocolate in the world, with China as its primary market. Even within the Group's overall sales, pralines are the most important segment, providing roughly 23 percent of consolidated sales (as shown in data from 2011–12), followed by Nutella (20 percent, an increase compared to just a few years ago, when it stood between 15 percent and 18 percent) and, tied for second place, snacks and chocolates (20 percent), then chocolate eggs (Kinder Surprise) with 16 percent, chilled snacks (8 percent), baked goods (5 percent), Tic Tac mints (5 percent), and drinks (with 3 percent Estathé, an iced tea sold in single packets or in plastic bottles, available only in Italy).

THE FOURTH LARGEST GROUP IN THE WORLD

When chocolate first arrived in Europe, at the beginning of the seventeenth century—initially at court and in monasteries, then in coffee houses—it was the privilege of a fortunate few. The foodstuff's "democratization" began in 1847, when Englishman Joseph Fry created the first chocolate bar. A little over a century later, Ferrero began producing chocolate specialties that practically anyone could afford. This prompted a revolution in food habits for billions of consumers, which in turn earned the global chocolate confectionary market (industries that essentially produce chocolate specialties) estimated sales of $105 billion (80 billion euros). Sixty percent of this market is controlled by six multinationals: three are American, one is Swiss, and the last is Italian, Ferrero (see the following table).

Global chocolate confectionary market share

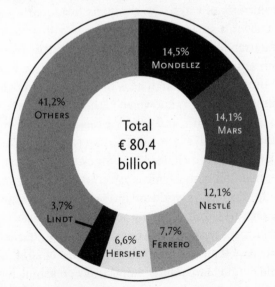

*Source: Euromonitor/*Wall Street Journal

In first place stands a relatively unknown company: Mondelez. The company's name is a blend of the French word for "world," *monde*, and *delez* as in "delicious." It was chosen through a referendum held in 2012 by the company's employees in the wake of a merger. Mondelez's headquarters are in Deerfield, Illinois, near Chicago, and it controls a number of famous brand names, including Kraft (the company's previous name), Cadbury, Milka, Côte d'Or, Toblerone, Oreo cookies, Jacobs coffee, Nabisco, and Lu. Baked goods and chewing gum are excluded from the classification drawn up by Euromonitor, an agency that specializes in economic analyses of large companies. Second place goes to another American company, Mars. Based on other rankings, Mars would be in first place, because the company can also rely on significant earnings from Wrigley, the number one chewing gum company in the world.

The story of the Mars company is similar to that of Ferrero in a number of ways. The company headquarters are in Hackettstown, a small town in New Jersey with a population of ten thousand, and it's run by the founder's heirs (almost all of whom are women). Forrest Edward Mars passed away in 1999 at ninety-five. Although he is the inventor of M&M's, in 1939, almost nothing is known about him. No one ever managed to interview him, and even the news of his death went unconfirmed for days. The Mars Group (which has factories in England as well) includes Mars, Snickers, Starburst, Twix, and Bounty. Company policy is extremely reserved, and rapports with the outside world are limited. No one is allowed to visit its factories, and company governance is based on Five Principles that everyone must respect: "Quality, Responsibility, Mutuality, Efficiency, Freedom." In August of 2014 John Elkann and Sergio Marchionne, respectively president and CEO of FCA (Fiat Chrysler Automobiles) chose Anne Valerie Mars,

Forrest Edward's granddaughter, to sit on the board of their new company.

The data included for Nestlé only takes into account sales generated from the company's chocolate products; its total business volume is much higher, close to 80 billion euros per year. Headquartered in Vevey, the Swiss multinational is the largest food company in the world. Ferrero comes in fourth among these big companies, just ahead of its direct competitor, the American company Hershey, producer of the famous chocolate Kisses, a teardrop-shaped treat created in 1907. In fifth place stands the Swiss company Lindt, which is celebrated for having created the first dark chocolate bar in 1879—thanks to Rudolph Lindt, who purportedly left a chocolate machine turned on by mistake. All of Ferrero's competitors are storied companies: Lindt was founded in 1845; Nestlé in 1866; Hershey in 1894; Mars in 1911; Kraft in 1923 (founded as the "National Dairy Products Corporation").

This chocolate oligarchy buys up roughly half the world's cocoa, 70 percent of which is cultivated in Africa. But demand is forever on the rise, and four million metric tons (4,409,000 tons) of cocoa are no longer enough to cover the needs of the entire industry. According to the International Cocoa Organization (ICCO), this deficit is destined to last until 2018, driving up the average price of cocoa and creating difficulties for companies in the sector. Ferrero "consumes" roughly 120,000 metric tons (132,277 tons) per year, compared with 100,000 metric tons (110,231 tons) of hazelnuts.

The swift development of the small factory built in the Langhe region is unequaled anywhere else in the world, at least in the food sector. From the day it first opened in 1946, it has grown only through self-financing, and has refused any takeover attempts or purchase offers from other groups. In 2009 Ferrero's attempt to purchase Cadbury stopped no sooner than it started. There were hints of at least two significant attempts to purchase Ferrero, published in the media but never confirmed by the Ferrero family: the first came in 1998, put forth by tobacco giant Philip Morris (then owner of General Foods and Kraft); the second by Nestlé, in October 2013. This latest attempt, which made a big splash in international financial newspapers, was categorically denied by then-CEO Giovanni Ferrero through a press release he wrote personally and sent to newspapers all over the globe, and even published as a full-page ad in some Italian newspapers. The title read, "We Are Only on Sale to Our Customers." Beneath the title, the image of a jar of Nutella and two proud, decisive lines: "Ferrero categorically denies having received any buyout offers. Ferrero is not up for sale for anyone."

At the start of 2014 the Ferrero Group announced it had closed the fiscal year (on August 31, 2013, according to a calculation that has become traditional in the company's fiscal reports since 2004, and which is designed to take into account the seasonal nature of some of its production) registering turnover of 8.1 billion euros, doubling the figures it had reported just ten years earlier.

Seventy percent of these sales were achieved through its "big brands" (see the table on page 191). In the chocolate confectionary market, Ferrero is the number one leader in six different countries: Germany, Italy, France, Portugal, Singapore, and Taiwan, as well as in Hong Kong. Ferrero is in second place in an additional five countries: Austria, Romania, Greece, China, and South Korea. In Europe, the company's market share stands at just over 17 percent (in value). The Group encompasses seventy-three consolidated companies with twenty factories around the world, with a total of thirty thousand collaborators (including 5,308 interim employees, mostly outside Italy). Its French and Italian facilities compete for the title of "Nutella City": the

Villers-Écalles factory, in Normandy, produces the most Nutella each year. But Italy registers the most overall production, counting both jars of the spreadable cream produced in Alba as well as those produced in Sant'Angelo dei Lombardi.

A PRECIOUS ALLY: BREAD

Available worldwide in a thousand different forms and varieties, bread remains Nutella's number one "companion." The global bread market in Europe's twenty-seven EU countries stands at thirty-two million metric tons (35,273,962 tons), but consumption models vary considerably from one nation to the next. On average, each European eats around 50 kilograms (110 pounds) of bread per year. In the UK the industrial sector accounts for 80 percent of production; while in France and Germany it's merely a third, because in those countries small bakeries continue to thrive. Germans love to eat sliced bread at breakfast (an excellent base for Nutella), while Italians enjoy cookies and zwiebacks. Together with Romania, Turkey is one of the countries with the highest pro capita bread consumption in the world: every day roughly 101 million 250-gram (just under 9 ounces) loaves of bread are produced there. Unsurprisingly, Nutella sells quite well in those nations. In the United States, total retail sales of bread were 1.4 billion in 2010, according to Euromonitor (2011), with a compound annual growth rate of 1.6 percent since 2006. And Hispanics—accustomed to eating toasted or cold slices of bread at breakfast—represent 17 percent of the American population. In Arab countries families are usually quite large, and a few years ago Ferrero began registering a rise in sales of Nutella—spread on their thin, particular kind of bread—during Ramadan, when breakfasts need to be rich and fulfilling. In India people eat it on *roti*—

made from stoneground whole meal flour—and *chapati*, un-leavened flatbread.

Elsewhere in the world there are bagels, waffles, doughnuts, pancakes (which people in the UK and Australia even celebrate in spring, on Pancake Day), crêpes (on February 2 in France, for La Chandeleur, or Candlemas, people spread literally tons of Nutella on crêpes around the nation), Italian *piadine*, or Mexican corn tortillas. You might say that by now, with the globalization and spread of the hazelnut cream all over the world, the slice of bread that appeared in Italy on Nutella jars and in the very first ad in 1964 has found plenty of original alternatives. Ferrero's marketing teams emphasize this aspect everywhere, even more so than mere nutritional value, because the "Global Consumer"—a person who turns to food multinationals for sustenance—has no interest in a message that tries to "explain" what he or she should eat, but is happy to be "inspired" by an emotion.

From this point of view, the Group's CEO Giovanni Ferrero, during his traditional speech to top management held at the end of the year at the Foundation in Alba (December 2013), noted that "we need to find an ethical balance between 'local to global' and 'global to local,'" adding that "Nutella, first created in 1964, continues to be a global success today. Therefore it would be easy for us to rest on our laurels and congratulate ourselves for everything we've accomplished. But there's a detail missing from this equation: endless fields for potential development stretch out in front of this brand. Did you know that out of one thousand breakfasts consumed around the world, just 25 have something spreadable on the table; and that of these 25, just three have Nutella spread on bread?" To be honest, there's still plenty of competition out there in the world for Nutella: in addition to marmalades, maple syrup in Canada and the United States, peanut butter, and yeast derivatives like

Marmite (UK) and Vegemite (Australia), there are also plenty of salty foodstuffs and cheese. In Saudi Arabia and many other countries in the Middle East, people spread *labneh*, a tangy cheese; in Mexico they spread *cajeta* (caramelized goat's milk); in Brazil it's *requeijão* (a kind of salted ricotta cheese); in Argentina *dulce de leche* (caramelized milk).

In Europe. Spreading Nutella on bread is a daily tradition for millions of German, French, Belgian, and Italian families. And while in France Nutella's market share is extremely high due to a lack of competition (with the exception of private labels), in Germany there's only one real competitor: Nudossi, produced in Saxony and considered a nostalgia brand because it was extremely popular in East Germany prior to the fall of the Berlin Wall. After Germany was unified, production of the spread ceased, but was reignited in 1999 to the joy of consumers across eastern Germany. There was a tougher battle for supremacy in Spain, where during the 1960s the Italian company Star (today in Spanish hands, part of the Gallina Blanca group) successfully launched Nocilla in three different versions: hazelnut and chocolate, white, and two-color. In 2013 Nutella got a measure of revenge, taking first place in market share over the "classic" hazelnut version produced by its competitor.

Ferrero has had a fair amount of success in England as well, where Nutella has even made its way into the homes of many Brits: in 2013 penetration of the hazelnut cream doubled with respect to figures registered six years earlier. Even England's traditional orange marmalade had to wave a white flag: a market survey conducted by the magazine *The Grocer* in 2011 showed that Nutella sales had grown by an average 8 percent per year. Another survey, this time by the agency Millward Brown, underlined the perfect success of the company's ad campaign in the UK. The campaign was based on three messages: Nutella's delicious, unique taste; the cream's versatility (since it can be consumed both with porridge and with fruit); and the validity of a foodstuff that can be eaten by the whole family, not just by children. Breakfast remains a ritual for almost everyone on the British Isles, especially during weekends.

Nutella's perceived image in the UK (%)

	in 2007	in 2013
A product you can eat every day	33	51
A product appropriate for breakfasts	10	45
A product you are happy to serve to your children	39	63

Source: The Millward Brown Survey

In Australia. If a global brand wants to register appreciable results in new markets, it has to be ready to shoulder years of hard work, constant effort, and coherence in its marketing strategies. The understated style of Ferrero's management, which to some degree contrasts with the strength of their iconic, now legendary brand, has made it easier for them to adhere to the basic tenets of good branding. Results are being achieved in many countries once considered "difficult." In 2013 the Australian Ferrero company generated a total revenue of 166 million Australian dollars (US$ 135 million), including sales and other revenue. Ferrero Rocher is the leading praline in Australia, and the production of Nutella—which began in 1979 in the factory in Lithgow, in New South Wales, and has grown every year since—is now exported to nearby countries as well, including New Zealand, Singapore, Japan, and China. In the past two years in particular there have been significant increases in Nutella consumption inside Australia, with peaks near 10 percent per year. The company's 2012

"Rise & Shine" TV campaign has begun to bear fruit. As the Australian Trade Commission recently wrote, "Ferrero has revolutionised the global confectionery market by making premium chocolate brands available to the masses at reasonable prices, while simultaneously upgrading consumers from everyday to more luxurious products."

In South America and emerging countries. The start of on-site production of Nutella in Brazil and Mexico helped drive consumption: improved economic conditions for the middle classes in both of these fast-developing countries made it possible for the hazelnut cream to gain strong increases in domestic penetration. In 2014 in Brazil Ferrero celebrated its twentieth anniversary, hosting a large competition that increased Nutella sales and the number of fans registered on the brand's local Facebook page. The competition had consumers use famous paintings by Vermeer, da Vinci, and van Gogh to create entertaining images "enriched" with a jar of the legendary cream.

In Ferrero's internal organization, the so-called emerging area may well be the future the company is betting on most heavily, with no fewer than thirty-seven business units in just as many countries, spread out across Africa, the Middle East, India, China, and the Far East. Nutella's greatest success in this area has been in the Arab world: a community of 280 million consumers with a shared cultural and linguistic fabric, 150 different television stations, some of which broadcast across the Middle East, and generally numerous families with lots of young kids. Qatar is the country with the highest GDP in the world ($98,000 per capita; source: FMI, 2013), and the city-states of Doha, Kuwait, Abu Dhabi, and Dubai aren't far behind, all boasting modern economies and Western consumer habits. Ferrero operates in this region through four different product categories: Kinder Chocolate; Raffaello and Ferrero Rocher; Tic Tac; and Nutella. Sales of Nutella now account for 30 percent of Ferrero's local sales volume in the Middle East: from 2000 to 2012 sales of Nutella multiplied by a factor of ten. It's also worth noting that these are all countries where people do not traditionally eat sweets at breakfast. The company is about to initiate a roll-out in grand style with an integrated TV marketing campaign aimed at mothers, as well as at young people via social media. Another success story is the opening of a Nutella Bar—a space where they serve countless flavorful specialties made with the hazelnut cream—at the Dubai Mall, the largest of its kind in the world, with over sixty million visitors per year. It was inaugurated in the summer of 2014 inside the store Eataly (operational since November 2013), modeled after similar spaces that had opened in the United States in Chicago and New York.

THE US "GOES NUTS ABOUT NUTELLA"

"Women in sleek black dresses and men with messenger bags checking their smartphones, hipsters in flannel and sunglasses, parents with babies strapped to their chests, and lucky tourists lined the perimeter of New York's Madison Square Park on Monday. But the crowd wasn't gathered for a concert, club opening, or celebrity sighting. This was a fiftieth anniversary celebration for Nutella. Pietro Ferrero of the small Italian town of Alba likely never could have imagined that his hazelnut spread would draw such a loyal and diverse following in one of the most cosmopolitan cities in the world," wrote fashion journalist Emily Shire in her entertaining article entitled "How Nutella Conquered America," published on the website *The Daily Beast* (May 21, 2014), founded by Tina Brown. The article detailed the party organized to celebrate Nutella's fiftieth anniversary, held outside the Eataly store in Manhattan.

In the United States, business is good for Ferrero: sales have tripled over the past eight or nine years, reaching $700 million. Nutella and Nutella & Go (an enormous, and to a certain extent unexpected, success) account for more than 40 percent of the Group's overall business volume, in part because Kinder Chocolate is still not sold in the United States. Tic Tac has been sold in America since 1969, but now even families have become familiar with Nutella. In August 2014 radio station 101.5 in New Jersey ran the following online poll: "Nutella or peanut butter—which do you prefer?" Everyone was surprised when the hazelnut spread won, garnering 43.6 percent of the vote compared to 40.0 percent for peanut butter. The next day, several newspapers wrote: "Americans go nuts about Nutella."

All you need to do is walk around Manhattan in order to see just how widespread the hazelnut cream has become. On West 35th and Broadway, near a small garden, you'll find one of the many sales points for the chain eatery Wafels & Dinges. Giulia, an employee at the store and a fan of Nutella, explains, "Waffles are a Belgian specialty that you cook on a hot griddle, and *dinges* means 'things' or 'whatchamacallits" in Flemish. We sell several different kinds of *dinges*: dulce de leche, *speculoos* spread (made with classic cookies from Brussels), Belgian chocolate fudge, and maple syrup. But our best seller, especially around breakfast time, is Nutella. And that's true not only here at my shop, but for all the trucks and carts we have spread out around Manhattan." While the company Wafels & Dinges—inspired by the original waffle sold in a horse-drawn carriage in Brussels in 1831—started in New York City in 2007, the chain eatery Vive la Crêpe!, which has five locations spread out around Manhattan, including one in the city's prestigious

Plaza Food Hall, was founded in 1996. French in style, the eatery provides a number of different crêpes, and naturally the most popular (together with one filled with apples and cinnamon, cream cheese, and *noir*, or dark chocolate) are its *crêpes à la Nutella*.

In 2005 the city also welcomed Piada—the first New York store dedicated to the popular Italian thin flatbread—which opened a new space on the Plaza Hotel's concourse level, inside the Todd English Food Hall, in January 2014. Nadia Tadè, one of the team members of the store, explains, "The good thing about importing the *piadina* to New York City, is that people happened to love it. Our customers really like the fact that it's a healthy, casual, and light meal stuffed with authentic Italian ingredients. So Piada has become a popular place where midtown New Yorkers can have a little Italian escape from their very busy working days. Of course, the reason why we decided to put the *piadina alla Nutella* on our menu is because part of our mission is to offer some of the Italian classics and this is definitely one of them." Nadia goes on to point out, "A very interesting thing is that both New Yorkers and tourists from all over the world know Nutella. They often mispronounce the name and need us to explain to them what it is; however, as soon as we show them the Nutella jar, they immediately recognize it and can't keep themselves from delivering a loud 'yummy!' Everybody loves Nutella and we have to have it on our list: we spread Nutella all over the *piadina*, grill it, and then serve it warm with a little powdered sugar on top. People, especially Americans, love the spreadable characteristic of Nutella. It is something that makes its intense hazelnut flavor and creamy texture even more enjoyable. Put Nutella on your menu and success is guaranteed!"

Nutella has even found its way into American cookbooks. Famous Italian-American chefs including Lidia Bastianich (owner of several famous restaurants in New York City, including Del Posto and Felidia, as well as others in Kansas City and Pittsburgh), Tony May (owner of SD26 at Madison Square Park), Cesare Casella (executive chef at Salumeria Rosi), or fans of Mediterranean cuisine like Jimmy Bradley (The Red Cat and The Harrison) and Jonathan Waxman (owner of the New York City bistro Barbuto), have all prepared original recipes for the book *Nutella Passion* (2010), by Clara Vada Padovani. Acclaimed food historian, New York food writer and journalist Francine Segan includes a recipe for pizza with Nutella in her book *Dolci: Italy's Sweets* (2011). She notes that when interviewing hundreds of Italians about their favorite desserts "after the predictable favorites like *cantucci*, *panettone*, and *tiramisú*, I'd hear, almost apologetically, '*pizza bianca con Nutella*'—plain baked pizza dough smeared with the popular chocolate-hazelnut spread." Nutella has conquered New York City. Says Segan: "In America we love Nutella. It's creamy and delicious and is really changing a lot of the ways that we snack. We love everything Italian in America, and it is for us a sort of Italian equivalent of peanut butter, so we spread it on bread and use it on crêpes, or use it as quick icing for cakes or muffins. For us it has become a pantry staple right next to ketchup. A little jar of Nutella on a kitchen table in an American home is really a great way to get the family to stay together for a meal." Among the reasons for Nutella's popularity in the States is America's increasing appreciation for hazelnut flavor, which is now popular in coffee, chocolates, drinks, and cakes. Explains Segan: "So when we traveled to Italy, or when we tasted Nutella, it was a great surprise flavor combination and hazelnuts suddenly shot to the top of our 'nut list'! We love hazelnuts—they have a great flavor that we mix into all sorts of desserts, and with chocolate it is a winning combination. Americans love the taste of hazelnuts and chocolate."

While the first Nutellausa.com website provided a store lo-cator so that visitors could figure out where this new prod-uct—first "discovered" in Germany by soldiers stationed on American bases and students backpacking across Europe—could be purchased, today distribution of the legendary jars has gone national, and for many families it has become an en-joyable addition to the breakfast table. The massive TV com-mercial campaign Ferrero initiated to support Nutella's roll-out focused on educating people about breakfast, including all the different things you could pair it with, in order to dif-ferentiate Nutella from other spreads. Marketing management in particular wanted to avoid branding Nutella as something to be used only with desserts or as a cake topping. In order to prepare the national TV campaign, Ferrero conducted initial tests in two limited areas: Albany (New York) and Providence (Rhode Island). Both are relatively small cities, with between 100,000 and 150,000 inhabitants, and capitals of their respec-tive states. Ferrero invested the same sums in two different media strategies. In Albany, the company broadcast a constant, nonaggressive campaign that ran for an entire year. In Prov-idence it ran four bursts, powerful waves of advertising that have a strong peak followed by long silence. The results con-vinced the company to use the strategy applied in Albany. In the US Ferrero enjoyed major success with Nutella & Go—a pack with a cup full of hazelnut cream accompanied by a small bundle of breadsticks for dipping and spreading, designed to be consumed while out on the go. The snack pack didn't need any advertising to be successful, surprising even the folks at Ferrero USA. For the American launch Ferrero gave the su-permarket chain Walmart exclusive rights to sell its products, taking advantage of the chain's 3,600 stores spread out across the entire country. It quickly became the store's biggest seller in the checkout area.

These results drove Ferrero's competitors to move quickly. Even the American giant Hershey took to the field to challenge Nutella. The "spread wars" officially started on January 15, 2014, when Pennsylvania-based Hershey presented three different spreadable creams entitled "Hershey's Spreads": chocolate, chocolate and almonds, and chocolate and hazelnut. The company used its website to launch a massive campaign to try and educate consumers. Using the hashtag #SpreadPossibilities, Hershey invited Americans to post photographs of their favorite combinations: with strawberries (an image used on the jar's label as well); on toast or waffles; and even on carrots, celery, popcorn, and French fries. A few media commentators even went so far as to claim in American newspapers that Hershey might, thanks to these products, steal a little market share from Ferrero in emerging areas like Turkey and South America.

NUTELLA BAR: CHICAGO & NEW YORK CITY

When it first opened in downtown Chicago, near the Magnificent Mile, local media described it as an "Italian theme park." Spread out over 63,000 square feet, with twenty-two bars and themed restaurants (pizza, meat, *rosticceria*, pastas, fish, and so forth), Eataly brings the best tastes of Italy to the American Midwest. The inauguration took place during "one of the coldest winters in the history of Chicago, in December 2013," according to Cristina Villa, head of PR for Eataly USA, "It was very challenging for us, but it was definitely better than what we expected." Eataly is the brainchild of Italian entrepreneur Oscar Farinetti, who opened his first store in 2007 in Turin, in northern Italy, inside an abandoned warehouse. Today there are almost thirty Eatalys around the world, in Italy, Japan, Turkey, the Arab Emirates, and the United States (New York in 2010 and Chicago in 2013), employing approximately 3,200 people. In the United States, Eataly Italia is the majority shareholder, along with the Batali-Bastianich Hospitality Group (which owns a quarter of the company), and two young New York financiers, Alex and Adam Saper. When visitors walk into the ground floor of Eataly Chicago, just past the information desk they see a large white wall upon which an image of the jar created in Alba is emblazoned. This is home to the Nutella Bar, a unique experiment realized in partnership with Ferrero: a new concept space that has been wildly successful and will be repeated all over the world. As Cristina Villa notes, "The Chicago Nutella Bar was the first one in the world and Chicago was proud of it. For crêpes this winter we had forty-five-minute lines!"

Since the bar opened, on December 2, 2013, lots of people have gotten in line to taste the specialties it offers, illustrated in Italian on a large billboard: *pane con Nutella, brioche con Nutella, saccottino con Nutella, muffin con Nutella, crostatina con Nutella, bacio di dama con Nutella, crêpe con Nutella, piadina con Nutella*. Katia Delogu, the pastry chef for Eataly USA and the person who oversaw these flavorful recipes, explains, "We start with a *pane e Nutella*, which of course is the best; everybody loves *pane e Nutella* because it is easy and simple. Then we make brioches and *saccottino*, which is a kind of croissant to mate with Nutella—really good too. During the day you can also have cookies or you can have a gluten-free cookie called *bacio di dama*, which is Italian style. We also make the *tortina*, which is a kind of breakfast cake, but everything comes with Nutella absolutely, and the best sellers of course are the crêpes." All the raw ingredients used to accompany the hazelnut spread are of the highest quality. In fact, the store of *alti cibi* (literally "high food," as the logo reads) invented by Oscar Farinetti was designed as a place

Above: The Giandujot, the Italian "ancestor" of Nutella, was a solid block of hazelnut and cocoa paste wrapped in aluminum foil that could be sliced and eaten with bread. The photograph above, which was taken in 1947, shows the first Ferrero plant where the company was founded, in Alba, in northern Italy.

Below: The first branded packaging used the image of Gianduia, the traditional Carnival character of Piedmont, who lent his name to the hazelnut and cocoa product. Gianduia was used in Ferrero advertising until 1954.

Above: The hazelnut paste became spreadable in 1949 with Supercrema.

Below: Models of vintage Ferrero trucks. The Ferrero fleet of vehicles that distributed its products in Italy was second in number only to the Italian army's. Photos courtesy Eaglemoss Publications Ltd.

The first advertising for Nutella, produced in 1964 by Studio Stile in Milan, showed a slice of bread, the perfect partner for the hazelnut cream.

Italian newspaper advertisements published in 1964 emphasized eating Nutella for breakfast, stating "Serve it in the morning."

depuis **nutella**
les noisettes ça se tartine

LE LAIT, LE CACAO, LE SUCRE AUSSI.

De mémoire de mère de famille, on n'a jamais vu ça : des noisettes, du lait, du cacao, du sucre sur une seule tartine. Pourtant ça existe.
Une tartine de Nutella, c'est un vrai goûter complet. Plein d'énergie. Et de l'énergie,

vos enfants en ont besoin toute la journée. Donnez-leur Nutella au goûter de 4 h, au goûter du matin à 10 h, au petit déjeuner ou au dessert. Avec Nutella, c'est toujours le goûter.

Dulcéa. SA. (76)

FERRERO

In the 1970s, Nutella advertising in France also paired the product with bread, suggesting that it can be eaten in the morning, as a snack or as a dessert.

German and Dutch advertisements focus on mothers as providers of Nutella for breakfast or an afternoon snack.

Nutella's most famous tagline was created in 1994: *"Che mondo sarebbe senza Nutella?"* ("What would the world be like without Nutella?") "Nutella parties" exploded as a trend, as shown in a popular TV commercial of the time.

16 de octubre 2013
Día Mundial del Pan
Con el soporte de:

nutella   ceopan

A todos los panaderos, gracias

Above: Nutella newspaper ad for World Bread Day in Spain in 2013.

Right: The combination of bread and Nutella is an important element on Facebook, too.

nutella

Left: Italian design has also been inspired by Nutella, such as the chest of drawers designed by Michelangelo Giombini, Matteo Migliorini, and Marco Sarno for the Salone del Mobile in 2006.

Below: The Andy Warhol–style image dates to 2003 and was produced by Ferrero France.

Today there are eleven factories worldwide that produce Nutella. From the top: views from Vladimir, Russia; Belsk, Poland; and Brantford, Canada.

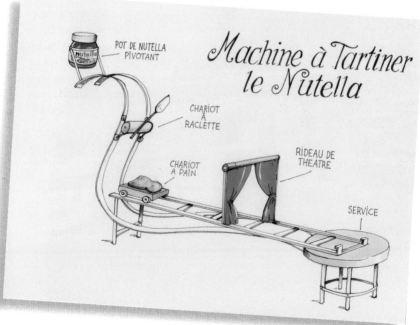

Top, left and right: In 2007, an Italian-American blogger, Sara Rosso, invented World Nutella Day, which is celebrated on February 5.

Bottom: The popular *machine à tartiner*, a playfully designed machine for spreading Nutella, was unveiled in 2004 at the Carrousel du Louvre (www.lamachineatartiner.com).

In May 2014, Nutella's fiftieth anniversary celebrations were held across the world: a truck tour crossed the United States, stopping at many locations.
Above: The first stop in New York.
Right, top and bottom: New York and Westfalenpark in Dortmund, Germany.

Above and right: The highly successful Nutella Bar, which opened inside Eataly Chicago in December 2013, was duplicated at the Eataly store in New York in 2014. Fans were offered many specialties made by Nutella.

Opposite: Just a few of the thousands of images posted by Nutella fans on the Nutellastories.com website, which went live to celebrate Nutella's fiftieth anniversary.

"Rund 94 Prozent aller Männer finden Frauen in Stöckelschuhen besonders attraktiv."

(DE) Germany, 28/02/2014

TAGS : KREATIVE GESCHICHTEN

SEGNALA UN ABUSO

6 ♥ MI PIACE

"15/5/2014 MY Engagement Nutella Ring"

(SA) Saudi Arabia, 15/05/2014

TAGS : قصص مؤثرة|الحب إبداعي|الكاهي العائلة

SEGNALA UN ABUSO

2 ♥ MI PIACE

"радужный ночник "Nutella""

(RU) Russia, 30/05/2014

TAGS : СЕМЬЯ ДЕТИ

SEGNALA UN ABUSO

2 ♥ MI PIACE

"Матрешки"

(RU) Russia, 28/04/2014

TAGS : ДРУЖБА ПРАЗДНИКИ ЮМОР

SEGNALA UN ABUSO

12 ♥ MI PIACE

1964

ITALIA

€ 0,70

nutella
FERRERO

2014

I.P.Z.S. S.p.A. - ROMA - 2014

Above: In 2014,
the Italian postal service
issued a postage stamp
to commemorate Nutella's
fiftieth anniversary.

Below: The Nutella
community on Facebook is
growing constantly:
here is the image published
to celebrate having reached
30 million fans around
the world.

30.000.000

MERCI

TAK

DANKE

СПАСИБО

GRAZIE

THANK YOU

DZIĘKUJĘ

ευχαριστώ

GRACIAS

OBRIGADO

TESEKKUR EDERIM

谢谢

blahn

nutella

where "niche," artisanal food specialties selected by consultants for Slow Food could be presented to the general public. Farinetti, the owner of Eataly, was just ten years old when the first jar of Nutella went on sale in Italy. "In Italy, Eataly introduces people to cheeses, cookies, prosciuttos, and gelatos made by SMEs, or small- and medium-sized enterprises. But out in the world we wanted to present the beauty and deliciousness of large Italian agri-food businesses too: Barilla, Lavazza, Mutti, and Ferrero. These are companies that use the highest possible quality raw ingredients, and still manage to sell their products inexpensively, precisely because they're big and can work with large volumes. I was born in Alba, and people from Alba always have to thank Ferrero for everything it has done for our region. It was my idea: I sought out managers inside Ferrero and together we created this extraordinary thing. Among all the small and large restaurants in the store, the longest lines always form outside the ones dedicated to Nutella."

After Chicago, the next Nutella Bar opened in Eataly New York, for six months, as a temporary shop in May 2014, attracting long lines of curious shoppers on 23rd Street, across the street from the Flatiron Building. Eataly's New York location is the third-most visited place in New York City, after the Statue of Liberty and the Empire State Building, and registers business volume of around $80 million a year. As Alex Saper says, "Nutella? We knew it would be popular, but we didn't expect everyone to be talking about the Nutella Bar when we first opened Eataly. The first thing that people were saying was that Eataly opened and that they had a Nutella Bar. Really we didn't expect the amount of success that it brought; we had lines and we still have lines all day long, every day. The amounts people consume in both Chicago and New York are very similar, between 100 and 120 kilos [220 and 244 pounds] per week. In each door we do roughly fifteen thousand crêpes per week.

High-quality ingredients are of the utmost importance. I think that what's so great about Ferrero is it's a very simple product, and that they use only the highest quality ingredients. The reason they're successful is because it's not filled with fifty different ingredients. It's very simple and it's just about the hazelnuts, and they do a great job."

The next step in collaboration between Ferrero and Eataly, both in the United States and in the rest of the world, will be to open new Nutella Bars: after Dubai, in the Arab Emirates, in São Paolo in Brazil, then Boston, Los Angeles, London, and Paris. Dino Borri, of Eataly—the person who oversaw the project together with Ferrero—says, "American people and also [people] in Dubai like the simplicity that we have in Italy; we didn't invent anything new, all we did was make crêpes, simple crêpes with just the right ingredients and with Nutella, or brioches with Nutella, or bread with Nutella or muffins, something super simple and super tasty with a little bit of Nutella. That's what people like the most, because here they usually put on a lot of toppings, a lot of other ingredients, so we decided to keep things as simple as possible. We want to re-create the Nutella Bar concept in every Eataly that we'll open in the future all around the world.

BRAND EXTENSION?

The Nutella Bar, which focuses on quality preparations to blend with the spreadable hazelnut cream, is different from the *Nutellerie* (literally, Nutella Shops) that opened toward the end of the 1990s. These were not as successful as people had hoped because they were seen more as being fast food restaurants than as a meeting place for people who wanted to enjoy eating fine food together. Now that project, in addition to others dedicated to bakeries, are the focus of a company in the Ferrero Group that is relatively unknown to outsiders and remains shrouded in secrecy. The company's experts are "geniuses" when it comes to sweets, who test new specialties, experiment with confectionary goods and study campaigns designed to reposition products. The company is named Soremartec—which stands for *Società di ricerca di mercato e tecnica* (literally "Research Company for Markets and Techniques")—and is Ferrero's Fort Knox, where the multinational company's future development plans are drafted and safeguarded. Official company documentation describes Soremartec as follows: "Working out of its new Alba headquarters inaugurated at the end of 2006, Soremartec supplies the entire Ferrero Group with performance, information, and studies in both the technical research department and in marketing, for the invention and launch of new products as well as to ensure the continued process of innovation and improvement for existing products and processes." The company is operational in all directions: in the sensorial analysis of products; in laying out marketing mix plans for the company's major brands; and in studying new kinds of packaging. It is an autonomous structure, responding directly to the ownership, and amounts to the heart of Ferrero's business innovation. In addition to Alba, Soremartec also has two other offices: in Monte Carlo, where there are offices and laboratories near Fontvielle Port (created by Michele when he moved there); and in Luxembourg where Soremartec's parent company is based.

It's not easy to glean more information about the secret projects these aforementioned "geniuses" are working on. Undoubtedly the experiences garnered at Eataly Chicago have opened people's eyes to the potential inherent to the HORE-CA sector (an acronym that stands for "Hotel-Restaurant-Catering"). Simply put, they proved Nutella can prosper outside the supermarket as well. For Ferrero, this doesn't necessarily mean jumping into the restaurant sector. Inside the company people have always said, "It's not our business; it's as if Airbus wanted to open its own airline company."

Just how far can a brand's territory expand? This is a hotly debated issue among marketing experts. In general, marketing theories detail three possible brand extensions:

1. *Line Extension*. This is when a product is presented with a new flavor or ingredient (something Nutella has never done); or when it is repositioned and redesigned. When it comes to logo and packaging for the Nutella jar, Ferrero refuses to make any changes. At most, the company has changed its "way" of presenting the product for consumption, adjusting messages either emotionally or rationally.

2. *Brand Extension*. This is when someone launches a product with the same "distinctive benefit" (a Starbucks coffee liquor or Nutella-flavored gelato); when the product is "complementary or an accessory" (for example Barilla pasta paired with Barilla sauces); when the product is different from a merchandise point of view, but retains the "same entrepreneurial and productive experience" (for example Parmalat fruit juices and Parmalat milk); when a product has the same stylist or design (for example Armani or Giugiaro sunglasses, by designers who also create clothing and cars, respectively);

3. *Brand Stretching*. When the brand moves "dangerously" far away from the company's core business (one of the few success stories is Virgin), while still remaining connected to the same values and philosophy that characterized the original brand.

Inside Ferrero, brand extension is viewed as a dangerous practice because it could detract from the company's original brand equity. In truth, a few things have been accomplished in this direction, as the winning example of Ferrero's Nutella & Go demonstrates. (In Italy, these are also sold in an Estathé version.) Soremartec has been studying a new "Ferrero Professional" line for some time now, which will include a specific product for artisan gelato makers. In May 2014, at the Gelato Festival, the company presented a new, partially processed product called Nutella Professional Line that can be used to make truly Nutella-flavored gelato. This kind of "D.O.C." Nutella gelato is a way to finally close the book on all the court cases the company has had to engage in with artisanal gelato makers who have previously appropriated the name and logo in an unauthorized manner. Ferrero will supply these gelato makers with its partially processed mix so that they can use it to make their popular specialties.

Lastly there is a third, even more important project in the works: a loaf of bread filled with Nutella, which has been experimented with for a few years now through a number of different area tests. The snack actually already launched in Italy in September 2014, and is called "Nutella B-ready." The name, which can be used all over the world, is based on word play between the English word "Bread" and the verb "to be ready." The product is being advertised as "a new way to make you happy at breakfast," insofar as it is "a unique product that blends the crunchiness of a waffle with all the creaminess and unique flavor of Nutella."

Throughout experimentation phases, Soremartec's main guideline has stayed the same: never abandon the characteristics that have made the brand successful. This means taste—therefore avoiding different flavors, for example almond, which companies like Hershey have experimented with—and creaminess, which should always stay the same, regardless of whether Nutella is served spread on a waffle or mixed into an ice cream. Inside Ferrero, this kind of placement is defined as a "power brand." It's a form of power that has yet to fail.

10
A family business

"Stay hungry, stay foolish," is a famous bit of advice Steve Jobs shared with Stanford University students during a speech he gave in 2005. In the wake of the destruction of World War II, Italy was undoubtedly hungry, also in the sense that the founder of Apple intended: unsatisfied and unhappy with what it had. But the country was also just a little bit "foolish," characterized by a desire to take risks, to seek out new dreams. The optimism and a can-do attitude that "courageous captains" like Michele Ferrero, Pietro and Gianni Barilla (pasta), Mario and Giuseppe Lavazza (coffee), Ernesto Illy (coffee), Ermenegildo Zegna (fashion), and Leonardo Del Vecchio (Luxottica eyewear) demonstrated during the 1960s have become a memory for most of Italy. During those years, Italian society was poorer than it is today, perhaps even more unjust and less educated. But it was undoubtedly less divided and insecure than today's society, because it had a clear, shared objective: to improve living conditions across the nation. The core of that "old economy" was family business. Michele Ferrero was the son of a pastry chef, born in a little town in the Langhe region, and ran an empire worth 8 billion euros that employs more than thirty thousand people all over the globe. The Barilla family, after having sold their business to an American company, managed to buy the whole thing back again. Lavazza and Illy espresso cups have spread out all over the world, and represent a way of life implicit in the Italian espresso. Thanks to his success with eyewear, Leonardo Del Vecchio competed with Michele Ferrero for several years for first place in the annual list of the wealthiest Italians published in *Forbes* magazine (both overtook Silvio Berlusconi). The Zegna family is now in its fourth generation of bloodline entrepreneurs and can boast clothing stores from China to the United States.

Many famous Italian brands are now in foreign hands: Krizia has become Chinese; Frau is owned by the American company Haworth; Fendi, Emilio Pucci, and Acqua di Parma are run by Bernard Arnault's French luxury multinational LVMH, whose rival Kering (previously PPR), owned by François-Henry Pinault, has purchased Gucci, Sergio Rossi, and jewelry company Pomellato. In the agri-food sector the foreign shopping spree has been even more all-encompassing: French company Lactalis now controls Galbani and Parmalat; Bertolli olive oils is in Spanish hands; Perugina and Buitoni are owned by Nestlé (Lausanne); Caffarel is owned by the Swiss company Lindt; Averna and Pernigotti have been taken over by the Turkish group Toksöz; Gancia is now the property of Russian oligarch Rustam Tariko.

Ferrero is one of the few Italian multinationals left. It is an almost unique example of a family business of this size without any other partners. In Tuscany, in the wine sector, a number of family businesses have prospered for centuries—for example, Barone Ricasoli (since 1114) and Marchesi Antinori (since 1385)—and are among the oldest in the world. Even though it is a relatively "young" company, the Ferrero family has solid traditions and a strong bond with its origins.

Nutella is extremely famous, but the brand owners have always kept a low profile, keeping their names and images out of the papers. It's difficult to find a photograph of them in newspaper archives; they don't give interviews and they maintain a privacy policy that might appear excessive in today's connected world.

In recent years a number of universities have conducted studies on the concept of "family business," and set out different parameters for defining one: evaluating, for example, if the family owns a controlling share and the company is publicly traded; if family members are or are not part of the management; and how the passage from one generation to the next has taken place. Ferrero, one could say, is a family business par excellence, both when it comes to strategic decisions and concerning control of the company's capital. Franzo Grande Stevens—famous in Turin as the personal lawyer for Giovanni Agnelli, the former president of Fiat, who passed away in 2003—was a trusted confidante of the Ferreros for years, held various positions on the company's board of directors, and helped guide the company during its financial development and the early years of its internationalization. In an interview published in Italian magazine *Panorama* in June 2012, Grande Stevens claimed that in family companies, the company identifies with its founding entrepreneur: "I've known quite a few of them, and I'm one hundred percent certain that they are catalyzed by the need to guarantee a better future for the creature they've created. For example, I know Michele Ferrero quite well, and I know he's not interested merely in conserving his patrimony, but in guaranteeing a future for his company. This is why men like him need to find a way to make sure that those who will lead the company in the future have the same love of the job, the same skills and the same qualities."

In Italy, 85 percent of all companies registered with the

Camere di Commercio (the Italian chamber of commerce)—half of which have sales exceeding 50 million euros—are still controlled by families. Recently these companies suffered a great deal during the economic crisis, but as long as the principles that inspired the company's creation and guided it during its growth phases are protected, they can survive rough economic waters better than public companies run by managers who are primarily interested in achieving positive results in the short term.

The Ferrero family has now reached its third generation of ownership, without any major shocks or governance issues, even though some of the people running the company have passed away when they were very young and unexpectedly, bound by the same tragic destiny. Giovanni, Pietro, and Michele are recurring names in the Nutella dynasty. The factory itself was founded by the brothers Pietro and Giovanni Ferrero, but fate stole away first one and then the other when they were in their fifties.

At that point Michele, Pietro's son, took over the company and until his death, in February 2015, Michele continued to be the true *deus ex machina* of the family company. His sons are Pietro and Giovanni.

Michele's son Pietro also died young, tragically stolen away by a heart attack in April 2011, when he was just forty-seven, while bicycling through South Africa on his beloved bike: he was in Johannesburg, together with his father, following developments in one of Ferrero's social enterprises. Pietro had been living in Alba, after studying in Brussels and Turin, earning a degree in biology. He oversaw innovation, industrial organization, and finance within the company. He was married to Luisa Strumia, and the couple had three young children: Michael, Marie Eder, and John. Here are a few words from an interview he gave in the monthly magazine *Capi-*

tal for an article written by Antonella Rampino (June 1995): "Even today, when my brother and I have taken over operational management, our father's influence remains important. Every once in a while we travel as a group—the Ferrero family together with our closest collaborators—and we visit a bunch of cafés and supermarkets. We talk to consumers, asking them what they think about the chocolates or snacks they find on sale. We do a little marketing in the field and then spend our evenings talking about our experiences; we have wonderful discussions! It's an older, more traditional way of working. We make decisions during the weekend, when we're all together."

GIOVANNI FERRERO: NUTELLA WILL LEAD OUR GROWTH

Giovanni Ferrero studied marketing in the United States, and started his management career primarily in sales: beginning in 1997 he took on the role of CEO for the family holding company, in equal partnership with his brother. For years now he has been writing literary fiction and has published five novels.

He is married to Paola Rossi, an official with the European Commission, and the couple have two children: Michele and Bernardo.

After the premature death of his brother Pietro, Giovanni has run the company on his own.

"Don't reduce all that to a dollar value, please! It requires constant effort, at every level of responsibility, doing things in such a way that everybody vibrates with tension and is focused on improving, on a never-ending search for excellence... It requires an unflagging determination to make teamwork, and a greater awareness of the importance of shared goals, prevail over individual interests, which are like an obscure cancer that can eat away at a business, whenever that business lacks the right motivations. . ." The author of these words is an "expert on the African continent," a man named Collins brought in by a brilliant British manager, Charles Bates, who is about to travel there and wants to learn everything he can about that corner of the world. Bates is the main character in one of Giovanni Ferrero's novels, *Il giardino di Adamo* (Adam's garden), in which the theme of comparing development models between advanced countries and emerging nations is told against the background of a love affair that unfolds out in the open savannah.

These concepts, present in all the fiction the multinational CEO has written, are an interesting indication of the author's thinking, and betray specific cultural and ethical references, as well as others related to marketing. In an article published in the Group's newsletter a few years ago, Giovanni said, "I deeply believe that successful companies will be those that go 'glocal,' in other words, the ones that work on both a global and local level, satisfying local consumers in the best manner possible, anywhere and everywhere they may be. 'Think Global, Act Local' is anything but an empty slogan." Speaking to the *Wall Street Journal* in November 2013 during one of the rare interviews he has given, Giovanni Ferrero said, "We were born as a family of entrepreneurs, and we intend to remain as such," adding that he felt no need to sell "to just anybody," nor to take the company public: the Ferrero Group's intention is to continue to grow thanks to autonomous decisions, just as it has always done, with the goal of doubling the Group's sales in ten years thanks to geographic drivers like Asia and the United States, and with Nutella as its primary product. He's confirmed the same concepts in an interview he gave for this book.

Why did you set the headquarters of Ferrero International in Luxembourg, where you have lived for a number of years?

"We chose Central Europe because this is where people consume the highest volume of chocolate and 'off-hour' products like snacks and milk-based sweets. Furthermore, our competitors have their headquarters here too: this allows us to work with a global perspective. Here we feel like we're connected with the entire Group, as if we were bound by an enormous umbilical cord."

The Organisation for Economic Co-operation and Development identified Nutella as a winning example of globalization. But Nutella remains different from global brands like Coca-Cola or McDonald's. Is its longevity simply the product of a perfect formula?

"The foundation of Nutella's success is its inimitable recipe, which appeals to everyone: the irresistible, unbeatable flavor of a slice of bread spread with Nutella has won over generations of children and parents, and is recognized the world over. Compared to the brands you've mentioned, we can certainly identify a few common elements: like the fact that they're trans-generational and appeal to families."

What would you say are the differences?

"One difference deals with Ferrero's ability not only to generate a unique flavor for Nutella, but to maintain a significant qualitative advantage over its imitators. This has limited our direct competitors' development on a global level. The reasons for this are connected with the Ferrero system, which is impossible to replicate in terms of absolute top quality and the way we process ingredients, starting from the vast experience we've garnered in processing hazelnuts."

You've stayed faithful to your origins, the hazelnuts of Italy's Langhe region . . .

"Of course, but there aren't enough hazelnuts in the Langhe to satisfy our needs anymore. We're the only producers able to use, throughout the calendar year, the freshest (and therefore most flavorful) hazelnuts. All our competitors use hazelnuts gathered during the autumn harvest. But once spring arrives we can depend on extremely fresh produce arriving from the southern hemisphere, where it's autumn and people are harvesting new hazelnuts. My family began cultivating hazelnut orchards in countries like Chile, South Africa, and Australia over twenty years ago precisely in order to obtain this qualitative advantage."

You've said that Nutella is well made and uses quality ingredients. But that may not be enough to explain its transformation into a lovemark . . .

"I'd point out another difference with respect to the other major lovemarks. Behind Nutella stands a true family company, and this can be seen in its focus on the long term, and the refusal to accept any compromises on quality. I believe that consumers can see this too. Finally there's another fundamental element that Nutella, unlike other major, globally popular brands, has built up patiently and over time: its association with breakfast and with waking up in general. Nutella enters the home and builds a careful, deep relationship with the family over time. Proof of this unique bond with consumers can be seen in the fact that every single day Nutella garners, online and elsewhere, spontaneous 'love declarations' from its fans, creating a true content archive (text messages, photographs, drawings, videos, creative initiatives) that is unequaled anywhere else."

Europe is increasingly sluggish in terms of economic growth. India, China, Brazil, and other countries will be the protagonists of future development. Today most Nutella is sold in Italy, France, and Germany. You told the Wall Street Journal *that Ferrero hopes to double sales over the next ten years, expanding in new markets where Nutella can drive company development. Will your growth model be the same you've used during the first fifty years of Nutella's existence? Will you be paying any special attention to the HORECA sector?*

"First of all, I like to point out that our fourth-largest market after Italy, France, and Germany is the United States. Ten years ago just 9 percent of the Nutella we produced was sold outside Europe. Today that number has risen to 28 percent, and our five-year plan calls for even stronger growth outside European borders. Up until today we've never needed to make any major changes in our growth model in order to develop outside Europe. For example, we emphasize Nutella eaten together with bread as part of breakfast in every geographical area on the planet, as recent launches in Brazil, Russia, and the United States confirm. Obviously, in countries where eating habits are considerably different from our own—for example, in Asia—we may need to identify a slightly different approach. No doubt in all these countries we'll be carefully evaluating out-of-home opportunities wherever they present themselves, especially in markets where eating food outside the home is a strong cultural characteristic."

The tendency toward understatement that has always characterized the family comes through in this interview with Giovanni Ferrero as well, confirming some of the fundamental characteristics of a singular Italian family business: the search for unique products; attention to the quality of raw ingredients; the bond with the Langhe and the land where the family was born; pride in having always developed the company from within, without any outside assistance; and determination to continue to do so in the future. There are new developments, like the company's vast investments in the United States; its expansion plans for Asia and emerging countries; and its willingness to look closely at future opportunities in the out-of-home sector. Most importantly, at the heart of everything lies a company ethic proudly rooted in another era, at the very foundation of Italian capitalism, when the economic boom inspired general optimism and a desire to tackle new challenges: two attitudes which, unfortunately, have become rare commodities indeed.

PART FOUR
Nutella Graffiti

11

A love story lasting fifty years

Guests blew out the fifty candles set atop a long baguette spread with the hazelnut cream, rather than a traditional birthday cake. Instead of the famous song, "Happy Birthday to You", music in several cities around the world was provided by famous pop stars. Congratulations kept coming in for months, in one continuous flow, via the Internet: almost eighty thousand memories in the form of videos, photographs, drawings, and declarations of love that came pouring in from fans all over the planet. It wasn't just a party for friends and relatives—it was a party for more than half a million people in ten different countries. "Fifty years of a great story of love," as Nutella summed up the event in a video posted in social media to thank fans of the spread, who in 2014 had helped make the initiatives set up for Nutella's anniversary such a resounding success. In newspapers and news websites, 1964 was remembered not just as the birthdate of American First Lady Michelle Obama, the founder of Amazon Jeff Bezos, of actors and actresses like Russell Crowe, Juliette Binoche, Nicolas Cage, Monica Bellucci, and Sandra Bullock, of the singer Courtney Love, the model Elle Macpherson, Japanese author Banana Yoshimoto and cycling champion Miguel

Indurain; nor would that "magical" year be celebrated merely as the first time songs by The Beatles or the Rolling Stones hit the airwaves, or iconic films like *Goldfinger* and *Mary Poppins* hit the theaters. Nutella's fiftieth anniversary was now an official member of the global history of cultural customs. In Italy the event was even celebrated with an official postage stamp: a 70-euro cent (roughly one US dollar) issued by the Italian national postal system.

If it is true, as some marketing experts claim, that brands have now become like "people" that earn human love and respect, then during the first months of 2014 Nutella proved itself beyond all expectations. Can a birthday truly be transformed into an opportunity for the brand? It's not always the case, although lately plenty of companies have begun taking advantage of birthdays in order to promote special marketing plans. There's a simple reason for this: birthdays are something that each and every one of us celebrates together with friends and family. But it hasn't always been this way: the birthday tradition is a relatively recent phenomenon, at least in Western culture. In truth, celebrating the day one was born became popular in Europe only at the beginning of the nineteenth century, first among aristocrats and then among the middle class. To a certain extent the culture of celebrating saints, at least in the Catholic faith, had kept birthday celebrations on the back burner. But it was a practice already common in ancient Rome and Asia, especially in China, as the famous thirteenth-century merchant Marco Polo recounted in his *Travels*.

Brands have helped make anniversaries relevant again. Even one of the most authoritative financial newspapers in the world, the *Financial Times*—first founded in London in 1888—celebrated its 125th anniversary in 2013 with a global marketing campaign designed to highlight the event. During the same year consumers saw Harley-Davidson motorcycles (created in 1903) celebrate 110 years of activity; beer company Heineken (founded in 1863) celebrate 150 years; and Hellmann's mayonnaise (1913) celebrate one hundred years. Coca-Cola, another powerful global lovemark, celebrated its 125th anniversary in Atlanta in 2011 with what it claims is the largest building illumination ever—lighting up its headquarters tower in Atlanta with nearly one million lumens of light every night during the month of May. A brand's decision to celebrate its birthday can prove to be a good strategy, but there's always the risk that nobody will be particularly interested in the event, when and if the conditions outlined by Kevin Roberts for authentic lovemarks are missing. He presented these conditions in detail in a drawing the author called "the Love/Respect Axis."

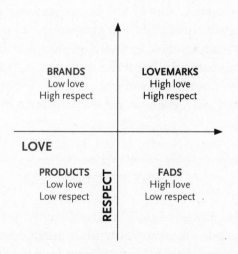

Source: *Kevin Roberts*, Lovemarks: The Future Beyond Brands *(New York: Powerhouse, 2005), page 149.*

The first condition, explains Roberts, is respect: "Without Respect there is no foundation for any long-term relationship." Therefore, in the top left-hand corner of the image we find traditional respected brands, for example automobiles. In the lower left-hand corner, with "low Love and low Respect," we find "products," in other words simple commodities that people can't do without but that are common for everyone. The author describes these as follows: "Sand, iron, salt, gravel, that sort of stuff. Some of them make it out of the shade and work their way up. Basmati rice is one example." Last but not least, "the bottom right-hand area had to be the home of fad, fashion, and infatuations: loved for fifteen minutes . . ." In his analysis of this axis, Roberts concludes with the top right-hand corner, where "the sun always shines: high Respect, high Love . . . Virgin is there. United would like to be. The iMac? Yes. The ThinkPad? Don't think so."

Roberts' analysis is relatively ruthless, and denies lots of products the possibility of ever becoming lovemarks. The case history of Nutella's fiftieth anniversary shows that the hazelnut cream invented by an Italian pastry chef has made it across this particular finish line, because it has earned love and respect from its consumers, and won official certification, for the first time all over the world, between January and June of 2014.

THE BIG IDEA

In the 1980s, British ad executive David Ogilvy, the founder of one of the world's most important advertising agencies, wrote: "Unless your advertising contains a big idea, it will pass like a ship in the night. I doubt if more than one campaign in a hundred contains a big idea." His observation is even more relevant today, bearing in mind the stimuli bombardment consumers are subjected to by modern media. Ferrero certainly didn't need a "big idea" in order to decide *whether* or not to celebrate Nutella's fiftieth anniversary, but it did need the "right idea" for *how* best to do so.

The decision to create a single anniversary celebrated all over the world wasn't by any means a given. When Nutella celebrated its fortieth anniversary in Europe, the company didn't stick with just one date. In Italy, celebrations were held in 2004, while in Germany and France they took place the following year. Each Ferrero business unit counted the years not from the first jar produced for sale in Alba, but from when the first jars went on sale in each national market. Three events held on separate dates were organized for Nutella's three "cornerstone countries," as they're referred to inside the company. In Turin, Italy, the company held a VIP party along the banks of the Po River on April 20, 2004, inviting actors and writers, broadcasting videos and bringing out a giant baguette with forty candles that was featured in all the newspapers and on TV. In Paris, starting on May 14, 2005, and continuing for exactly forty days, the company opened a temporary Nutella Bar called "Table Nutella" that offered crêpes and other snack spread with the hazelnut cream to endless lines of fans. In Westfalia-Renania, in Gelsenkirchen, the company organized a world record breakfast on May 29, hosting 27,854 people inside an athletic stadium in order to celebrate their favorite flavorful specialty. These three anniversaries proved that Nutella lovers were enthusiastic about the experience, and the company couldn't afford to pass up the occasion. So Ferrero began working on a "big idea" to celebrate half a century of Nutella well in advance.

In the little town of Findel, near the Luxembourg airport, stands the company's global headquarters, home to more than seven hundred employees. Already in 2012 an international team was at work on the concept for Nutella's fiftieth. What should they start with? Inside the company, people were thinking about a fundamental element: "For five decades Nutella has received love and adoration from its consumers, together with plenty of spontaneous declarations. It wouldn't be incorrect to say that the jar enters peoples' homes as part of a deep, intimate relationship. It's as if Nutella could see people in their pajamas, without any makeup." Therefore in Luxembourg, the work team began to conceive of the 2014 event as an opportunity to share this love with everyone, and to thank people for having given it.

They identified several guidelines around which to build the anniversary:

- For this first time in the history of Nutella and Ferrero, it would be important to create a marketing mix campaign that took advantage of every channel on a global scale, all at the same time and involving at least fifty countries.

- It would be important to find a unique, easily recognizable logo that could be put on jar labels, the web, and into TV commercials.

- They needed to convey brand content through a graphic design and video that fully expressed brand values: togetherness, care, enthusiasm, dynamism, vitality, and love.

- They had to create a unique claim, through which to share the memories, feelings, and passions hidden within each slice of bread spread with Nutella (the expression "fifty years full of stories" was chosen).

- It would be important to let fans talk about the hazelnut cream, so that they could tell their own stories about their relationship with Nutella.

That was the "big idea": the history of Nutella is the history of its consumers. Within this concept, the company identified a claim along with help from the McCann Worldgroup agency (which then won the contract for the global campaign)—and the Ferrero Group's internal packaging division management came up with the graphic design and logos. The campaign got underway through a two-step process. The first step, in summer 2013, invited Nutella fans in five different countries (Italy, France, Germany, the United States, and Canada) to upload their stories onto the website www.nutellastories.com through texts, photographs, drawings, and videos. It was a low-profile beginning, with no extra advertising, and targeted at the brand's most diehard fans in nations where Nutella consumption was already strong. It was also open to employees. The second step came in at the end of January 2014, when this online platform was opened up to the entire world, flanked by a simultaneous launch in print media, on TV, and on social networks. The objective? To communicate a single date for celebrations all over the planet, set for May 18, 2014, fifty years after the first jars were first placed on store shelves.

NUTELLASTORIES.COM

At a party, a mother gives a group of children a cake baked in the form of the iconographic Nutella jar. Then the party moves on to a merry table of young adults in the middle of a beautiful, sunlit day. Naturally there's plenty of bread spread with the legendary cream, forming the word "Nutella" in seven cutout letters. Then comes a river of impressionistic images: childhood drawings, a sand castle in the form of a Nutella jar, even a young girl's fingernails decorated with the brand's lettering. The iconic jar reappears on a skateboard, T-shirts, rings, wool sweaters, and even as a colorful clay sculpture: the video condenses as much creativity as possible, spontaneous and joyful, all provided by fans who want to celebrate their lovemark. This was the first "call to action," a classic TV commercial shot by Italian director Giuseppe Capotondi. In order to create the video, Capotondi drew his inspiration from authentic love declarations posted online by Nutella fans. The video was launched on the TV and via the Internet, on social websites and on www.nutellastories.com. The website's homepage explained: "In 2014, Nutella celebrates its 50th birthday. It has been 50 years shared with you. 50 years full of stories, big and small. And we would love to see and read them. To make this celebration really special, we're asking you to share your most memorable moments that involve Nutella. Early mornings gathered around the breakfast table, birthdays with friends, special events . . . We've all experienced a special moment with Nutella." The anniversary year had just begun, and Ferrero was making its bid to get Nutella finally, definitively recognized as a global lovemark.

A small, elite work team including people from twelve different countries gathered together for the first time in Luxembourg in April 2013. Their task? To get the website online in just a few months. Usually a global platform destined to become a container for UGC, or user-generated content, requires far more design time. The company basically built a social network that put the consumer front and center, like Facebook or Twitter, but limited to a single brand. The goal was to create a website that could aggregate and allow the upload of individual content in such a way that it would all be visible together, making it possible for users to interact with it (anyone uploading had to sign up and respect the website's policies). The website www.nutellastories.com was localized in eleven countries, plus an international section, and in eighteen different languages. It could be navigated via different devices, including desktop computers, laptops, tablets, mini-tablets, and smartphones. The site was made as accessible as possible, with just five sections, making it easy to jump from one to the other: stories, the fiftieth anniversary, world, news, events. The designers opted for a simple graphic design, with a white background and red and black lettering, just like the logo, favoring a linear motif that echoed the layouts of most modern social networks.

But just sticking the website up online wasn't enough. Ferrero needed to start gathering content and publishing it online, ahead of the celebrations scheduled for May 18. Every digital strategy includes a call to action, otherwise it would be like organizing a concert featuring a famous rock star, but never advertising it in posters, announcements, or events. Ferrero's plan called for several distinct phases:

- Reach: call to action, inspiration and traffic generation.

- Engagement/Interaction: love upload and contest participation; moderation and contest validation.

- Advocacy: insightful rewards; how we say thanks.

The plan aimed to make the anniversary as visible as possible through classic media, digital media, and public relationships. Facebook helped too, since Ferrero set up twenty-two fan pages in thirty-nine countries, as well as on the Russian social website VK, or VKontakte. The result was a deluge of posts on Facebook walls from almost thirty million Nutella fans. The posts dedicated to "fifty years" were displayed in almost 112 million Facebook user feeds. The company even calculated the engagement ladder, measuring how much fans got involved: 4.5 million interactions among the 624 posts for "fifty years"; 3.8 million posts clicked; 649,000 likes; 73,000 comments; and 61,000 shares. When a user shares a link to content, marketers achieve a higher step on the ladder: it becomes advocacy.

Overall, the birthday operation was entirely positive. Inside the company, the results were considered complimentary, even flattering, especially in qualitative terms and compared to other "call to action" campaigns launched on analogous digital platforms for UGCs, for example Coca-Cola's "Happiness Flag" for the 2014 FIFA World Cup in Brazil; or the extreme sport photo contest sponsored by Red Bull. The initiative generated a broad, continuous echo, like a long wave lasting several months, well into 2014. Ninety thousand users—the diehard core fan base—signed up on the website www.nutellastories.com. They were spread out all over the world, and not limited merely to countries targeted with the "call to action." While users had to sign up in order to share content (an option that was closed at the end of summer 2014), the website remained open and free to all comers for the entire anniversary year. During the first eight months, 2.6 million users visited the site. Even those who were merely curious stopped at the site for a relatively long time, two full minutes on average (the average stop at a given website is less than one minute), and viewing a total 6.7 million webpages.

In the end, 76,422 "Nutella stories" were shared on the platform, with ten countries leading the classification for most posts.

The people who designed the platform expected users to follow the social media model to a greater or lesser degree: immediacy, speed of uploading content, a photo or quip to share with friends without needing to spend too much time thinking about it. But on www.nutellastories.com people wound up

Posts published online at www.nutellastories.com by country

Italy	21,978
United States	15,170
UK	11,544
France	8,800
Germany	4,835
Canada	3,621
United Arab Emirates	2,923
Russia	1,290
Poland	1,250
Belgium	590
Other Countries	4,421
Total	**76,422**

taking a little more time than usual so that they could talk, almost as if it were a confession, about their relationship with the brand. Perhaps the experience of remembering is too rich and profound to be condensed into just the few type spaces permitted in a tweet. In the end, the results surprised marketers, both in terms of richness and for the depth of the relationship established through the platform. It is a trend supported by other data as well: 76.9 percent of the posts were text stories, compared to 19.8 percent pictures and an extremely small percentage of video: proof that the written word—in a Babel of languages and typesets—can still triumph, even in an image-driven society.

Even the country-by-country flow of data exceeded expectations. Italy came out on top, which may have been expected. But Americans were not far behind, despite the fact that Nutella hasn't been there nearly as long, followed by relative new comers, the UK and Canada. Perhaps Anglo-Saxon "digitalization" is greater than in France or Germany, above and beyond brand popularity. Last but not least, the Nutella team was satisfied with the quality of the "Nutella confessions" it collected. There were numerous touching episodes, divided by tags organized with the somewhat simplistic logic of social networks: creative/ funny; families, friendship; holidays; mornings; touching stories/love. There was also an opportunity to "Like" different posts, and forty-six thousand users did so. The users may have been people located at different ends of the earth, but via the web they discovered a common passion, "speaking" to one another about Nutella and thereby becoming brand ambassadors in their own right.

A WORLD HERITAGE

The photographs and sketches posted online by fans for Nutella's fiftieth anniversary highlight what may perhaps be an excess of love. There was a Canadian couple who decided to hand out jars of Nutella as wedding gifts; two German *fiancés* who posted a photograph of their faces spread with Nutella and wrote, "If you want to be beautiful . . ." One American mother shared an image of her daughters' smiling faces and wrote, "My girls lovin' them some Nutella! Puts a smile on their faces." In Italy, a user named Stefano posted a photo of himself as a child, a slice of bread spread with the hazelnut cream on the breakfast table, accompanied by a shot of him today, bearded and smiling, plunging his spoon into a jar of the cream. Other people proudly shared images of the glasses they've gathered from a "Nutella collection" extended over decades. One Italian lady made a cake in the shape of the iconic jar to celebrate her husband's birthday, filling it "with 4 kg of Nutella!" In Belgium, Emeline photographed her *"fondants alla Nutella, miam miam..."* A vast assortment of smiling faces, some sporting hazelnut cream "moustaches," were posted to share daily moments that made them happier than most, accompanied by lots of creative drawings, cakes, fake tattoos, and parties with friends and families. One has to wonder just how a brand could become such a reassuring presence, helping people all over the planet get past their daily difficulties. "Because it's good," Nutella's many fans might respond. Here is a selection of posts gathered on the website, authentic testimonies that show what it's really like to be a lovemark.

> "I first got Nutella on my 13th birthday as a present. I was really mad because I wanted video games but I got a jar of Nutella. So I put it next to the TV where I played video games and I didn't look at it for at least 2 days. It just sat there. One day I was looking for a snack in the house but we didn't have any. So I picked up the jar and opened it, I got a spoon and took a bit, then I fell in love with it. After that day I bought a jar every chance I got. :) Thank you!!!"
>
> Ryan, United States, May 18, 2014

> "When I first came to Dubai I was single without even a cup to drink my tea. After I moved to my first humble home, I went out for some quick shopping. While passing by the shelves where Nutellas were stacked, I noticed those small Nutella cups. 'This is what I needed' I thought, and bought. Within two days I had my first teacup! Over the years I kept on buying them. Now I'm married with a 2-yr-old daughter. We grow our basil by the window in a Nutella cup, my daughter drinks her milk with another one, my wife enjoys that exact amount of coffee latte, and I use another one of those to grow my sourbread yeast, which I use for baking our daily bread . . . the bread we love the most with a generous spread of Nutella!"
>
> Bedebu, United Arab Emirates, July 3, 2014

"Nutella . . . You're there when we go wrong, you comfort us with your delight. You listen to us and make us melt with your chocolate hazelnut taste. You're still better than any man! NUTELLA, I LOVE YOU!"

Cindy, France, June 8, 2014

"I discovered Nutella during a visit to Poland in 1999. I loved it, and brought a jar back home because I'd never seen it in the stores in Calgary. Since then, it's become available everywhere, much to my delight. It's more than a spread for your toast—Nutella makes simple things a treat. I love spreading it on apples and dipping raspberries and cherries in it. It turns delicious snacks into divine moments."

Susan, Canada, June 30, 2014

"Throughout my childhood, every time I didn't want to obey my parents, they used Nutella to punish me. They'd tell me I couldn't eat Nutella for a week. It was the worse punishment ever! And finally, for my 20th birthday, my parents figured out how many jars of Nutella I'd eaten so far. I don't remember the exact number but it was insane. This is what I call my love story with Nutella."

Jonathan, United States, May 6, 2014

"I met my soul mate in a wonderful *creperia* . . . Everything was magical, overwhelming, sublime . . . Our love blossomed amid the infinite sweetness of Nutella, and between one crêpe and the next, we fell in love. Thank you, Nutella!"

Loirs, Italy, May 3, 2014

"One day I asked my little sister: what percentage do you love me? She answered 50%. I was amazed—why only 50%. She said: The other 50% is for Nutella. If Nutella didn't exist I'd love you 100%. So I told her, if I buy you a jar of Nutella, would you love me 100%? And she said, I'd love you more. This is my story with my little sister J."

Salma, Morocco, Facebook post, 2014

"For me, bread and Nutella was that moment after school, when right after I got home and I'd put away my backpack and just before *Le Club Dorothée*, my favorite kids' show. Because if Nutella is

50, today I'm 30! For me, Nutella was a gift, a poignant moment at the end of a long day. I still carry that flavor with me today. It's really simple, but maybe that's why I love Nutella so much."

Gregory, France, April 5, 2014

"I was 18, and in order to celebrate the last day of classes, my classmates and I decided to make a mega bread-and-Nutella. Unfortunately, we hadn't thought how we were going to pick it up and move it! So on the day of the party, a friend of mine and I wound up holding onto a 2-meter-long Nutella sandwich while riding a scooter, with the risk of losing it at every curve! Fortunately the trip went okay, and the sandwich made it to its destination. It was the sweetest way for us to celebrate the end of school and the beginning of a new season in life."

Elisa, Italy, March 10, 2014

"When I was a kid, I used to eat so much Nutella I'd almost always end up with some of it left over on my hands. One day, my mom told me to wash the Nutella off my hand and I scrubbed and scrubbed but it still wouldn't come off. That's when we learned my Nutella stain was actually a birthmark on my right palm!"

Denise, United Kingdom, March 7, 2014

"If you were ever to ask me what I did during my first year in college, the first thing on the list would be 'I ate way too much Nutella on toast at 3 a.m. with my best friend.' Mostly after nights out or the night before essays were due, or just because we were watching films late, not that we ever really needed a reason. Four years later that same best friend and I still buy each other Nutella. And once, she even brought me a 1-kg jar all the way from Italy. I actually have a pink spoon I only use to eat Nutella straight out of the jar."

Giulia, Canada, August 7, 2014

"The power of Nutella: my mother, who will be turning 100 this August, eats at least five spoonfuls of Nutella every day after her regular snack. She's always loved it, and it makes her smile. Last week I snuck in a couple of spoonfuls before she did, and she said (in perfect Milanese dialect), 'Damen vun anca a mi' (Give me a spoonful too.) I couldn't help but hug her, feeling very moved because she hadn't been able to complete a full sentence for quite some time. Thank you, Nutella, for the joy you give my mamma!!!"

Giorgia, Italy, February 28, 2014

"If when you were a child you never ate Nutella with a spoon from the Nutella jar, you never had a real childhood. :)"

Wilde, Germany, July 4, 2014

"Nutella is what makes toast joyous. Nutella spread in the morning gives us a lot of strength for the rest of the day."

Raphi, France, June 9, 2014

"For me Nutella is the taste of my childhood. My mom used to prepare little portions, no bigger than my mouth, on untoasted white bread, and place them in a line around the plate rim. I'd pick them up one by one and enjoy them with a layer of butter between the Nutella and the bread. 20 years later and I'm still having Nutella in exactly the same way. Nutella is the best!"

Saba, United Arab Emirates, April 9, 2014

"When I had my first baby, I was stuck at home and couldn't get out a lot. I saw a TV commercial for something that looked so good that I kept raving about it. My husband decided he would learn how to make it (without my knowledge). He looked up a basic recipe online, and the next thing I knew, I had a plate of Nutella & banana-filled crêpes, with strawberries on top & syrup. It was the best thing I ever ate! That's love."

Starlite, United States, May 13, 2014

"You can't buy happiness, but you can buy Nutella, which basically means the same thing."

Tony, Greece, May 29, 2014

A POSTAGE STAMP AND THE FLUO JARS

In the space dedicated to stamp collectors in a post office in the center of Rome, not far from the Trevi Fountain, a folder appeared on the morning of May 14, 2014, that immediately attracted the attention of collectors. It was a stamp, at the center of which was the image of a jar of Nutella, with the year of its birth (1964) above it, and the current year (2014) below, all of which set against a gold background. The collector's item could also be stamped with the date of emission. The stamp also displayed "ITALIA" and its value (70 euro-cents, approximately one US dollar), making it legally valid and not simply a collection piece. It was printed at the Istituto Poligrafico e Zecca dello Stato (Italy's State Mint and Polygraphic Institute) in rotogravure on white paper, neutral coating, self-adhesive and non-fluorescent, for a total run of no fewer than 2.7 million individual stamps.

Nutella has officially entered Italian history. The decision to print the iconic hazelnut spread on a stamp was made at the beginning of 2014 by the Ministry of Economic Development as part of a series themed "leading examples of Italy's production and economic system." At the press conference organized to celebrate the presentation, held in the foreign press association in Rome, dozens of journalists representing newspapers from all over the world took part, listening to presentations given by Federica Guidi, Italy's minister for economic development; Luisa Todini, president of the Italian postal service; and ambassador Francesco Paolo Fulci, president of Ferrero S.p.A. The conference marked the official launch of global festivities to celebrate fifty years of Nutella, and was followed by a VIP event organized that afternoon at Teatro Adriano, a theater dedicated to the famous Roman emperor Hadrian. People entered a large hall by passing between eleven Corinthian columns, providing an austere and glorious framework for a celebration that hosted nutritionists, journalists, sociologists, actors, and politicians, including the mayor of Rome. Those present made every effort to celebrate their illustrious guest of honor, sharing their most intimate memories of snacking on Nutella. Everyone had a chance to appreciate a personal message from the company's CEO, Giovanni Ferrero, which was also published in the illustrated pamphlet that accompanied the postage stamp: "A tribute that constitutes an important recognition of the value of Nutella as a leading example of Italy's production and economic system."

Such an epic anniversary would not have been complete without special commemorative jars of Nutella destined, along with the postage stamps, to become collector's items among the product's numerous fans. These included jars from the "Fluo Jar" collection, on which the Nutella logo and its legendary image of a slice of bread spread with the cream were screen printed in relief, in four different fluorescent colors. The year (2014) was set in relief on the back for a limited edition of 3.5 million pieces. This collection was accompanied by the "Celebration" glass series, sold in Italy and Middle Eastern countries, as well as a special series created for the United States and Canada using plastic jars accompanied by a special sleeve designed to emphasize the graphic design.

THE B-DAY IN TEN COUNTRIES

In the United States the "Nutella Jubilee" got underway a few days after the Italian press conference. On May 12, in the shadow of the Flatiron Building—a striking triangular edifice built in 1902 at the intersection of 23rd Street, Fifth Avenue, and Broadway in New York City, fans patiently waited in line for their turn to taste a slice of bread spread with the hazelnut cream, given away as part of the inauguration ceremony for the Nutella Bar in Eataly. Guests of honor included the actress Whoopi Goldberg, who has never hidden her love of Nutella, and the official host was Joe Bastianich, famous "restaurant man" (the title of his book) and international judge for the TV program *MasterChef*, together with his mother Lidia Bastianich, a chef, writer, and ambassador of high-quality Italian cuisine in the United States. While speaking to the media about how Nutella had started out in the Langhe region and travelled all the way to Manhattan, Joe remarked, "Nutella represents all the best of Italy." His mother Lidia added, "These two Italian-tasting ingredients—chocolate and hazelnut—are winning Americans over. And it's very easy to use, so people just love it." Interviews ended with Bernard Krielmann, CEO of Ferrero USA, who said, "Here in the US, people skip one out of every two breakfasts: we can help moms in their struggle to bring kids back to the breakfast table."

American celebrations for Nutella's fiftieth anniversary got under way the following Monday, May 19, on the sidewalk outside Eataly on Broadway and alongside Madison Square Park. Visitors were given a chance to taste Cronuts, a croissant-donut hybrid created by French-American pastry chef Dominique Ansel, in a limited Nutella edition: a form of sweet street food offered over the counter of a colorful pastry kitchen truck that would later hit the road on a Nutella Truck tour. The road show crisscrossed the entire United States, making sixty-four stops including Chicago, Minnesota, Boston, Baltimore, Washington, Philadelphia, Raleigh, Greensboro, Atlanta, and towns in Florida and Kentucky. The final stops were Dallas and New Orleans, concluding in October 2014.

Nutella created a special tagline, "Spread the happiness," for the entire campaign. This expanded to "spread the party" across five continents, involving hundreds of thousands of people on the weekend around the B-Day. Here's a look at some of the significant locations for this global party, celebrated in parks, piazzas, and malls all over the planet.

Italy. Naturally the party was held in Alba, in southern Piedmont, where festivities got underway on Saturday, May 17. Eight hundred stores, two hundred stalls, and two hundred and fifty houses in the town's historic center were "decorated" in the brand's famous white and red colors. There were street artists, breakfasts offered free in local bars, and a grand celebration that evening with twenty-five thousand people in the main piazza, outside the municipal building and Alba's cathedral: a concert with gospel choirs and a ceremony to put out a luminous "candle" set atop the tallest medieval tower in the city. But perhaps the biggest Italian festival was held in Naples, with a mega-concert featuring numerous pop stars: an "award" given to the southern city for having sold more jars of Nutella than anyone else. The marathon concert lasted from the morning until late at night, and attracted more than one hundred thousand people to Piazza del Plebiscito, a 25,000-square-meter (6-acre) public plaza that often hosts entertainment in Naples. Organized by Filmmaster Events, the concert was a joyful, entertaining party during which roughly three tons of bread and Nutella were distributed to hordes of people playing, singing, and dancing together. After Italian singers like Arisa, Giuliano Palma, and Almamegretta finished performing, the candles were blown out by international pop star Mika (born Michael Holbrook Penniman, Jr.).

France. During a beautiful sunny day in the Parc de Sceaux in the suburbs south of Paris, people gathered to celebrate Nutella's French birthday party, publicized extensively in the social media and the press. The morning of May 18 began with the distribution of twenty-five thousand Nutella breakfast kits, accompanied by a mass Zumba, a group-fitness activity set to Afro-Caribbean rhythms, and other games and competitions. A vast lawn inside the park hosted an enormous picnic replete with colored balloons, entertainment for children, and "Bread and Nutella" mascots. A number of singers went onstage to perform for the crowd, including Zaho, Brice Conrad, Alex Hepburn, and Louis Bertignac. One hundred and fifty thousand single-portion Nutella packs were given away for free, and just as in Italy and Naples, the Parisian event (organized by the SoonSoonSoon agency) was shared live on YouTube and Nutella's Facebook page, with roughly fifty thousand users connected on each social network.

Germany. Famous personalities from German showbiz celebrated the anniversary in Dortmund, in the Ruhr, at the Westfalenpark: live music, breakfast recipes, and stories provided by fans and posted on the www.nutellastories.com platform broadcast live on giant screens. At the end of the day, a group of celebrities in attendance (including Anna Loos, Matthias Schweighöfer, Til Schweiger, Nazan Eckes, and Verona Pooth) distributed five Nutella Fan Story Awards. Schweighöfer, the director and star of the successful film *What a Man* (2011), in which he plays a young man struggling to keep two separate love stories afloat, had this to share with the ten thousand fans who had come to the park for the celebrations: "Nutella went with us on vacation, no matter where in the world we were eating breakfast. It's a beautiful childhood memory." The program for the festival included plenty of sports, subdivided into thirteen areas: everything from early morning yoga to rock-climbing walls and trampolines. An enormous jar of Nutella, 20 meters (60 feet) tall and 14 meters (46 feet) wide, towered over the party displaying a giant LED screen that let visitors follow all the different events live.

Dubai. Ferrero Middle East and North Africa organized the party for Arab fans, setting the festival in an extremely popular location in the city-state—the Dubai Mall. This legendary shopping center is one of the most popular tourist attractions in the world, drawing 65 million visitors per year. For one whole week, from May 18 to 24, the mall atrium hosted the "Nutella Story Machine," essentially a giant fiberglass jar of Nutella, 4 meters (13 feet) tall, into which fans (whether there by chance or responding to an invitation shared via social media) could insert an empty glass Nutella jar containing their own handwritten message and Nutella story. In exchange, the Nutella Machine gave back a full jar with the fan's name on the label. This minor "magical miracle" fascinated young and old visitors alike, drawing more than five thousand people to the giant jar, and garnering three thousand handwritten contributions. While the machine was working, music played and fans were invited to sing "Happy Birthday, Nutella" in a language other than their own, accompanied by a karaoke video. There were also a number of other activities, including photographs taken with a "magic machine" that could be shared instantly via social media, and a flash mob involving a group of young dancers that put a smile on everyone's face.

Russia. Gorky Park, set along the banks of the Moscow River, is the most popular entertainment park in the Russian capital, made internationally famous in a novel written by Martin Cruz Smith. On May 17 and 18, Nutella gathered roughly 120,000 people there to celebrate the brand with warm slices of toast spread with the hazelnut cream, colored balloons, and music and dance performances. Over the course of a pleasant spring day, thousands of children gathered to express themselves through drawings, or have their pictures taken with their parents and entertainers dressed up as Nutella jars, or watch videos. The festival also featured some karaoke machines, dancing, live music, and plenty of happiness. At the end, visitors were presented with a mega-birthday cake weighing 50 kilograms (over 110 pounds) and shaped like a Nutella jar, cut up into fifty thousand slices and served to fans young and old alike.

USA. The stage was set in New York City for breakfast, with people getting in line as early as 6:30 a.m. on Monday, May 19, on the sidewalks outside Eataly, at the corner of Broadway and Fifth Avenue. All eyes were on Dominique Ansel, the gourmet star of American social media, with plenty of fans stopping by to have their photo taken with the famous pastry chef. Roughly seven thousand people participated in the event, including local New Yorkers and visiting tourists, all of whom were given a chance to sample Nutella served with strawberries, banana popsicles, mini bagels, apples slices, or waffles. The singer Holley Maher hosted the event, performing her hit "Waffle Truck" (used as the soundtrack for Nutella's ad campaign in the United States). Even those who couldn't be physically present at the event were given a chance to participate online, generating 440 million hits and more than 18 million mentions via social media.

Canada. Nutella has been sold in Canada for a number of years, so the festivities organized to celebrate the hazelnut cream's fiftieth anniversary lasted a long time, almost an entire month, and included stops in all the major cities. The party got started in Montreal on April 25, 2014, then moved to Quebec City for May 2 and 3, Vancouver for May 9 and 10, and Toronto for the finale, held (as throughout the rest of the world) on May 17 and 18, 2014. Approximately 120,000 Canadians participated in this affectionate birthday celebration, while thousands of photographs and personal stories were posted online on social media. These ended up on the www.nutellastories.

com platform, which offered a trip to Italy as a grand prize, as well as thousands of instant prizes including Nutella earbuds, photo frame magnets, key chains, and USB keys. The main attraction in this coast-to-coast Nutella Party tour was a large, Nutella jar-shaped space that hosted a crêperie offering a range of different things to eat: fifty thousand crêpes were distributed to visitors across Canada. While they waited in line to taste a crêpe, fans were given a chance to watch a half-century retrospective about the story of Nutella. Canadian Olympic figure skater Joannie Rochette was the party's special guest in Toronto and Montreal. One young girl came to the party to celebrate her eighth birthday and won a set of Nutella-printed pajamas. She later wrote Ferrero an email to happily proclaim, "I wear them to bed every night!"

Poland. In Warsaw celebrations were organized inside Ujazdów Park, a popular public garden that many newlyweds use as a setting for their wedding photographs. More than five thousand people gathered here on Sunday, May 18, following open invitations published on www.nutellastories.com and Ferrero's local Facebook account. Numerous special events were organized for the younger visitors. An open breakfast was prepared for everyone, including restaurant service: roughly eighty tables were attended by dozens of waiters, and more than one thousand jars of Nutella were consumed along with crêpes, fresh bread, croissants, fresh fruit, and fruit juices. Guests of honor included famous actors, athletes, and journalists like Omenaa Mensah, Charles Daigneault, Kinga Paruzel, Martin Gimenez Castro, and Diana Volokhova.

The United Kingdom. Ferrero's British Nutella team sent out an open invitation for a special breakfast, held inside Alton Towers, a giant entertainment park located in Staffordshire, to be served on Saturday, May 17, to the winners of a competition run by the website www.nutellastories.com. Inside the amusement park, Ferrero set up a mega-gift pack, complete with a giant screen upon which thousands of stories shared by fans were broadcast. Later in the day, partygoers gathered together to unwrap the giant gift box, which housed a giant jar of Nutella built using 1,335 400-gram (14-ounce) jars of the hazelnut cream. Thirteen thousand people attended overall, and a similar event was also organized in Dublin, Ireland, where a big gift box was set up inside Dundrum Shopping Centre, this time built of eight thousand jars of Nutella.

Australia. Down Under, Nutella's birthday came in the fall, rather than in the spring, and the company celebrated in Lithgow, New South Wales, where Ferrero's facility is located. This time the party was reserved for company employees, their families, and friends in the local community, and was held inside a giant tent, where waiters served a special breakfast to several hundred people. The company's managers and the town mayor acted as hosts for the event. At the end of the celebration those gathered sang a merry "Happy Birthday" to the spreadable cream while chefs divvied up a traditional Nutella jar-shaped birthday cake.

* * *

If all the stories sent to the website as part of Nutella's fiftieth anniversary celebrations were to be published, the pages would fill up one hundred books as large as the one you're reading right now. They constitute a global "heritage" of optimism, edible enjoyment, and personal passion that few other brands in the world can claim. In the ten countries in which the mega Nutella Parties were held, hundreds of thousands of people gathered to sing a joyful and carefree happy birthday song to the hazelnut cream. As Giovanni Ferrero, CEO of the company, emphasized at the Foundation in Alba during the anniversary celebrations, people everywhere produced a worldwide wave of positivity: "I'm happy to be able to tell you that every morning millions of families sit down for breakfast together, starting their days with optimism for life."

12
Nutella Playlist

What could Lady Gaga, Maria Sharapova, Alain Ducasse, Rafael Nadal, and the current and former Italian prime ministers possibly all have in common? Their passion for Nutella, of course. It's a group that cuts across divisions, including celebrities, writers, journalists, artists, entrepreneurs, politicians, and many others. Unlike the words that decorate the walls and cars of the subway, their words are an elegant kind of graffiti, the heartfelt declarations of affection, at times ironic, often allusive, that consecrate the success of this delicious longseller. This explains this composite list of thoughts uttered by a "who's who," people who publicly admit their endorsement for this hazelnut and cocoa cream. The marketing strategy thus achieves its best results: acknowledgements earned, which are worth much more than product placement in a movie or a video clip on the Web.

This short collection from the world of entertainment, sports, literature, and business, divided geographically and chronologically, does not seek to be complete, nor can it be so. It is, however, proof that the legend is truly a national one, from the frivolous to the intellectual: what language would it be without Nutella?

THE WORD ITALIANS LOVE THE MOST

In studies on linguistics, among the four hundred Italian neologisms that have entered the language of journalism, politics and television, Nutella was singled out as being "the word Italians love the most."

"Nutella is the perfect cure when you're nervous."
Christian De Sica, actor, son of film director Vittorio De Sica
Grazia, March 6, 1988

"My breakfast? A latte, two sandwiches, and Nutella."
Kristian Ghedina, skier, downhill ski champion
Agenzia Ansa, February 3, 1990

"Why don't they give the Nobel Prize for literature to the person who invented Nutella?"

Fabio Fazio, TV host
"The Greatest Questions," *Cuore*, July 8, 1992

"I love to eat and what gives me the most pleasure is eating a salami sandwich followed by a Nutella sandwich right after that."

Monica Bellucci, actress
La Repubblica, July 5, 1994

"So what are we going to do, spend our whole lives regretting Nutella?"

Leonardo Pieraccioni, actor and filmmaker
in his movie *I laureati* (The Graduates), 1995

"I'd say that culatello is right-wing / Mortadella is left-wing / If Swiss chocolate is right-wing / Then Nutella is left-wing."

Giorgio Gaber, singer-songwriter
in the song "Destra-sinistra," 1995

"People wonder whether Nutella is right-wing or left-wing, but I refuse to take part in this game."

Gianni Morandi, singer
La Repubblica, February 11, 1995

"Depriving [the holding company] Fininvest of a television network would be like depriving Ferrero of Nutella."

Silvio Berlusconi, businessman and former prime minister
of Italy, *Corriere della Sera*, March 22, 1995

"That night in Atlanta, after I won the Olympic gold medal, I
dipped my spoon into a jar of Nutella."

Jury Chechi, athlete, Olympic rings champion,
La Stampa, July 30, 1996

"Michele Ferrero was a pâtissier, and with great insight he invented several products, starting with Nutella, [a brand that] became
a world leader thanks to his creativity, capacity to understand the
public's tastes, and great entrepreneurial courage."

Luca Cordero di Montezemolo, businessman, former president
of Ferrari, *Agenzia Ansa*, October 12, 2005

"At night I dream of Nutella."

Filippo Magnini, athlete, swimming champion
Agenzia Ansa, October 18, 2005

"This morning I had Nutella, but I can't go overboard. You'll see,
I'll know what to do . . ."

Francesco Totti, soccer player
Agenzia Ansa, February 20, 2006

"Fruit, vegetables, yogurt, but, every now and again, a few forays
into Nutella."

Emma Marcegaglia, businesswoman, former president
of Confindustria, *Corriere della Sera*, March 13, 2008

"I liked Nutella so much that I'd use it to treat my injuries; if I happened to fall and scrape my knee, I'd spread some Nutella on it
and the pain would go away. That's where the expression 'to lick
your wounds' comes from [. . .] Why, mothers everywhere, would
you always buy Nutella and then hide it? [. . .] Nutella isn't just a
chocolate hazelnut spread, it's a whole world."

Rosario Fiorello, entertainer
Sky TV, May 16, 2009

"My secret? Sit-ups and Nutella. I adore it."

Flavia Pennetta, tennis player
Corriere dello Sport-Stadio, November 10, 2009

At a meeting for the primaries of his party
"Have you seen how you can get personalized Nutella now? The idea of putting a person's name on the jar is amazing. The party we shall make, if I win, will have to call people by their first names. You are not consumers, you're not users or just people. You are you, men and women with an identity. The Democratic Party will have to call its members by their names, like the individual pieces of a community, and not as though the party were made up of an anonymous society."

Matteo Renzi, politician, prime minister of Italy
La Repubblica, October 6, 2014

"While I was eating a fruit salad yesterday I kept imagining that it was drowned in Nutella."

Vanessa Ferrari, gymnast
Corriere della Sera, November 2, 2013

"You know what it's like when you taste Nutella, don't you? One spoon is never enough."

Antonio Cassano, soccer player
Corriere della Sera, January 3, 2014

"I'm absolutely crazy about pizza and Nutella and it isn't always easy to resist."

Sara Errani, tennis player
Tennisworlditalia.com website, January 25, 2014

EUROPEAN LOVERS

Race car drivers, royalty, singers, and European sports champions are all joined by a common passion.

"What's the secret of my success? Nutella and individually wrapped madeleines, to make sure they stay fresh."

Stéphane Peterhansel, French racing driver
of the Paris-Dakar Rally, *Action Auto Moto*, February 2004

"Thanks to my crêpes sprinkled with sugar or spread with Nutella I'm always Super-Mom!"

Caroline Barclay, French actress,
Hola, November 17, 2004

"Nutella is one of Italy's major industrial symbols, like the Vespa or the Fiat 500. There are some who say it's a sort of Italy in miniature."

Eric Jozsef, French journalist
Libération, January 29, 2005

"Nutella! I love jam, but it's Nutella I eat every day."

Lorie, French singer,
Too Much, April 2005

"I adore Nutella. Whenever I'm in my restaurant in New York I make sure I have a large ten-pound jar of it around."

Alain Ducasse, French chef
LaStampa.it, April 19, 2009

"Chocolate! Nutella! French fries! But I eat them when I am not close to a match and I never overdo it."

Rafael Nadal, Spanish tennis player
Webmd.com, May 25, 2011

"What's my dream if I win the Wimbledon tournament? To take a bath in Nutella."

Novak Djokovic, Serbian tennis player
Agenzia Ansa, July 4, 2011

"Real men drink coffee and eat Nutella on toast."

Jack Wilshere, English soccer player
Talksport.com, July 15, 2011

"I have snacks throughout the day as well, but they aren't as structured, so it's things like peanut butter or Nutella on toast for a hit of carbohydrates. The kind of thing I would've had in my student days, but the difference is now I'll have it because I need energy as opposed to because that's the only thing in my cupboard."

Dai Greene, English 400-meter hurdles world champion
Theguardian.com, January 20, 2012

"Yum! This chocolate hazelnut spread is delicious! I love it on toast in the morning, but honestly, it's so good I could eat it straight from the jar."

Heidi Klum, German model and actress
Shape.com, May 17, 2012

"I can't resist Nutella. I eat it right out of the jar."

Rebecca Ferguson, English singer
Ibtimes.com, May 29, 2012

"I like to eat Nutella straight from the jar."

E.L. James, pen name of Erika Leonard, English writer
(*Fifty Shades* trilogy), Telegraph.co.uk, August 7, 2012

"These are irresistible to both adults and children and so easy to make. Nutella isn't just for spreading on toast!"

Pippa Middleton, English author and columnist (from her cookbook *Celebrate*), Marieclaire.co.uk, October 31, 2012

"Working on piece for *La Repubblica* about my trip to Ferrero factory. In the spirit of authenticity, I should eat some Nutella now. Right?"

Joanne Harris, English author
A tweet from November 20, 2012

"I love Nutella—I loved it as a kid, being half Italian . . ."

Marco Pierre White, English-Italian chef
Athomemagazine.co.uk, November 29, 2012

"Cruz loves Nutella on a croissant. And I have any scraps that are left over."

David Beckham, English soccer player
Dailymail.co.uk, February 2, 2013

"Eating Nutella straight from the jar! Catch me when I'm hungry and there's nothing else around, and I'll just demolish the whole pot! I can't resist it."

Rob Damiani, English musician and member
of the band Don Broco, Reveal.co.uk, April 23, 2013

"Nutella is my obsession . . . I love it. It's my favorite food. Do not put a tub of Nutella anywhere near me!"

Sophie Anderton, English model
Reveal.co.uk, September 21, 2013

"We eat bread, Nutella, bananas, apples, kiwis, apricots. We also prepare whole grain rice with tuna."

Pierre Casiraghi, son of Caroline, Princess of Monaco (setting
sail from Monaco for Cape Town for the Cape 2 Rio Regatta)
Hola.com, January 26, 2014

"Morning, Love! Nutella with strawberries just makes my day ;)."

Yolanthe Sneijder-Cabau, Spanish-Dutch actress and TV host
A tweet from March 8, 2014

When asked what his favorite after-match snack is.
"A Nutella sandwich."

Gerard Piqué, center back for the Spanish national team and FC
Barcelona, Libertaddigital.com, September 25, 2014

AMERICAN FANS

It seems hard to believe that Nutella has only recently conquered the American public, as the declarations of love by celebrities are already countless.

"Defining Nutella as a hazelnut-and-chocolate spread is a bit like describing the David of Michelangelo as a large carved piece of marble"

Andrea Lee, writer
The New Yorker, March 6, 1995

"Nutella is the essence of Italianness: it's goodness that you can spread."

Elisabetta Povoledo, journalist
Herald Tribune, December 10, 2004

"I was afraid I wouldn't find the things I was used to having. Here in America you can even find Nutella now."

Tom Waits, singer-songwriter and actor
Corriere della Sera, July 21, 2004

Question: What are the three things you can't live without?
"My cellphone, Nutella—I love Nutella. And this necklace . . . I am addicted to Nutella, the chocolate hazelnut spread. I can't live without it."

Michelle Trachtenberg, actress
Kidzworld.com, 2005

"My kids aren't really big sandwich eaters, so I'll give them taco meat they can dip chips in, Nutella and fresh fruit, sliced sausage."

Brooke Burke, actress and dancer
Celebritybabies.people.com, May 8, 2009

"Ok. Firstly, yes I love Nutella (with Banana + Wonderbread) who doesn't..."

Lady Gaga, singer,
A tweet from January 26, 2011

"I have a relationship with Nutella beyond normal people's. Eating Nutella was one of the few good memories I had as a kid."

Fabio Vivian, chef
Today.com, February 5, 2012

"Ooh, yummm! For the kids, usually chunky peanut butter and Nutella with bananas. Brings me right back to my childhood."

Jennifer Behm, MasterChef winner
People.com, June 29, 2012

"I love the combination of shortbread, roasted hazelnuts, and chocolate. The shortbread can be baked in advance, wrapped with plastic, and then filled with Nutella just before serving."

Ina Garten, Emmy Award–winning author
People, November 18, 2012

Holding a ten-pound jar of Nutella in a photograph she posted on Twitter.
"Breakfast, anyone?"

Hayden Panettiere, actress
Dailymail.co.uk, July 3, 2013

"Yummy! My favorite thing to eat when I travel to Holland. The Dutch pancakes with strawberries & Nutella are amazing!"

Paris Hilton, actress and model
Reveal.co.uk, September 21, 2013

Accompanying a Facebook post of a photograph of her looking lovingly at a jar of Nutella.
"This is ♥"

Caroline Sunshine, actress
Dis411.net, June 1, 2014

"I believe Nutella and Popcorn should each be their own food group on the pyramid. I'm addicted to Nutella!"

Kate Stoltz, model
Usmagazine.com, June 26, 2014

FROM THE REST OF THE WORLD

Nutella is spread all over the world—actresses, models, sports champions from Canada, Russia, South America, you name it, have no qualms about confessing how much they love to eat it.

"My breakfast menu before a Formula One race: Nutella, maple syrup, yogurt, and a glass of milk."

Jacques Villeneuve, former Canadian Formula 1 racing driver
La Repubblica, October 26, 1997

"I really love Nutella, I've had it since I was a kid and until this day I can just eat it out of the jar. Once I start I can't stop. I think it is just delicious and I love introducing it to people who have never had it before because I've never met anyone who doesn't like it."

Emmanuelle Chriqui, Canadian actress
People.com, January 21, 2010

"What would I take with me to a deserted island, or things I could not live without: a jar of Nutella."

Joannie Rochette, world champion Canadian figure skater
Joannierochette.ca, 2010

"My only temptation was coffee with crêpes. The best crêpes with Nutella were made there."

Kseniya Sobchak, Russian TV anchor
Ksenia-sobchak.com, March 11, 2012

"On rainy afternoons, everyone should be let out of work to watch movies that have talking animals in them and eat a whole jar of Nutella."

Dani Calabresa, Brazilian actress
A tweet on April 11, 2012

"My little pleasure. Don't blame myself for eating a little bit of Nutella. I know that other sportsmen love Nutella too—for example, Rafa."

Anastasiya Pivovarova, Russian tennis player
Gotennis.ru, May 3, 2012

"I eat quite well. Really like vegetables and salad, but when I'm oversensitive, sometimes, I eat a whole bar of chocolate or Nutella."

Fiorella Mattheis, Brazilian actress and model
m.terra.com.br, August 6, 2012

"My weakness: Nutella has a taste of my childhood."

Nataliya Turovnikova, Russian DJ
Tatler.ru, November 1, 2012

"My balm for the soul? Crêpes with Nutella."

Maria Sharapova, Russian tennis player,
Corriere della Sera, November 28, 2012

"Those of you that regularly read my blog know I'm a self-confessed chocoholic. Chocolate chip cookies, cakes, brownies, icing . . . and I've even been known to eat Nutella straight from the jar when I'm having a cheat meal."

Harley Pasternak, Canadian-American personal trainer
People.com, June 19, 2013

Question: What's on your kitchen counter?
"Lots of fruit and usually some Nutella."

Shakira, Colombian singer,
MarieClaire.com, 2014

13
The timeline of a success

Nutella's history officially begins in 1964, but the story behind the product cannot overlook its ancestors, Giandujot, Supercrema, and perhaps most importantly, the family of artisans who put those specialties on the market: the Ferreros, who originally came from a small village lost amid the hills of the Langhe region, in the lower Piedmont area of northern Italy. This chronology goes back over the key phases, starting from when Pietro Ferrero opened the family's first store, and ends with the worldwide celebration of the product's fiftieth anniversary. It is almost a century of events, during which Nutella has taken a leading role in the last fifty years, earning a place among the world's best loved brands.

THE ANCESTORS

1923 – A pastry shop in the Langhe

After working as an apprentice baker for a few years, twenty-five-year-old Pietro Ferrero opens a pastry shop in Dogliani, in the Langhe region (a hilly area near the Tanaro River in Piedmont, northern Italy). Under the porticoes of that small town where Pietro's shop is located, his cakes soon win over the heart of Piera Cillario, four years his junior. They will wed in 1924.

1925 – Michele Ferrero is born

The pastry-maker couple soon experiences the joy of the arrival of an heir, Michele, born on April 26, in Dogliani. Monsù (the word in local dialect for "Mister") Pietro is a determined and ambitious worker, but that town in the hills is simply too small for him, so he decides to move his family to the capital of the area, Alba, and starts working in a shop that is already well established.

1933 – The first shop in Turin

The enterprising pastry maker takes a big leap and moves to Turin, where he opens his pastry shop close to the Porta Nuova train station. Five years later he will try his luck in Somalia, selling *panettoni* (a traditional Italian dessert bread cake) to Italy's colonial troops.

Pietro Ferrero's adventure lasts just two years. Having been unsuccessful, he moves back to Turin.

1937 – Giovanni Ferrero founds his department stores

Pietro has a brother, Giovanni Ferrero (photo), seven years his junior. Giovanni grows up in Dogliani and moves to Alba, the capital of the Langhe region, in the 1930s, where he starts his own business.

On November 2, Giovanni opens a company for the wholesale of foodstuffs, confectionary products, and brewer's yeast. The business is in his wife's name: Ottavia Amerio is a young salesgirl he had met in Canelli, a hillside town not far from Alba. They will marry in 1930. Giovanni Ferrero is the company's *procuratore speciale*, which gives him the power of attorney.

1940 – Seven shop windows

In an elegant part of Turin, Pietro and Piera Ferrero open a pastry shop that boasts seven shop windows: business is good, their customers are loyal, and their products are very popular.

World War II breaks out and bombs are dropped from the skies: the family decides to move back to Alba permanently.

1942 – The workshop in Alba

Pietro and Piera, in spite of the problems related to the war, manage to resume their pastry-making business. Pietro invents some new specialties on the small premises located inside a courtyard in the historic quarter of Alba.

Piera works behind the counter of a shop called Rava, a liquor-confectionary-pastry shop owned by her relatives, the most beautiful one of its kind in the city. The shop is located on the main road, known as via Maestra.

1945 – A *Pastone* called Giandujot

In the fall, the Ferreros' artisanal activity takes off, thanks to Pietro's talent at creating a "cake for the humble," a *pastone* (the name it would be given by Pietro's son Michele a few years later): it is a surrogate made with very little cocoa, hazelnuts, sugar, and vegetable oil.

It is the debut of the Giandujot, a delicious ingot wrapped in tin foil that's meant to be sliced and eaten with bread. It is an instant success.

1946 – The Ferrero Company is established

On May 14, "P. Ferrero owned by Cillario Pierina previously owned by Giuseppe Ferrero, situated in Alba, and the producer of chocolate, nougat, and confectionary products in general" is registered at the Chamber of Commerce in Cuneo. This is the official act that establishes the company.

At the end of the year, the company's production moves, along with its thirty workers, to a warehouse in Alba close to the Tanaro River. The Ferrero plant is still located there today.

Giovanni Ferrero and Pietro become partners, with Giovanni overseeing the commercial side of the business.

1947 – The hazelnut-flavored wedge

To try to forget the miseries of war, Ferrero starts producing a small delicacy: the Cremino, an individually wrapped hazelnut-flavored specialty as big as a wedge of spreadable cheese. Although most Italians had been left with little money in their pockets, everyone could afford to pay five lire (twenty cents out of a dollar today) for 21 grams (nearly .75 ounces) of rediscovered sweetness.

1948 – The company is flooded

On the morning of September 4, 1948, in Alba, a small river overflows its banks and floods the Ferrero premises: the 120 women who are there working when it happens clamber onto the roofs and are rescued. Pietro does everything in his power to save the company, working, alongside his employees, shoveling mud for three days and three nights.

Production starts up again, but Pietro's health has been greatly affected.

1949 – Pietro Ferrero dies and Supercrema debuts

On March 2, just when he is finally starting to taste the fla-

vor of success, Pietro Ferrero (photo) dies of a heart attack at the age of fifty-one. The company, vigorously managed by his brother Giovanni, and his widow, Piera, continues to prosper, also thanks to a new speciality.

It is the debut of the spreadable Giandujot. Called Supercrema, it is the real ancestor of Nutella. The label on the 1-kilogram (2.2-lb.) jar reads: "A delicious, genuine product with high energy value, it in fact has no fewer than 5,100 calories." A version called Nusscreme also exists, which is sold in large tin containers: it is a "preserved food product having a high energy value."

1950 – General partnership

After Pietro's death, on May 5 in Turin, the Società P. Ferrero & C is registered as a general partnership. It is the first real restructuring of the company, leaving behind its artisanal phase once and for all. It has three members, each one with an equal share: Pietro's widow, Piera Cillario Ferrero; their son, Michele; and Pietro's brother, Giovanni. The family divides up the work that is to be done: Michele, age twenty-five, deals with production; "Uncle Giovanni," with sales; while "Mamma Piera" oversees the skilled workers.

The results of the industrial activity are brilliant: there are three hundred workers with an output of 15.8 metric tons (17 tons) per year, which will double by 1957.

1951 – Sultanino, the first product invented by Michele

The Sultanino is the first product invented by the young, twenty-six-year-old Michele Ferrero: it is a new kind of treat, a low-priced candy bar conceived to be eaten by children as a snack. He invents it by himself to surprise Uncle Giovanni, buying a new piece of equipment to be able to do so. This new product is instantly successful, and in just one year, production grows from 0.6 metric tons at the start to 2.8 metric tons (.7 to 3.1 tons) by 1952.

1952 – Giovanni creates the Società Caffè Ferrero

Giovanni Ferrero's business activity continues, in the company of several partners, independently of the confectionary company that had been created by his brother.

The SAS Caffè Ferrero is founded, again owned by Giovanni.

Giovanni Ferrero buys shares of other Italian food companies, such as Venchi Unica.

1953 – Cremablock

Another product invented by Michele begins production in Alba: Cremablock, 36 grams (1.5 ounces) of chocolate with hazelnut filling, sold for about 70 cents out of a dollar.

The young confectionary business beats the competition, thanks to its choice of simple packaging with small quantities, instead of expensive luxury packaging.

1954 – Good-bye, Gianduia brand

Until now the company logo had been Gianduia, the Turinese masked character who smiled as he embraced two children, with the words: "I was the first, and I'm still the best." The design is replaced by a stylized Ferrero logo, written in small italics and topped by a stylized crown symbolizing Alba, famous for being "the city with a hundred towers."

A new product appears in Italian stores: Cremalba. Sold in small chunks it costs 30, 50, or 100 lire (between 70 cents and two dollars today). The product is made from powdered milk, coconut butter, eggs, and sugar, and it comes in several flavors: cocoa, coffee, zabaglione, or with candied fruit.

1955 – Ferrero picture card albums

In Italy, it is the start of the *"Grande concorso a premi 'Caccia Grossa'"* ("Big Hunt" Prize competition): contestants who succeed in completing an album with all one hundred picture cards of wild animals (there's an elephant on the album cover), are awarded plastic toy animals, dolls, or watches.

The picture card collection will continue into the 1970s.

1956 – Mon Chéri conquers Germany

The first Ferrero praline makes its debut: a praline with a liquor cherry heart, surrounded by a crust of sugar and coated in dark chocolate. Its name is Mon Chéri, and it is wrapped in red paper to express the idea of it being a special gift.

The first Ferrero plant abroad is built in an abandoned factory that had manufactured war materials in Allendorf, Germany, just two hours north of Frankfurt. "Assia GmbH", its name, immediately begins producing Mon Chéri, whose slogan is "some of the fiery charm of the South." The praline is sold individually close to the checkout counter, and it costs 50 cents out of a dollar today. From an initial 0.9 metric tons (1 ton) per day in 1957, the following year a total of 20 metric tons (22 tons) are reached. It gradually becomes the best-selling chocolate in Germany, with 500 million pieces per year.

1957 – Giovanni Ferrero dies

After being awarded an Order of Merit for Labor in 1955, Giovanni Ferrero becomes an important figure of reference in Italy's confectionary sector. He also attempts to establish a trade association to bring together the most important companies in that period, such as Motta, Alemagna, Venchi Unica, and Pavesi.

At the peak of his life as an entrepreneur, Giovanni Ferrero dies suddenly on October 25, 1957. His share of the Ferrero company does not go to his wife, who is instead given a payoff as had been established in the company agreement underwritten in 1950.

After her husband's death, Ottavia Amerio Ferrero dedicates the rest of her long life to charity. She will die in 1992 at the age of eighty-five.

1958 – Ferrero in Belgium and Austria

The company continues its attempt to conquer other European countries: a Ferrero commercial headquarters opens in Belgium. While Brussels becomes famous the world over for its World's Fair, on April 29, Ferrero launches Mon Chéri, competing on a par with the many companies that are part of the history of the praline, and eventually conquering a lead-

ing position on the Belgian market.

The business company Ducalba Susswaren Import GmbH is established in Austria.

In the Lombard city of Pozzuolo Martesana, 25 kilometers (16 miles) east of Milan, Ferrero starts experimenting with baked products and syrups, so that it can get a share of the nascent children's snacks market.

1959 – Germans like the Hanuta wafer

A new Ferrero product appears on the shelves in Germany: the crunchy hazelnut-flavored Hanuta wafer. One of the secrets of its success is the set of collectible picture cards that comes with every packet.

1960 – The French factory in Normandy

Dulcea is set up in France, at first as a distribution company. In Villers-Écalles, Normandy, 25 kilometers (16 miles) from Rouen, Ferrero buys an old textile factory and turns it into a production plant. It will become one of the most important in Europe.

The hazelnuts that grow in the Langhe are no longer enough: the variety known as *avellane* (cobnuts) that are grown in southern Italy are needed, too, so Ferrero opens a factory in Lauro, in the Nola area, south of Naples, where they can be processed. The warehouses will be handed over to a local businessman in 1985, when the company opens up two new plants in the Campania area hit by the earthquake in 1981.

1961 – Brioss, the first snack

After much testing, the first Ferrero snack arrives in Italian pantries. The name of the snack is Brioss: a slice of sponge cake filled with apricot or cherry preserves that's still being produced today.

Ferrero has three industrial sites in Italy, for a monthly production of 4,700 metric tons (5,180 tons) of confectionary products.

1962 – Villa Piera is born in Germany

Villa Piera opens in Allendorf, Germany, providing accommodation for young Italian women who emigrate to Germany to work for Ferrero. At the start, it has three hundred young women as guests, many of whom come from Sardinia. Social workers and doctors are also hired to assist them.

Ferrero becomes a joint-stock company with its business headquarters in Turin: Piera Cillario is appointed president, a post she will hold until 1980, the year of her death.

Her son, Michele Ferrero (photo), not yet forty, is the company CEO. All the shares have always remained in family hands.

1963 – Tartinoise debuts in France

A spreadable hazelnut cream makes its debut on the French market. It's called Tartinoise, and it comes from Supercrema, Nutella's ancestor.

Ferrero consolidates in Germany: in Sachsenhausen, the area south of Frankfurt just past the Main River, an eleven-story building is the new German management headquarters.

In Rozenlaan, near Breda, Ferrero Holland also begins its activity: its offices are located in a small shop and Mon Chéri is the first product sold there.

On September 11, in Turin, Pietro is born, the first child of Michele and Maria Franca Fissolo, who were married the year before.

NUTELLA AND FERRERO PRODUCTS

1964 – The first jar in Italy

Nutella is officially launched on April 20, when production starts at the company plant in Alba. In May, this hazelnut cream is introduced to consumers across Italy, sold in an eight-sided glass container and advertised on billboards.

Ferrero transfers its marketing and administration to the new management headquarters located in Pino Torinese, on the hills close to Turin. A new logo is patented: the small italic lettering is replaced by a more impelling representation of the name FERRERO, now in golden capital letters with an attractive typeface. Within two years' time, the same logo will be used for all its products.

On September 21, in Turin, Maria Franca and Michele's second child is born, Giovanni Ferrero. He will become the Group's CEO.

1965 – Nutella is spread in Germany

A year after its launch, Nutella takes on the German market.

The hazelnut cream is introduced in a new, distinctive jar, which will become as famous as the Coca-Cola contour bottle.

1966 – The product's debut in France and mini containers

Nutella is sold in France. The new brand, pronounced with an accent on the final "a," is popular across the Alps, too. Hazelnut cream is sold in handy *coupelles* (fruit salad bowls) as well as in decorated glasses to be kept and used as glassware.

The first novelty is introduced in Italy: handy packaging that includes three plastic 30-gram (1-ounce) mini containers, so that consumers can eat Nutella even when they're outside their home.

The moment has come to find a place in the home of chocolate, Switzerland, with the company called Miralbana, in Zurich; Ferrero United, in the United Kingdom, is also set up. By this time, a third of the turnover accrues from foreign partners.

1967 – Debut on Italian television

In Italy, Nutella debuts on *Carosello*, a TV program that's broadcast every evening and consists of five two-minute sketches during which the product cannot be named directly, followed by an advertising thirty-second coda  ("tail"). The commercial claims that four thousand vehicles transport hazelnut cream "to millions of children who spread Nutella on bread."

The first sports sponsorships also begin, with the fiftieth Giro d'Italia, won by cyclist Felice Gimondi: after each stage the winner is awarded a prize marked Ferrero. Following cyclists all over Italy is the "*Trenino dei bimbi Ferrero,*" a large truck fitted out like a locomotive that hands out confectionary products.

1968 – Kinder's debut

Children like Nutella, especially as a snack. Thanks to the baby-boom generation, children born between 1945 and 1964, these young consumers turn into a veritable army. Hence, Michele Ferrero conceives a product for them that will especially convince their parents: Kinder Chocolate, chocolate bars filled with milk, which come wrapped in small individual portions.

The company opens a commercial operating headquarters in Malmö, Scandinavia.

The Ferrero family moves from Alba to Pino Torinese so that they can be closer to the management headquarters.

1969 – Tic Tac for Americans

After creating many sweet products made from hazelnuts and cocoa, the confectionary company invents a mint that in a few years' time will become a worldwide success. The mint is named Tic Tac. Just like Nutella, it's a unique product that has been analyzed in great depth; it takes its name from its innovative pocket-sized packaging.

Ferrero also goes overseas and lands in the United States. Its first headquarters is in Yonkers, New York. In the space of fifteen years Ferrero USA reaches a turnover of $10 million, with its most successful product being Tic Tac. A catchy jingle is used to advertise the product: "Put a Tic Tac in your mouth and get a bang out of life!"

Michele Ferrero is awarded the Goldener Zuckerhut prize by the German food magazine *Lebensmittel Zeitung*.

1970 – A multinational with 7,700 workers

In France, Dulcea becomes Ferrero France, with its headquarters in Mont-Saint-Aignan, Normandy, just a few miles from the plant.

Thanks to Nutella, Mon Chéri, and Tic Tac, Ferrero's global turnover is close to $1.2 billion in today's money, with 7,700 workers and a daily production of 500 metric tons (551 tons) including spreads, pralines, candy, and snacks.

Piera Ferrero and her son Michele inaugurate the new location of Ferrero Olanda in Riethil, 25 miles south of Rotterdam.

In Pino Torinese, close to Turin, the company advertising division, called Pubbliregia, is set up, where both Italian and foreign creatives work on the advertising campaigns. Pubbliregia will become an independent company in the 1990s.

1971 – Michele Ferrero is awarded an Order of Merit for Labor

Italy awards Michele Ferrero an Order of Merit for Labor. The president of the Italian Republic Giovanni Saragat makes the following inspiring statement: "The personal impetus given by Michele Ferrero, after the death of founders Pietro and Giovanni when he was just twenty-four years old, has taken the company to a leading place in Italy in terms of the quantity of output, and of considerable importance abroad for the ever-growing diffusion of its products."

1972 – The office on Park Avenue, New York City

Ferrero in the United States begins its New York period, which will last until 1994, when company headquarters will be relocated to New Jersey, where it is still today. But the company's first offices are on Park Avenue in Manhattan; later, it will move to Fifth Avenue, and, after that, to a whole floor on Madison Avenue and 41st Street.

A real tea brews in a single-dose cup with a straw: it's the Estathé revolution, the first industrially produced iced tea in Italy. The age-old tradition of drinking hot tea in a cup at five in the afternoon is completely revolutionized. Thirty years later, the "marriage" with Nutella will take place with the invention of Snack & Drink packages.

1973 – The international holding in Luxembourg

The Ferrero International SA holding is constituted in Luxembourg: all the foreign stakeholders will join it, except for the German Ferrero GmbH.

Michele Ferrero is awarded another international prize, and he is the first European to receive it: it's the Kettle Award given by the American publication *Candy Industry Magazine*.

The turnover of the Ferrero Group continues to rise, with fifty-six direct sales outlets in Italy, 3,000 distribution workers, 1,500 vehicles supplying 300,000 points of sale, and 6,500 employees.

1974 – With Kinder it's Easter every day

What is it about Easter eggs that kids love the most? The gift inside the egg. Well then, why should they experience this thrill only once a year? Why not every day . . . Thanks to this idea, "Signor Michele," which is what everyone at the company calls him, creates the highly successful chocolate egg known as Kinder Surprise.

The Kinder Division debuts, an umbrella company brand that includes chocolate bars, Brioss snacks, and now the eggs.

Nutella production is equal to over 20,000 metric tons (22,000 tons) in the world. Today, it is almost twenty times that.

Ferrero Australia opens in Sydney, and Ferrero Canada is set up in Toronto, which in the 1970s and 1980s mostly operates in distribution.

1975 – Ferrero Ireland and a factory in Ecuador

On July 22, Ferrero Ireland Limited is born, and in Cork, just a three-hour drive south from Dublin, a plant is built to produce Tic Tac. It is currently the company's largest mint-producing plant, with exports all over the world.

That same year, a laboratory where cocoa is analyzed is built in Quito, Ecuador; a plant will soon be built there, as well.

In September, the Ferrero family moves to Brussels.

1976 – Nutella lands in Australia

Nutella's gradual expansion to the East begins. A Ferrero plant is built in Lithgow, Australia, about 150 kilometers (90 miles) from Sydney, in New South Wales, with lines for the production of hazelnut cream and Tic Tac.

For the development and production of patented machinery dedicated to the packaging of specialties, Ferrero OMS is founded, later to become Ferrero Ingegneria.

1977 – A headquarters in Hong Kong

Ferrero is the leading company in the Italian confectionary sector: in top place for the production of chocolate bars, second after IBP (Industrie Buitoni Perugina) for chocolate treats (Rocher had not been invented yet), and at the top for spreadable cream.

Operating headquarters open up in Hong Kong.

1978 – Ferrero Japan

In order to supply Central America with Tic Tac, the first machines that make the mints arrive in Quito, Ecuador; this will be followed by a Ferrero plant completed in 1990.

A new sign appears on a building in Tokyo: Ferrero Japan Limited.

1979 – In Germany: there really is Nutella inside

In Germany, Ferrero replies to its competitors with a claim destined to become part of everyday language: "Nur wo Nutella draufsteht, ist auch Nutella drin" ("You know there's Nutella inside only if the label actually says Nutella").

1980 – Farewell to Piera Cillario Ferrero

In May, Michele Ferrero steps down as CEO and hands the post over to the managers: Virgilio Motta and Luciano Chiesa.

On December 3, 1980, at the age of seventy-eight, company founder Piera Cillario (photo) dies.

Nutella output is over 50,000 metric tons (55,000 tons) in the world.

1981 – Ferrero international debuts

From January 1, the company restructuring becomes operative: Ferrero S.p.A. and Ferrero Sud S.p.A. are created in Italy, while Ferrero International B.V. is set up as the holding. The latter's headquarters are in Amsterdam and it has control over the shares and coordinates all the companies.

1982 – Ferrero Rocher, the most sold praline in the world

To safeguard its consumers, the Nutella jar that ends up on the tables of Italian families is capped with a golden foil seal that consumers peel off, which makes the jar even more enticing to open.

A whole hazelnut immersed in a velvety cream similar to Nutella is encased inside a spherical wafer, which is covered with chocolate and hazelnut grains: this is Ferrero Rocher, another of Michele Ferrero's ideas, and he is also the inventor of the complex machinery needed to produce it.

Today, it's the best-selling chocolate praline in the world, with China at the top of the list of consumers.

Among the ingredients of its success are the gold wrapping paper and the decision to place it inside a paper cup, making it a luxury chocolate available to everybody.

1983 – The first jar of Nutella in New York

Nutella takes its first step to conquer the United States: it is imported in the northeastern part of the country.

In Italy, in a castle near Alba, Michele Ferrero presents an "Opera Sociale" named after his parents with the intention of offering a point of reference to the elderly who have collaborated with the company for at least twenty-five years.

The following year *Filo Diretto*, the house publication, will be published periodically and addressed to all the company workers. Maria Franca Ferrero—who still runs it today with passion and energy—will become its president in 1990.

1984 – A movie for the legend

Nutella turns twenty. It is very popular with baby boomers, who are well past their adolescent years by now. The movie *Bianca* is released, directed by Nanni Moretti. Thanks to a thirty-second scene, it will turn Nutella into a legend with the public at large, the Holy Grail of happiness. From that moment on, Nutella becomes the representation of Italians dreaming about eating something delicious.

1985 – After the earthquake, two plants built in southern Italy

In the Irpinia area, in southern Italy, which had been struck by the November 1980 earthquake, work begins on two new Ferrero plants: half of the investment was funded by State contributions.

The first of these is located in Balvano, Basilicata, and it makes white bakery products. The second one is located in Sant'Angelo dei Lombardi: at first it is dedicated to the production of Nutella and Duplo, but these products will soon be followed by Tronky and Kinder Bueno.

On September 28, in Alba the new ultramodern Ferrero Foundation headquarters, built according to the family's wishes, is inaugurated, complete with recreational spaces available for former employees, outpatient clinics, and workshops.

1986 – Ferrero celebrates its fortieth anniversary

The company celebrates its forty years in business, reaching 6,677 employees and a turnover of 926 billion lire (equal to $1.5 billion in today's money), having almost doubled in just five years.

1987 – Duplo is launched in Italy

The Alba factory produces a new chocolate snack: a wafer with three domes filled with cream (similar to Nutella) surrounding a whole hazelnut. The name of the snack is Duplo, and its success will be long lasting.

1988 – Ferrero Iberica in Barcelona

Ferrero Iberica opens in Spain, and it will also manage the Portuguese market. The offices are located in Barcelona and have just five employees. The challenge for Nutella is all uphill, as Spanish children have been raised on an imitation hazelnut spread, called Nocilla, taken there by the Italian company Star.

1989 – Ferrero Ardennes is launched in Belgium

In Arlon, a city with a population of 25,000 in the region of Wallonia, Belgium, not far from the border of the Grand Duchy of Luxembourg, is the Ferrero Ardennes plant, occupying an area of 77,000 square meters (19 acres). The plant mainly produces Kinder Surprise, Schoko-Bons, a praline with a soft center of milk and crunchy hazelnut grains inside a chocolate shell, and the coconut-flavored praline called Raffaello.

Ferrero decides to enter the Easter egg market in Italy by producing Maxi Kinder Surprise.

1990 – A French book: "Proustian Madeleine"

The French love Nutella as much as the Italians do. This is proven in the book by the writer and journalist Rita Cirio, *Qualità: scènes d'objets à l'italienne*, published in Paris, in which Nutella is defined as "a sort of spreadable and collective Proustian Madeleine": this is the certification of its "social" nature.

Ferrero pralines have always been withdrawn from the market in the warm months, to reappear in the fall. One of the goals Michele Ferrero seeks to achieve is the de-seasonalization of chocolate, which tends to be sold less in summer. This is why Kinder milk-slice is commercialized, followed by Kinder Pinguí in 1992, and by Kinder Paradiso in 1994: for the first time these Ferrero products require cold storage. The coconut-flavored Raffaello praline makes its debut in Germany.

1991 – The Ferrero Foundation becomes a charitable trust

The Ferrero Foundation of Alba is recognized as a charitable trust by the Italian government, and it is one of a group of nonprofit organizations with social missions known in Italy by their acronym ONLUS.

An agreement with Warner Bros. allows Ferrero, in Italy, to reproduce the characters of children's best-loved cartoons, from Sylvester the Cat to Tweety and Daffy Duck, on Nutella glasses.

1992 – First Tic Tac lines in Poland

Ferrero Polska takes its first steps in the Polish market and the construction of a first small plant for the production of Tic Tac begins in Wilanów, not far from Warsaw. Production will begin a year later.

Expansion also continues in South America with commercial headquarters in Mexico. Ferrero's first commercial offices open in China: consumers will especially love the Ferrero Rocher chocolate treat.

1993 – Ferrero enters Greece and expands to Barcelona

The presence of Ferrero in Spain has significantly grown, despite the fact that the sale of chocolate has been traditionally hampered by the country's high temperatures. Ferrero Iberica already has a hundred workers and a new, more modern plant is opened at El Prat del Llobregat, close to Barcelona, on February 18.

Ferrero Hellas is set up in Athens, and begins to penetrate the Greek market with the Kinder and Rocher lines. Harder, but slow and constant, is Nutella's penetration in the market, as another hazelnut-based cream, called Merenda (the branding is in Italian, in Roman lettering), already exists, produced by the Pavlidis company.

1994 – A plant in Brazil

Expansion abroad continues, with commercial offices in Hungary, the Czech Republic (the company called Ferrero Ceska sro), and in Scandinavia, where offices are in Mälmo, Sweden. The plant in Poços de Calda, in the state of Minas Gerais, Brazil, 240 kilometers (150 miles) from São Paolo, starts producing Nutella as well.

On November 5, there is another tragedy in Alba caused by flooding, which leads to the death of many people in Piedmont. The Ferrero plants suffer heavy damage and production is at a standstill for twenty-five days, but recovery is fast, thanks to the workers who volunteer to come to the factory.

At the Open Gate in Rome, a fashionable club in the Italian capital, the first Nutella Party is held in late November, with a huge sandwich and 30 kilograms (66 pounds) of hazelnut cream.

1995 – From New Jersey, Nutella made in the USA

In the United States, Ferrero opens a small factory in Somerset, New Jersey, which is inaugurated in June, with the Ferrero family in attendance. For many years it will also produce Nutella, until the large Canadian plant in Brantford starts production in 2006. The first Ferrero offices in Russia are opened.

In Poland, Nutella starts to be imported.

1996 – Production begins in Argentina

September 30 is the first day of production at the La Pastora plant in Argentina, in the city of Exaltación de la Cruz, an hour's drive from Buenos Aires.

In Paris, to celebrate its thirtieth birthday, an exhibition is held entitled *Génération Nutella*, in the prestigious space of the Carrousel du Louvre, with the work of artists, actors, and poets.

Tic Tac sponsors the Ferrari F1 team, and will continue to do so until 2002.

1997 – Pietro and Giovanni become Ferrero CEOs

Nutella spreads toward Eastern Europe: another plant that produces Nutella is opened at Belsk Duzy, 60 kilometers (37 miles) south of Warsaw in Poland. Now there are fifteen producing plants of the Ferrero Group, with a total of 16,000 workers.

The third generation makes its entrance in the company management: Pietro and Giovanni Ferrero, Michele's sons, become CEOs.

1998 – Sponsor of the Champions League

On May 20, in Amsterdam, Juventus Football Club loses to Real Madrid in the final of the Champions League. Along the sides of the playing field are Nutella billboards: the sponsorship continues for three years, with the finals of Barcelona '99 and Paris 2000.

On August 9, in Italy, the bakers of Bedona, in Emilia-Romagna, make it into the *Guinness Book of Records*, after baking a roll that is about 332,66 meters (363 yards) long: it is the longest sandwich in the world, filled with cured meats, cheeses, and Nutella.

1999 – The first Nutella website in the USA

For at least two years spontaneous groups of Nutella fans, such as the one on the platform called Tripod, have been forming on the Internet. The Ferrero legal office is adamant about preventing the illegal use of the brand. The first official site dedicated to the hazelnut cream goes online in the United States: www.nutellausa.com.

2000 – Nutella online in Italy and Germany

The Internet sites www.nutella.it and www.nutella.de go online.

From March 16 to 19, in Turin, a big Nutelleria with 16-foot-tall lettering is set up for Eurochocolate: it is a stand, measuring 1,000 square meters (3,289 square feet), where the hazelnut cream specialties, from appetizers to desserts, can all be tasted.

Another sports sponsorship begins, one that is still active today: Nutella becomes an official sponsor of the Italian national football team.

2001 – Nutelleria pilot stores open in Bologna and Genoa

On February 24, in Italy, the first official Nutelleria is inaugurated in Bologna. In December, another one is opened in a shopping mall. This trial will only last a few years: Ferrero will abandon the idea of opening a fast food chain, and will instead aim at fostering smaller "Nutella points" in coffee shops, and, later, Nutella Bars at Eataly.

In June, the exhibition called *Cento anni di prodotto italiano* is held in Padua, organized by the Galileo Science and Technology Park and by the Italian School of Design. One hundred Italian products that have made the history of design are on display, and visitors are asked to fill out a questionnaire placing them in order of importance. They choose Nutella first, followed by Vespa and by Fiat 500.

The Internet site www.nutella.fr goes online.

2002 – "TartiNutella," a designer knife in France

Even design is attracted to the legend. In France consumers are drawn to the spreading knife called "TartiNutella" designed by the renowned architect Patrick Jouin.

Kinder Joy starts production, which is meant to replace Kinder Surprise in the summer: the milk and hazelnut cream is inside a plastic capsule that protects it, while the surprise is in another capsule. After its success in Italy, Kinder Joy will soon become available in the warm countries of the southern hemisphere.

2003 – Snack & Drink and MyNutella.it

For the first time Nutella is sold together with bread sticks and Estathé. The package has three compartments for outdoor consumption.

On July 26, in Frankfurt, Germany, a Nutelleria opens at the Oberhausen shopping mall: it will close down after the Italian ones.

In Italy, in April, an Internet site makes its debut, anticipating social media: it is a virtual community of the product's fans called MyNutella, for which thousands of people register.

2004 – Nutella celebrates its fortieth anniversary in Italy

On April 20, in Italy, Nutella's fortieth anniversary is celebrated, with a party in Turin and a convention at the Ferrero Foundation of Alba, which also sees the participation of the family: Michele Ferrero blows out the forty candles on a baguette spread with Nutella (photo).

On October 7, in Rome, another birthday is celebrated: the Kinder egg turns thirty. A dedicated exhibition is held.

The program of Ferrero's social projects also gets off the ground; in June, the first plant to produce Kinder Joy opens at Yaoundé, Cameroon.

In Alba, refurbishment of a former spinning mill begins, which will be completed two years later. Since then it has hosted Soremartec, the Ferrero research center.

2005 – The anniversary is also celebrated in France and Germany

France celebrates the fortieth anniversary of Nutella's arrival. For forty days, in the heart of Paris, a "convivial, ephemeral, magical" temporary café named Table Nutella is the center-piece.

In Germany the final event of the celebrations is held on May 29 at the Arena AufSchalke in Gelsenkirchen, a town in the Renania-Westphalia region. As many as 27,854 people gather for a special breakfast based on Nutella, setting the Guinness record for the biggest breakfast in the world.

In the yearly report of the international advertising agency Young & Rubicam, which assesses the state of health of the brands through consumers' perceptions, it emerges that the best-loved brand by both young (ages eighteen to twenty-four) and old (over forty-five) is Nutella.

On April 26, Michele Ferrero turns eighty, and the president of Italy, Carlo Azeglio Ciampi, appoints him Knight of the Great Cross, Italy's highest honor.

2006 – The Canada plant is inaugurated

Two plants are inaugurated: a plant with a social mission in Walkerville, South Africa, and a major productive center in Brantford, Ontario, Canada, which is in full swing starting  October 20. The following year the plant will be further reinforced, and it will represent Ferrero's most important productive platform for North America.

On September 29, in Alba, in the former spinning mill, the new headquarters of the Soremartec research center is inaugurated. A master's degree is also instituted, named in honor of Mi-

chele Ferrero, and promoted by the Ferrero Foundation and the University of Turin, for the study of the science and technology of food and human nutrition.

Ferrero Rocher and Nutella, as design objects, represent Italy at the exhibition *50+2Y Italian Design*, held in September at the National Art Museum of China (NAMOC) in Beijing.

In April, in Milan, design trials inspired by Nutella are held on the occasion of the Salone del Mobile: the designers Michelangelo Giombini, Matteo Migliorini, and Marco Sarno at the Fuorisalone present their NutMobili ("NutFurniture") inspired by Nutella's jar, shaped like a Pelikan ink bottle: a retro chest of drawers, furniture made from polycarbonate, and a 1950s-style refrigerator.

Also, Giombini introduces a Gustanutella ("TasteNutella") metal spoon and a leather bag for carrying the jar around in case of sudden hunger pangs. Paolo Ulian displays his Finger Biscuit: a thimble-shaped biscuit that can be placed in the jar to be eaten in a single mouthful.

2007 – The first World Nutella Day is held in the USA

Sara Rosso, a digital strategist, and her friend the lawyer and blogger Michelle Fabio, both of Italian descent, create a World Nutella Day on the Internet for February 5 (a date that has no link with the history of the brand).

Ferrero's social undertakings continue to develop with a plant in Baramati, India, while a new plant is born in Cameroon, 5,000 square meters (1,640 square feet) in size.

Ferrero Energie is set up in Alba, to develop plant strategies for greater economic and environmental efficiency, in addition to the acquisition of the necessary energy for the Group's activities.

2008 – A Nuday in Italy to launch the Nutellaville website

On January 28, in Italy, an attractive brown-and-white calf-skin leather handbag is presented to the press, in the shape of a jar: it's the Gilli Nutella Cube, produced in a limited edition of one hundred.

On June 12, in Turin, to celebrate the arrival of summer, the first (and for now the only) Nuday is held in the town's historic squares, gardens, and other locations, where people can "share stories, passions, anecdotes and pieces of life inspired by Nutella."

On the same day, the website www.nutellaville.it is launched: a virtual city, "poetic and imaginative," where films, photographs, poems, and songs inspired by Nutella can be found.

2009 – Breakfast for the G8 leaders

In July, in L'Aquila, Italy hosts the G8 summit for world leaders: on their tables at the business breakfast is a snack consisting of fruit, milk, bread, and Nutella.

A new plant opens in Vladimir, Russia.

On May 6, the announcement is made that Ferrero is the most reliable company in the world, ahead of Ikea and Johnson & Johnson. The award is given to the two brothers, Pietro and Giovanni, in Amsterdam, on May 29. Every year the Reputation Institute of New York presents its Global Rep Trak Pulse: the reputation of the great world brands is calculated according to the responses of over sixty thousand people in twenty-seven countries.

In Villers Écalles, the city in Normandy where the Ferrero plant is located, the fiftieth anniversary of the company in France is celebrated, and Rue Pietro Ferrero is inaugurated in honor of its founder.

Breadsticks and hazelnut spread are sold together in a new package: this is Nutella & Go, the evolution of Snack & Drink, which, after its debut in France in 2008, is now sold in Italy and in other countries.

2010 – A Facebook page

On April 15, having abandoned the project Nutellaville, the first post on the Nutella Facebook page is published: in just three months the page exceeds 1.5 million fans, and on October 7, the milestone of 2 million "likes" is reached. The page had only been created one year before.

On May 26, the hazelnut and cocoa spread's first official tweet on Twitter is heard.

On July 5, in Rome, the first report on Corporate Social Responsibility (CSR) is presented.

On the same day, Italian Foreign Minister Franco Frattini gives the Winning Italy Award to brothers Pietro and Giovanni Ferrero: an award that is given to the figure or the company that has "been capable of promoting and valorizing Italy's image in the world."

2011 – The death of Pietro Jr.

On April 18, while in South Africa, where he is working on one of the company's social undertakings, Pietro Ferrero (photo) suddenly dies at the age of forty-seven. The funeral is held in Alba on April 27. The whole city and countless famous names are there to pay tribute.

After his brother's death, Giovanni Ferrero is the sole CEO of the Group. The ambassador Francesco Paolo Fulci, formerly vice president of the international holding, also takes over the post of president of Ferrero S.p.A. Italia.

Italy celebrates the 150th anniversary of national unification, and among the objects displayed at the exhibition *Making the Italians*, held at the Officine Grandi Riparazioni in Turin, is a red, white, and green jar of Nutella.

2012 – The favorite brand in Germany

The German magazine *Lebensmittel Praxis*, in a survey among the buyers, branch directors, and managers of large distribution chains, elects Nutella as *"Händlers Liebling,"* the favorite brand for distributors, one that they cannot do without.

In April, in California, a class action suit is brought against Ferrero USA by the mother of a four-year-old girl: she believes that the company's advertising is deceitful and the indications on the label concerning the product's nutritional characteristics are unclear. The company reaches an agreement with consumers for a symbolic award of four dollars for anyone who can show, having joined the class action suit, that the product had been purchased between January 1, 2008, and February 3, 2012.

2013 – Two new plants open in Mexico and Turkey

On June 18, in Mexico, with an investment of $200 million, a plant is opened in San José Iturbide, Guanajuato. This is followed by another one, the Group's twentieth, on September 8, in Manisa, Turkey, home to most of the hazelnuts used to produce Nutella.

On December 2, in Chicago, the first Nutella Bar in the world opens inside the Eataly store.

On March 13, a great party is organized to say farewell to winter in Moscow. Called *"Maslenista,"* it is organized by Nutella in Sokolniki Park: two thousand warm blinis are served with hazelnut cream.

In July, for the third consecutive time, Ferrero conquers the top spot in the dreams of job seekers in Italy: it comes first in the "50 Best Places to Work" ranking drafted by the American website Glassdoor based on employees' opinions.

On October 17, after several articles in the international press hypothesizing the possible sale of Ferrero to the Swiss giant Nestlé, the CEO Giovanni Ferrero denies any talks are in progress by publishing a full-page ad reading: "Ferrero is not up for sale for anyone." The family remains firmly at the helm of the Group: Giovanni Ferrero with his parents, Michele and Maria Franca (photo).

2014 – Celebrations for a worldwide birthday

Celebrations for fifty years of the brand are held on May 18, for the first time contemporaneously around the world, with just one big Nutella Day, and events in Italy, France, Germany, the United Kingdom, Poland, Russia, the United Emirates, Canada, the United States, and Australia. The website www.nutellastories.com receives more than 74,000 comments proclaiming affection for Nutella.

In January, Poste Italiane dedicates one of the year's stamps to Nutella's fiftieth anniversary. The stamp is released on May 14.

In July, the acquisition of Oltan in Turkey is announced, a company that specializes in processing hazelnuts, with its main plant in Trabzon: it has five plants that process 8,000 metric tons (8,800 tons) of hazelnuts, for a turnover of $500 million.

The Nutella brand is extended with a new product, which contains a cream and hazelnut filling. It is Nutella B-ready, "a bread wafer filled with Nutella." For now, it is only available in Italy.

2015 – The death of Michele Ferrero

On February 14, Michele Ferrero dies at eighty-nine in Monte Carlo. The funeral is held in Alba, on February 18.

Selected bibliography

Aaker, D. A. *Brand Relevance*. San Francisco, CA: Jossey-Bass, 2010.

Backer, K. D., and S. Miroudot. *Mapping Global Value Chains*. OECD (OCSE) Trade Policy Papers, No. 159, 2013. http://dx.doi.org/10.1787/5k3v1trgnbr4-en.

Bazzarini, A. *Piano teorico-pratico di sostituzione nazionale al cioccolato aggiuntovi un metodo economico-speculativo di sostituzione al caffè*. Venice: Fracasso, 1813.

Bosio, G. *Nutella: da prodotto di largo consumo a prodotto di culto*. Graduation thesis. IULM University of Milan, 1997.

Candler Graham, E., and R. Roberts. *Classic Cooking with Coca-Cola*. Nashville, TN: Hambleton-Hill, 1994.

Casalegno, C., ed. *Pubblicità istruzioni per l'uso*. Milan: Franco Angeli, 2012.

Cirio, R. *Qualità: scènes d'objets à l'italienne*. Paris: Éditions du May, 1990.

Collins, J., and J. I. Porras. *Built to Last: Successful Habits of Visionary Companies*. New York: Harper Business, 1994.

Condividere valori per creare valore. Responsabilità Sociale d'Impresa, Rapporto 2000–2010, 2011, 2012. Brussels: Ferrero CSR Office.

CoolBrands. London: Superbrands, 2006.

De Vecchi, S., A. Di Nola, and M. Tonelli. *Storia di un successo*. Turin: Aeda, 1967.

Fabris, G. *La pubblicità, teorie e prassi*. Milan: Franco Angeli, 1997.

Fabris, G., and L. Minestroni. *Valore e valori della marca*. Milan: Franco Angeli, 2004.

Fabris, G., and G. Padovani. *Nutella siamo noi*. Pino Torinese: Ferrero SpA, 2006.

Fenoglio, M. *Vivere altrove*. Palermo, Italy: Sellerio, 1997.

Ferrero 1946–1996. Pino Torinese, Italy: Ferrero SpA, 1996.

Ferrero, G. *Il giardino di Adamo*. Milan: Mondadori, 2003.

Ferrero, G. *Marketing Progetto 2000*. Milan: Franco Angeli, 1990.

Galloway, J. H. "Sugar." In *The Cambridge World History of Food*. Cambridge, UK: Cambridge University Press, 2000.

Ginzburg, C., ed. *Imprese sociali Ferrero*. Milan: Skira, 2012.

Ginzburg, C., ed. *Trent'anni di Fondazione Ferrero*. Milan: Skira, 2013.

Giono, J. *The Man Who Planted Trees.* 1953. Reprinted White River Junction, VT: Chelsea Green, 2005.

Johanson, P. *Lance Armstrong: A Biography.* Santa Barbara, CA: Greenwood Biographies, 2011.

Holt, D. B. *How Brands Become Icons.* Boston, MA: Harvard Business School Press, 2004.

Keller, J-P. *La Galaxie Coca-Cola.* Geneva: Éditions Zoé, 1999.

Klein, N. *No Logo.* Toronto: Random House Canada, 1999.

Kotler, P., and G. Armstrong. *Principles of Marketing.* 13th ed. London: Pearson, 2008.

Lavarini, R., and R. Scramaglia, *Lavorare creare donare.* Alba, Italy: Fondazione Ferrero, 2003.

Levi, P. *The Monkey's Wrench.* Translated by William Waver. New York: Penguin, 1987.

Marsero, M. *Dolci delizie subalpine.* Turin: Lindau, 1995.

Minestroni, L. *Il manuale della marca.* Bologna: Fausto Lupetti, 2010.

Off, C. *Bitter Chocolate.* Toronto: Random House Canada, 2008.

Packard, V. *The Hidden Persuaders.* Brooklyn, NY: Ig Publishing, 2007.

Padovani, G. *Gnam! Storia sociale della Nutella.* Rome: Castelvecchi, 1999.

Padovani, G., *Nutella un mito italiano.* Milan: Rizzoli, 2004.

Pavese, C. *The Moon and the Bonfire.* Translated by L. Sinclair. London: Peter Owen, 2003.

Pigna, A. *Miliardari in borghese.* Milan: Mursia, 1966.

Rizzini, M. *Origini, evoluzione e affermazione di un prodotto di successo: il caso Nutella.* Graduation thesis. IULM University of Milan, 1997.

Roberts, K. Lovemarks: *The Future Beyond Brands.* New York: Powerhouse, 2005.

Rogers, E. M. *Diffusion of Innovations.* New York: Free Press, 2003.

Sciannammè, M. C. *La comunicazione nello sviluppo della reputazione aziendale: il caso Ferrero.* Graduation thesis. University of Pavia, 2010.

Segan, F. *Dolci: Italy's Sweets.* New York: Stewart, Tabori & Chang, 2011.

Seglin J. *The McGraw-Hill 36-Hour Marketing Course.* New York: McGraw-Hill, 1989.

Semenzin, F., and M. Semenzin. *Un mondo di figurine 1946–1970.* Turin: Editris, 2008.

Stone, B. *The Everything Store: Jeff Bezos and the Age of Amazon.* New York: Little Brown and Company, 2013.

Vada Padovani, C., and G. Padovani. *Gianduiotto mania.* Florence: Giunti, 2007.

Vada Padovani, C., and G. Padovani. *Italia Buon Paese.* Turin: Blu Edizioni, 2011.

Vada Padovani, C. *Nutella Passion*. Florence: Giunti, 2010.

Upshaw, L. *Building Brand Identity*. New York: John Wiley & Sons, 1995.

Weber, L., and L. L. Henderson. *The Digital Marketer,* Hoboken, NJ: Wiley, 2014.

Acknowledgments

Many managers, marketing experts, university professors and journalists have helped me to write this book, an international version that is even broader than the text I recently published in Italy. Some of them prefer not to be mentioned, but they know I owe them my sincerest gratitude.

I would like to thank the interviewees cited in the book: Attilio Barra, Ferrero technologist; Cecilia Casalegno, professor at the University of Turin; Maurizio Chimenti, Ferrero technician; Vincenzo Cosenza of Blogmeter; Michele Di Capua, Ferrero technician; Oscar Farinetti of Eataly; Giovanni Ferrero, CEO of Ferrero International; Giuseppe Francone, retired Ferrero employee; Valeria Sandei, CEO of Almaviva; Alex Saper, manager of Eataly USA; Davide Scodeggio of Zodiak Active; Francine Segan, writer; Nadia Tadè, manager of Piada in New York; Cristina Villa, of Eataly USA.

I was given precious information, contacts and advice by: Dino Borri, Eataly New York; Alessandra Ciuccarelli of Cohn & Wolfe for Inalpi; Alberto Dal Sasso and Samantha Rovatti of Nielsen; Ilaria De Bernardis of Almaviva; Maurizio Fiumara and Dario Giaccone for the transcription of the English interviews; Paola Franchi of Assocom; Alessandro Galavotti, (for the Archive of the ANSA news agency); Peter Hesse and Marina Verna for their translations from the German; Maria Giovanna Migliaro of Audiweb; Lorenzo Montersoli, Minister of Economic Development; Massimiliano Ricci of Poste Italiane.

I am grateful to the generous collaboration I received at Fondazione Ferrero from its director Mario Strola, and from his collaborators, Cristina Manzone and Elena Torchio.

My gratitude always goes to the webmaster of my website, Angelo Saccu, and to the videomaker Roberto Ghisu.

Heartfelt thanks go to Ottavio Di Brizzi, Paola Rabezzana and Giovanni Ubbiali of Rizzoli, who believed in the book and supported me in my work, as well as to the translators Aaron Maines and Sylvia Notini.

I would like to thank Ferrero S.p.A. and the many collaborators who made the archival data and images available to me. The book is the product of my own research in complete autonomy with respect to the company.